International Business Systems Perspectives

Compiled and Edited by
C.G. Alexandrides

Professor of Management
School of Business Administration
Georgia State University

School of Business Administration
Georgia State University
1973

To Sophia

CONTENTS

FOREWORD

The complexity of our emerging world economy, resulting from international governmental actions and the decisions of multinational corporations, necessitates a systematic approach to the study of international business and world trade.

This collection of readings is designed to meet a need to inform both corporate managers and academicians regarding current developments in the applications of econometric analysis and quantitative methods to international business.

They are designed to stress the importance of a systematic approach to the study of international business and world trade through the use of simulation, model-building and computer methodologies. The editor has attempted to obtain the best works of internationally prominent scholars and researchers in this increasingly significant field of international business systems.

It is the objective of this volume to present a review of the integrated field of international business and world trade. Toward this end, readings were selected to concentrate on the current academic response to the growing challenge of international business. We hope that this new perspective in international business will be useful in stimulating further research and greater understanding.

Georgia State University
January 1973

Kenneth Black, Jr., Dean
School of Business Administration

PREFACE

International business as a discipline has been making strides in spite of the academic debate whether it is an extension of domestic business or a separate field. The growth of the discipline with its functional fields has been primarily generated by the internationalization of business and economic production.

At present, the U.S. academic community teaching international business courses or engaged in research numbers over 500 in about 150 colleges and universities. The courses range from undergraduate to doctoral level, using traditional teaching methods, cases and internships. An increasing list of textbooks, cases and articles on international business has been published in spite of the relatively short period of its existence.

In the area of econometric analysis and quantitative methods to international business considerable progress has been made recently mainly by members of the academic profession. In addition to the interest of the academic community, an impetus in this area has been provided by the concern of governments and international organizations due to increasing international economic interdependence. The computerization of international business research methodologies has been made possible by the present availability of international trade data and international economic statistics by governments, OECD and the U.N.

The collection of readings is an attempt to present the "state of the art" in the area of simulation, model-building and computer applications to international business and trade. It is hoped that these research methodologies and theoretical frameworks can contribute to a better understanding of the international environment within which international business operates and the interdependency of international economic and trade relationships of nations. Moreover, a systems approach to international business resolves the academic argument whether it is an extension of domestic business or a separate field.

My appreciation to the contributors and to Dr. James R. Miller, Director of the University's Bureau of Business and Economic Research, for making possible the publication of these articles, most of which have not been published before.

January 1973   The Editor

INTRODUCTION

International Business Systems in Perspective seeks to introduce econometric analysis, quantitative methods and computer applications to the field of international business.

The book is divided in the functional fields of international business with the first part on simulation and the concluding on the future of international business.

A brief summary of the articles under the six main parts follows:

International Business Simulation

Professor Hans B. Thorelli examines INTOP (International Operations Simulation) as a simulation of the problems that many international firms face in the diverse environments in which they operate. INTOP blends the functional areas of production, finance and marketing to the complexity of international business operations.

Professors John Fayerweather and Ashok Kapoor describe the international business negotiation simulation as a pedagogic device in international business education. The negotiation simulations involve student teams representing business and government sectors interacting in commercial situations. The exercise attempts to bring the reality of international business operations to the classroom.

International Trade Econometric Models

The article by professors Hickman, Klein and Rhomberg describe the organization, plans and progress of Project LINK, a world trade system which links the various national models. It was constructed for the purpose of estimating world trade consistent with econometric forecasts of domestic activity in all the participating countries.

The article by F.J.M. Meyer Zu Schloctern and Akira Yajima describes the 1970 version of the OECD trade model along with changes from the original version, and outlines the extension of the model—tracing the "feedback" effect of trade on GNP. This model is designed to be a forecasting tool for aggregated commodity imports and exports of major countries.

Professor F. Gerard Adams and Helen B. Junz examine the effect of the business cycle on trade flows of industrial countries. The article examines the effect of macro-economic conditions, here and abroad, upon trade flows. Its purpose is to recognize and measure this effect in order to be able to anticipate, and deal with, the balance of payments effects on domestic policy decisions rather than to tailor domestic economic policy to external constraints.

International Finance

Professor Alan Shapiro examines how firms engaged in international business can manage their financial assets and liabilities, and protect themselves from exchange losses due to currency devaluations and revaluations. Several models and optional timing policies are used in determining when the danger of exchange loss outweighs the hedging cost, and in selecting among the various hedging options.

Professor David P. Rutenberg analyzes how to maneuver the liquid assets in a multinational company by the optimal use of tax havens, bilateral tax treaties, non-uniform treatments of income received from abroad, and national differences in income tax rates. This model attempts to forecast whether a national subsidiary of a multinational company will be a net source or sink of funds.

Professors Robert R. Miller and Dale R. Weigel test empirically some direct investment theories by using elaborate investment data on Brazil. For this purpose, a two-stage linear discriminant model is used. The study finds positive and negative factors inducing direct investment in Brazil.

International Management

In this article Professor S. Benjamin Prasad assesses the significance of the Harbison and Myers, Farmer and Richman, Negandhi-Estafen comparative management models. He makes a case for the need of empirical comparative studies to build foundations for theoretical frameworks.

Professors Musbau Ajiferuke and J. Boddewyn analyze the correlation of selected socio-economic indicators in comparing attitudes and motivation among managers in fourteen countries found in the survey by Haire, Ghiselli and Porter. In the study eight variables were considered to be representative indicators. Even though the analysis strengthened the validity of the findings of the survey, the availability of more indicators still makes the ground for comparative management research highly attractive and fertile.

Dr. John S. Schwendiman investigates the subject of international strategic and long-range corporate planning. The article examines some key dimensions which distinguish international strategic and long-range planning from purely domestic planning, and proposes a process flow model of international corporate planning.

International Marketing

Professor C. G. Alexandrides' research is focused on how to identify potential export markets for disaggregated products. For this purpose, he described the methodology and models used in the computerized international market information system. A case study is also presented with findings to demonstrate the capability of the system. The ranking of potential export markets for each commodity is based on projected import demand, the anticipated market share performance in each market by exporters, and the degree and trend of international competition.

Professors James D. Goodnow and James E. Hansz examine the hypothesis that a firm will tend to pursue an entry strategy involving greater control of overseas production and marketing activities as the country's environment becomes more politically stable, higher in market opportunity, economic development and performance, and cultural unity, and lower in legal barriers, physiographic barriers and geocultural distance.

Professor Jose R. de la Torre's thesis is that the marketing characteristics of a product are major determinants of its export potential from developing countries, particularly as these characteristics affect how, by whom, to what extent, and under what conditions successful export efforts are undertaken. The research analyzes the relationships which exist between a product's marketing characteristics and various indices of export performance.

Professor Warren J. Keegan maintains that the continuing measurement and evaluation of marketing performance presents formidable problems in the multinational enterprise. The environmental differences in markets are associated with problems of communications related to geographical distance and differences in language, practices, and customs. In multinational companies environmental complexities and geographic distances result in the creation of geographically dispersed intermediate headquarters which add an organizational level to the control system. The objective of this article is to build a descriptive model of the multinational marketing control process employed by large, successful firms.

In this article Judd Polk examines the internationalization of economic production, and its implications in our emerging world economy. He sees this economic interdependence as the result of international investment and its resulting annual output of some $450 billion. This interdependency will become stronger as direct international investment continues to grow, and internationally produced output increasingly becomes a larger portion of the gross world product.

Professor Ernest W. Ogram examines the future path of multinational corporations, the environmental factors affecting such a path, and the firms' impact upon the economies in which they operate. He contends that the success of the multinational corporation, if it meets its social responsibilities and remains fully competitive, will contribute to higher standards of living for all.

Professor Richard D. Robinson examines the international direct investment patterns and their future development. He foresees a demand for international cooperation between governments and multinational firms to prevent increasing conflicts, but provide for mutual benefits in a framework of partnership. He speculates on world business as a driving force for world government.

The Editor

Simulating International Business Operations

Hans B. Thorelli
Indiana University

Introduction

Games as simulation and training devices originated with the military, who for several decades were the only interested party. The last twenty years have witnessed the emergence of business games as well as diplomacy and international relations games. Simulation by gaming is rapidly finding many other applications, ranging from the planning of state university systems via city governmental affairs to the determinants of public opinion.

Objectives

Games represent a form of simulation. The concept of simulation is not without its ambiguities in either popular or scientific parlance. We find it natural and useful to think of simulation as "a technique for studying the behavior of complex systems." Thus, it involves the use of a model of reality comprising a bundle of interrelated variables, and manipulation and/or observation of the behavior of this system over time. More often than not, it is impossible to represent in the simulation all variables at play in reality and to assign them their proper relative weights.

1

The International Operations Simulation (INTOP),[1] the subject of this article, represents the first application of a sophisticated game design to management problems in international operations and in coping with overseas-based competition in domestic markets.

Education

In the area of education three major types of purposes may be distinguished: to increase the student understanding of business problems at the functional level (marketing, production, etc.), of the inescapable interrelatedness of the functions and parts of a business and of the various firms in an industry, and to broaden the grasp of, and provide some practical training in the problems of organization and policy and the decision-making process. In these simulation exercises students get an opportunity to grapple with such functional and subfunctional problems as market research, forecasting, sales management, pricing, physical distribution, advertising, or investment policy, procurement of financial resources, budgeting and financial control. While the details of these problems will differ from any specific situation facing the students in real life, the principal elements, their general linkage and their dynamics will be sufficiently similar to offer the students a taste of closer to "the real thing" than that of almost any other teaching tool educators are in position to offer.

Research

INTOP was also deliberately designed to serve as an instrument for research business economics. The relative complexity of the model, which effectively forces a division of labor among decision-makers, also makes the game eminently suitable for research on leadership and task-oriented groups. The psychologist, the sociologist, and organization theorist alike will be interested in exploring the emergence and exercise of leadership in initially unstructured but heavily task-oriented groups. By changing parameters in terms of the game task environment, number and composition of team members and their assignments, we may also gain new insights into what is really meant by the assertion that leadership is largely situationally conditioned.

Business Planning

The third major area of application is business planning. Here a distinction seems useful between simulation of markets and business strategy on the one hand and administrative systems on the other. Simulation of the former kind typically aims at the examination of specific production, finance, marketing, etc., policies of the firm under game environmental circumstances which in some important respects portray real markets. Simulation of administrative systems may involve such matters as the analysis of centralization vs. decentralization of different types of decisions in an organization, the exploration of management information systems, and the indoctrination of personnel in new organizational patterns. For such uses it is necessary to resort to a sufficiently complex simulation, such as INTOP, which really poses participants with man-size problems of organization and utilization of data.

Orientation

While the main purpose of the simulation is to increase understanding of the problems of international operations in general, and those in multi-national corporations in particular, INTOP is so designed as to yield substantial pay-off in general management training as well. This is achieved by a balanced representation of such functional areas of real life companies as finance, marketing, production, and research and development.

Among the particular advantages of INTOP is that this simulation forces participants into a stream of truly entrepreneurial (top management) decisions of business philosophy and objectives, as opposed to the heavy strategy-tactics emphasis of most other games. This is accomplished by continually forcing the teams with the choice of representing national or international companies, and, if the latter, whether by exporting, licensing, or selling to overseas distributors, or overseas-based manufacture. In addition, there is a choice between being a single-line and a diversified producer.

A principal aim of the simulation is to focus the attention of participants on the challenging idea "that changing a business— finding it new roles, new customers, new markets—is even more important than operating it efficiently." Whatever the stance adopted, participants are necessarily faced with grouping for logic in the business objectives—strategy—tactics sequence.

The emphasis on entrepreneurial decisions makes it imperative that the top management level be represented in the organization of participating teams. However, the purpose is also to make ample room for middle management simulation whenever desirable.

INTOP is a fast-moving exercise. This is assured by a model providing for vigorous competitive interaction in consumer markets in combination with opportunity for intercompany selling, borrowing and licensing. The dynamics are further emphasized by a number of time-lags and scheduling functions. A prime purpose of the game is to stress the role of long-range planning as an indispensable instrument in this context.[2]

An important consideration in the design of INTOP was its future use as a business planning and research instrument. In particular, it has been built with simulation of multinational corporate organizations in mind. However, the game by analogy is equally applicable to the internal coordination problems of any dispersed and diversified concern operating exclusively in domestic markets. The International Operations Simulation is currently being used in company and university executive development programs on all five continents.

Figure 1: Overall View of INTOP FORTRAN Operations

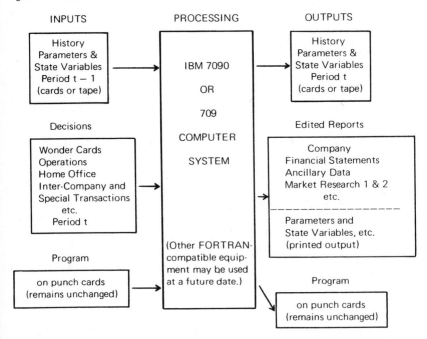

Simulated International Business Negotiations*

John Fayerweather and Ashok Kapoor
New York University

The simulated international business negotiation has been developed as a pedagogical device to contribute to the special needs of education for international business. It was first used by Professor Kapoor in the Spring of 1968 and has since been employed in a variety of other courses with substantial success. It appears to have considerable promise in development both of intellectual capacities for formulation of international business strategy and development of personal behaviorial skills in dealing with international environmental situations. This paper will outline the main characteristics of the simulations and discuss their practical utilization.

Purpose

The negotiation simulations relate to two major distinctive characteristics of international management: adjustment of strategy to varied environmental conditions and behaviorial sensitivity and adaptability. The importance and nature of these two elements have been sufficiently documented elsewhere so that there is no purpose in elaborating on them here.[1] The key point in the present discussion concerns the limitations of other pedagogical methods in

*Reprinted from the *Journal of International Business Studies*, Vol. 3, No. 1, Spring 1972 by special permission.

accomplishing major learning progress in these areas. The key to the limitations of lectures and even good case studies is the problem of conveying sufficient sense of reality and particularly of personal involvement to accomplish the desired types of learning. The negotiation simulations also have real limitations in this regard but they appear to be a significant step ahead. The essence of the negotiation exercise is a role playing recreation of an interaction between an international management group and a foreign private and/or public group to discuss a business problem. This sort of classroom situation brings into play the same sort of student dynamics which are involved in management games and other types of substantial role playing exercises. Typically there is a high degree of personal motivation encouraged by a sense of competition and group study satisfaction.

These are valuable components in the process but the unique values for international business study lie in the substantial sense of reality and of personal involvement which is created. The negotiation problems incorporate major elements of foreign national interests, nationalism, culture and other environmental factors. These elements are, of course, discussed at length in the literature and may be studied through cases and other means. The special role of the negotiation simulation in this study process lies in the extent to which grappling with the elements in a situation in which one is deeply involved as a role-player results in greater "take" of understanding of their character and greater capacity for personally sensing and adjusting ones behavior in their presence. Present indications are that a simulation is a very useful supplementary educational device for accomplishing this objective.

In addition to the fundamental purposes it should be noted that the simulation exercise also contributes directly to a specific skill of major importance in international business management, namely negotiating ability. Currently international executives estimate that 50% or so of their time is devoted to negotiating with foreign governments and further time to discussion with foreign businessmen, labor groups and others.[2] The various parties involved in international business transactions (foreign investors, host governments, local partners, international agencies, etc.) have entered into an era of negotiations. Confrontation is being avoided as evidenced by the U.S. government's decision not to use the Hickenlooper Amendment against Peru when it nationalized the International Petroleum Company. Increasingly the parties are recognizing that they have both common and conflicting interests which form the basis for negotiation.[3]

Thus a very large part of the responsibilities of men in this field are dependent upon their skill in negotiation processes. Much of this negotiation is concerned with moderate problems and often on a one for one basis, but a considerable amount involves substantial issues and group negotiation. For all sorts of interactions of this nature, specific skills developed by the negotiation exercise are a useful contribution. The students also develop an understanding of the relative role of the functional tools of business administration (financial analysis, accounting statements, quantitative measures, etc.) as they are actually used in support of a position.

Nature of the Exercise

On the basis of over three years of experience we can sketch a number of aspects of conduct of simulated international business negotiations. In doing so, however, we should stress that these points are only the result of early experimentation in our particular situation. The important elements of the simulations are their broad character as reproductions of real business interactions. With the passage of time and particularly different situations at other schools, it may that he details of execution will differ considerably.

So far our chief use of the simulated negotiations has been as part of established courses in International Business Management, International Marketing Management and Asian Business in the graduate school and Principles of World Business and International Marketing Management in the undergraduate school at New York University. This form of utilization typically calls for one to two classes per exercise and no more than five or six exercises per term. During the current year we have an experimental group of 20 students devoting a major effort to the negotiation simulations in lieu of their masters thesis. They will devote a great deal more time to each negotiation and pursue collateral studies related to the process as well.

In all of our applications of the negotiation simulation we have used real business cases. Theoretically it would be possible to create fictitious situations which might be desirable to emphasize certain points or for other reasons. However, it would appear to us impractical to achieve the primary objective of maximum reproduction of reality by this means. The objective is to confront the student with the same type of complex, imperfectly understood type of situation which is normal to international business. For many of our simulations we have used two major cases on which we already had a large amount of material available from our own research: the Western Industrial Corporation (WIC) negotiation with the Government of India for a $500 million fertilizer development and the conflict between the First National City Bank and the Canadian Government over control of the Mercantile Bank.[4] The book length versions of these studies running almost 400 pages in length offer detailed information on the dynamics of negotiations with condensed case versions providing basic information on the situations in a form suitable for distribution to all students. A study of these case analyses offers the student an understanding of the host of factors influencing the negotiation process. In addition, the wealth of information on project characteristics (financing, production, location, marketing, personnel, etc.) within the context of broader environmental forces permits students to immerse themselves in all features of a project. This is essential for it forms the basis for developing a feel for the dynamic process of negotiation.

However, we have also used some cases on which only limited information was available.[5] These also have been more productive we felt than simply discussing a similar case in the open classroom discussion normal to regular case teaching. We are considering for the intensive experimental project this year having the students in at least one instance go out to business firms and collect the raw material for the negotiations in part themselves. So far we have in most instances used situations where a multinational firm was negotiating with a host government. We find it is both practical and useful to have exercises involving other types of negotiations, for example within multinational firm and between multinational firms and foreign businesses. However, in practice it would appear that the firm-government negotiation is likely to be most productive in focusing on conflicts with national interests, nationalism and foreign cultures and it happens that cases of this sort are more readily available because of their public visibility. Thus we suspect that emphasis on them is most logical but the alternative types of negotiation should always be considered as possibilities. These points about the character of cases to be used in the negotiation suggest that there is substantial variety open to the instructor. The only essential point would seem to be that the case have sufficient depth and body to assure strong involvement by the student.

The existing body of written case material presents situations which took place in the past. Students often feel that negotiating a case which reflects a situation which occured in say 1960 is somehow outdated. This attitude can affect their sense of participation in case negotiations. Therefore, in many cases, we have instructed the students that the negotiations are taking place on the date that the class is to negotiate. For example, the unsuccessful WIC fertilizer negotiations in India took place in 1964-1965. The students, however, are instructed that the project proposal is being revived and the American consortium is sending a team to negotiate with the Indian Government as of the date on which negotiations in class are scheduled. In this way, the students feel that they are engaging in negotiations which are not dead and buried and that their decisions will influence the future course of events.

There are additional learning benefits of this approach. Environmental factors and the cast of characters within governments and investing companies change. Thus, the students will be dealing with a different Minister of Finance in 1971 than the individual named for 1965. Similarly, the senior corporate executives would have changed. Therefore, the students will have to recognize the importance of such changes in the cast of characters in formulating their strategies and approaches to negotiations. In addition, the environmental factors such as international relations or economic priorities within a country would have changed. Again, the students would have to recognize these features in formulating their negotiating strategies.

Yet another benefit of this approach is that the students develop two snapshot pictures composed of project characteristics and the broader environmental characteristics: first, as of the time indicated in the case; second, as of the time of the negotiations. This permits them to develop a point of comparison with the past, the likely reasons for direction of change in corporate or host country policies, and the likely pattern of evolution in the future. Having two snapshots permits them to engage in imaginative speculation on the reasons for change which constitutes a major learning process. Finally, by viewing the case situation in two time snapshots, students begin to realize the fact that the features of negotiations—basic processes and characteristics—remain relatively unchanged, and therefore, the skill they acquire in negotiating in the classroom will assist them some years hence when they might reasonably hope to engage in real life negotiations.

The stage of a course at which negotiation exercises should be used will vary by the nature and level of the course. At the undergraduate level at New York University, students are first exposed to the nature and importance of environmental factors and the manner in which functional skills are extended into an international business framework. Because of limited familiarity with the real world of international business, many of these concepts remain relatively abstract for the student. At this stage, one or two negotiation exercises are inserted. The student then thinks through the nature of a concept such as nationalism or national interest and begins to develop an understanding of its application in business situations. Thereafter, as the course progresses and new concepts are added and earlier concepts elaborated upon, the student can relate to given case situations in which he participated to grasp the essence of such concepts. At the graduate level the students are more mature, and in a metropolitan university such as New York University, a fair portion are practicing managers. Therefore, negotiation exercises are used relatively early in the course. Graduate level students with a practical orientation, begin to realize the practical usefulness of what they are exposed to in the classroom.

An additional advantage of conducting negotiations relatively early in the course is to encourage the development of a group feeling among the students. Of course, this assists in informal discussions among the group inside and outside of the classroom and enriches a student's overall educational process. This objective is particularly important for universities located in metropolitan areas with large enrollment of part-time students who seldom have the opportunity for developing such group relationships.

For the negotiations, the students are organized into teams representing different parties to a negotiation. Initially we had three teams representing the foreign company, the host government and the home government. However, sometimes the latter has been omitted or additional parties have been inserted depending on the characteristics of a given case. For example, for the WIC fertilizer negotiations this fall a consortium of Japanese companies was included competing with the American consortium. The Chrysler-Mitsubishi case, was also used this fall with a group representing the Japanese automotive industry included to show the important role of industry associations in Japan. In addition, a group representing Volkswagen of West Germany was included as a competitor with Chrysler for a joint venture with Mitsubishi. In this way, the students begin to think multinationally realizing that competition for American companies can arise from Western Europe in the case of Chrysler and from Japan in the case of the fertilizer manufacturing venture. It also points out that often host countries have the option of seeking resources from more than one source.

The home government presents a troublesome problem in the simulations just as it does in reality. It clearly has a part to play in relations between multinational firms and host governments but its specific presence in a case and particularly the physical presence at negotiations is often embarassing to one or both of the other parties. Since the prime objective in the negotiation is to recreate reality, it seems undesirable to leave the home government out of the picture entirely. Yet injecting it as a full fledged team comparable to the other two teams is not consistent with reality.

From a learning standpoint, it is highly desirable to have a team representing the U.S. Government in the form of the Agency for International Development or a U. S. Embassy overseas. Students playing the role of the U.S. Government have typically made comments that they were "frustrated" for several reasons. They realized that the U.S. Government could do very little in influencing the host government. Yet the American investors sought Embassy or AID representatives to exert pressure on the host government for a favorable response to a company's proposal. Or government representatives were placed under pressure from Washington because of representations made at that level by American corporations. Perhaps the most important learning experience for students playing the role of U.S. Government representatives has been the necessity to remain silent in the actual negotiations because they are between the devil and the deep blue sea, and to engage in informal explorations with the host government and the foreign investor.

The character of the negotiating teams is one of the very important elements in the success of the exercise. The teams may be expected to do substantial amount of study among themselves and this study process provides a sizable portion of the learning experience. The groups should therefore be of a size and nature which permits effective group study. We believe that the ideal group is somewhere in the range of six to ten students but obviously the size is substantially dependent upon the total class size and other elements of the school situation. It would appear, however, that the group should not be excessively large partly because this will limit the effectiveness of the small group study process and partly because there will be too limited opportunity for any individual to participate in the actual negotiation sessions. To avoid this problem where we have had large classes we have separated the students into major groups for different negotiation exercises to limit the negotiating teams to a maximum of 10 to 12 students which is clearly at the upper level of pedagogical desirability.

Particular attention should be placed on the composition of the group in terms of the various types of experiences and country backgrounds present in each group. At New York University, we have a good knowledge of a student's background from an information questionnaire he fills out the beginning of the course. Students with experience in the industry or the country in which the case is based are carefully distributed among the different teams. Foreign students especially from the country in which the case situation took place are also distributed.

For the execution of the negotiation it is essential that there be an allocation of individual roles within the teams. For example, the host government group will typically include a minister of finance, a minister of industry, etc. Each of these individuals will have a particular point of view and it is important that those individual points of view be brought out and made an explicit part of the negotiation process. The assignment of individual roles will also facilitate the preparation and small group study process in that it directs the study of literature, analysis of issues, etc., required. The actual assignment of roles may be done either by the instructor or by the groups. We have employed both processes. We incline at the moment to letting the students do their own assignment primarily because this increases the group motivation and benefits of group interaction. However, it does involve a certain inefficiency in the expenditure of time and direction of effort. If only a limited time is available for the exercise, it may be more desirable for the instructor to do the assigning.

The quality of leadership is the critical factor in the development of a team and its effectiveness in negotiations. Therefore, we have often played an important role in selecting as team leaders students who display qualities of leadership. When leaders are picked, an effort is made to maximize the learning process of the individual student. Thus, an American student working with an American company in the United States is assigned the role of senior host government minister, or a student from a foreign country, especially if his country is the one in which the case is based, is assigned the role of top corporate executive of the American company. The leaders learn more by swapping roles which are different from those they have or are likely to have in reality.

In some cases we have assigned students to prepare position papers before the negotiation session. In the paper the student is expected to state the strategy which he plans to follow in the negotiations. This has been done on an individual basis related to the individual role assigned to the student for the negotiation (e.g., finance minister of the Canadian Government). Such a paper could also be assigned on a group basis but that would require substantially more effort on the part of the group and the group performance will be more visible in the actual negotiation. The paper has been assigned in large part because of the difficulty of providing each individual with ample opportunity to develop his own concept of his role in the process. It also serves the incidental purpose of providing some evaluation of each individual's performance for grading purposes. To grade the performance in the actual negotiation is difficult in view of the group dynamics at work to which the individual should be subordinated.

It is both realistic and desirable that the opposing negotiating teams have some interactions prior to the formal negotiation sessions. These may be limited to having one or two spokesmen discuss the agenda for the negotiation sessions or they may even try out tentatively certain proposals on each other through informal "give and take". There is no limit to the amount of this preliminary negotiation which is useful. As a practical matter, however, the time allocated for the negotiations will probably restrict it to a moderate amount. A campus atmosphere is more amenable to such informal explorations than is true in a metropolitan environment.

For the most part our formal negotiation sessions have consisted of devoting a full class period (1¾ hrs.) to the complete negotiation of a case. These sessions have been quite effective. However we have had some variations on them which suggest that a number of alternatives may be both feasible and more desirable. The chief problem for major cases is that one class session is a very short time. Typically the students are just getting really warmed up to a subject and into some difficult questions when the time runs out. In light of this problem of which the students were well aware from a previous experience, we had one group on a volunteer basis devote six hours on a Saturday to extended discussion of a case. This experience was highly satisfactory for all concerned. We have also experimented with an arrangement in which half of one period is devoted to preliminary negotiation and then a full period to a final session. In the project which will be conducted in the spring of 1972 we will experiment with a series of negotiations to test the ultimate time limit which is productive for this purpose. The main point which would seem to emerge from our present experimentation is that the negotiation period must at least be long enough to allow the dynamics of interaction sensitivity and adjustments to come into play and that a single period is a minimum for this purpose.

The conduct of the negotiation session requires a certain degree of structuring for both reality and effectiveness. At the same time the structuring should be limited to provide maximum scope for individual student participation according to personal sensitivity, motivation, etc., since this is the essence of the learning process. The minimum overall requirements are a rough agenda and orderly conduct typically provided by control by the senior member of the host government or the corporation. The students are expected to conduct themselves with a reasonable respect for protocol and courtesy through various breakdowns in this process, which are to a degree realistic, provide useful learning experiences. For example, almost invariably a host government person will do or say something which results in a multinational firm executive or even the full team reacting in a way which is offensive to the national pride or culture of the hosts. There are likely to be some sharp counterreactions and the whole rapport of the negotiation may seem to be endangered. This will appear as a disruptive aberration in the negotiation but from many points of view it may be extremely valuable.

The negotiation may proceed continuously through the full period, but we have provided that each team may call for as many as three five minute recesses and generally at least 2 of these are employed. This of course is quite realistic as typically negotiations will extend over an extended period and there will be recesses and substantial gaps in time during which the teams can reevaluate their positions, and change their strategy and tactics. The recesses offer an opportunity for a shift in negotiation tactics. Members of opposing teams may try to work out informal understandings or attempt high pressure selling of an idea. U.S. Government representatives in particular use such recesses because they permit informal representations to foreign companies and to host government officials which they might not wish to do in open. Microphones may be placed at the table assigned to each particular team, and a review of the tapes subsequently reveals a fascinating account of the informal negotiation process which takes place.

Another useful device is for the instructor to inject changes in conditions and other variables into the negotiation, typically by sending messages to one of the teams or making announcements. This adds a vital element of reality which is hard to provide otherwise and it contributes to the dynamics of the negotiation. In a real negotiation the parties rarely are able to sit down at the table and work through to agreement without being subjected to substantial pressures from outside and from changes in conditions which force their negotiations to alter their course. The contributions from the instructor serve a purpose of creating some of these changes. For example, he may send instructions from the board of directors of the multinational firm which force the team to change its tactics. He may report that an opposition member of the legislature of the host country has made a speech which puts the negotiating government group under pressure to change their position or he may report that there has been a development in some other part of the economy which changes the assumptions on which the negotiations have been proceeding. From the point of view of the immediate dynamics of the negotiation, the instructor will try to time these messages to stimulate or redirect the discussion in a productive direction. For example, if the negotiators seem to be losing sight completely of an important factor he may inject a message on that point to redirect their discussion.

In practice it is very difficult to have more than four to five members of each team play a vocal part in the negotiation process. Where the teams are larger than this the other members of the team may, however, still benefit substantially from this phase of the exercise by sitting behind the vocal negotiators and contributing ideas to them and discussing tactics during the recesses. If the class is fairly large, however, there will still be a certain number of students who are audience to the negotiation process. As suggested above these students may have been assigned to direct participation in another negotiation exercise. However, they may also be brought in to a limited degree to benefit from the immediate exercise by giving them appraisal sheets on which to rate the negotiators and also by bringing them into a post-mortem discussion of the negotiation after it is completed.

We have devoted virtually the whole class session to negotiating to maximize benefits from what appears to be a fairly short period. However, we have always allowed ten to fifteen minutes at the end of the period for a post-mortem discussion which permits the students to observe and integrate their learning experience somewhat. Typically the negotiators, the "audience", and the instructor all make some observations appraising the performances. We have also made video tapes of the negotiations. These could be used in the post-mortem appraisal process. However, such a utilization requires a substantial amount of time and in the limited class periods available we have preferred to use that time for more actual discussion and other purposes. In the intensive project of the experimental group for next spring we expect to do more with the video tape appraisal.

A critical feature of negotiation is the difference between what you say and what is understood by the listeners. Several features have been inserted in the negotiation exercise to highlight this dimension. Often students come on a voluntary basis to review the tapes. Listening to the audio tape or viewing the video-tape upon conclusion of negotiations impresses upon the students the importance of effective communication. The typical reaction is "did I say that". Again, each team is asked to assign to one of its members the task of keeping notes of the meeting. These notes are typed and circulated to the entire class subsequent to negotiations.

More often than not, each rapporteur has a different understanding of what was said by his own group and/or the other groups. Of course, this feature highlights the critical importance of effective communication. We have also experimented with having the rapporteurs from the various teams meet after the negotiations to thrash out a common statement to which all sides would subscribe. Nine times out of ten, they are unable to emerge with a common statement which presents the respective statements and positions of the different groups into a unified document.

Preliminary Appraisal

From our present experimentation with the simulated international business negotiations we have arrived at a few preliminary conclusions.

The most obvious conclusion is that the exercises generate a high degree of student interest and consequent involvement and effort. After every negotiation some students have made remarks like, "this is the most exciting thing I have been involved in at the school so far". The expenditure of time and preparation for the negotiation is visibly far out of proportion with the preparation the student devote other class assignments. In informal polls in the class, the students have strongly endorsed the negotiation. All of this would indicate that from the student reception point of view and the generation of work and involvement the exercise is highly satisfactory.

From the point of view of performance, the accomplishments of the students are "satisfactorily imperfect". The point of that odd phrase is that they function sufficiently well as negotiators so that the negotiations proceed reasonably well but they show sufficient inadequacies in skill so that one can see that the potentials for learning are there. Furthermore these potentials are demonstrated in the increase in skill when we run a second negotiation with the same class.

Perhaps the most critical and interesting element is the ability of the students in the host government teams to integrate into their own behavior the point of view and even behaviorial characteristics of the host nationals. If this had not proved reasonably satisfactory, the whole process probably would be impossible. In fact we have been quite impressed with the ability of American MBA's to take on the coloring of Indian government bureaucrats in a chamelion manner. The process is not perfect but it is sufficient to provide the necessary reality against which the multinational firm executives can react and the latter seem to have no trouble in demonstrating from time to time typical American nationalism, bluff "lets be business like about this" attitudes and the like. The realities are, of course, enhanced if one happens to have a few foreign students in the group which we typically do at our school because we have a large foreign student population. However we are confident that, even where one has 100% American students, sufficient host national reality can be created.

The most important point of appraisal is the degree to which learning takes place in the negotiation exercises. On this we have very solid evidence as is so often true in complex learning processes. To a very large degree we are proceeding on faith and intuitive sense form talking with students, observing them during the evolution of the course, etc.

Future Development

There are possibilities for evolving the negotiation exercise into a more complex effort through involvement of groups outside of the university. We might establish working relationships with international divisions of commercial banks and students could be asked to actually negotiate with appropriate bank officers for loans for their projects. Similar arrangements could be made with the Agency for International Development for financing and risk guarantees, the International Finance Corporation for seeking venture capital and with other institutions which typically are involved in international business transactions. However, venturing in this direction while exciting and hopefully rewarding also entails a large expenditure of time for the instructor and the students. How much further complexity is added will therefore depend upon individual desires and local facilities.

While the possibilities of expanding the negotiation simulations into more sophisticated exercises are intriguing, it is well in closing this paper to stress that even in the simpler forms with which we started our work the negotiations were effective in their pedagogical goal. The sense of environmental reality and the dynamics of participation injecting the students into a moderately structured interaction of different international negotiating groups are the heart of the pedagogy.

FOOTNOTES

1. See John Fayerweather, Jean Boddewyn and Holger Engberg, *International Business Education, Curriculum Planning* (New York, Graduate School of Business Administration, New York University, 1966).

2. For Latin America, see A. Kapoor, "Business-Government Relations Become Respectable," *Columbia Journal of World Business*, July-August 1970. For detailed discussion of time devoted to government relations, see A. Kapoor and J. Boddewyn, *International Business Government Relations: A Study of U.S. Corporate Experience* (New York American Management Association, forthcoming).

3. For additional comments and discussion, see A. Kapoor, *International Business Negotiations: A Study in India* (New York University Press, 1970). pp. 3-18. See also Fred C. Ikle, *How Nations Negotiate* (New York, Frederick F. Praeger, 1967). Despite the importance of the subject of international business negotiations, the literature on it is very limited indeed. For reference to most of the literature in this field see Kapoor.

4. A. Kapoor, *International Business Negotiations* and John Fayerweather, *The Mercantile Bank Affair* (forthcoming). Condensed versions of these cases are available through the Intercollegiate Case Clearing House, Soldiers Field, Boston, Massachusetts, *Western Industrial Corporation* - ICH 14G15 and *The Mercantile Bank of Canada* - No. 9-371-678.

5. One case book, Richard D. Robinson, *Cases in International Business* (New York, Holt, Rinehart and Winston, Inc., 1962) has proved to be particularly effective for negotiation exercises because of the case situations it offers.

Background, Organization and Preliminary Results of Project LINK

Bert G. Hickman
Stanford University

Lawrence R. Klein.
University of Pennsylvania

Rudolf R. Rhomberg
International Monetary Fund

I. Introduction

Project LINK is a cooperative international research effort to integrate national and regional econometric models into a world system by linking their international sectors. This paper constitutes a description of the organization and long-range plans for the project together with a progress report on some results from the first year of operation.

Origin of Project LINK

The project was developed under the sponsorship of the Social Science Research Council. In 1968 the Council's Committee on Economic Stability concluded that the time had come for an international attempt to forge links between national econometric models. The feasibility of the proposal was examined at a planning conference held at Stanford University under the auspices of the committee on July 8-9, 1968.[1] The group decided that the time was indeed ripe for an attempt to establish the framework of a world model by integrating the research efforts of the various model building groups. The Committee on Economic Stability agreed to draft a research proposal and to recommend that the Council seek financial support for a realistic program.

19

The project got under way during the summer of 1969. In keeping with the cooperative international spirit of the entire enterprise, financial support has been forthcoming from several sources, with principal contributions from the International Monetary Fund and the National Science Foundation, and supplemental support from the United Nations Conference on Trade and Development, Japan Economic Research Center, the Bank of Japan, the Belgian National Science Foundation and other national bodies. The Social Science Research Council has responsibility for financial administration of the project.

Organization

Participants in the project presently include econometric model builders from North America, Western Europe, and the Orient.[2] Research is proceeding at each participating center, but provision is made for coordinating the efforts of the several centers at frequent intervals. The coordinating Center is located at the University of Pennsylvania, with Lawrence R. Klein as Project Coordinator. The Center serves as a repository for the associated models with complete data files and keeps participants informed about project research, meeting plans, and administrative affairs. Regional working teams in North America and Japan (under the Chairmanship of Rudolf Rhomberg) and in Western Europe (Chaired by R.J. Ball) meet once a year. An executive committee consisting of Bert G. Hickman (Chairman), R.A. Gordon, Klein and Rhomberg oversees the general course of the project from the vantage point of semiannual meetings. Finally, there is an annual working session of one or two weeks at which all participating research centers are represented. At each such session the work of the preceding year is reviewed and assimilated, and research plans are formulated on a cooperative basis for the coming year.[3]

Objectives

The basic aim of the project is to augment radically our factual knowledge of the nature and strength of the international economic relationships which bind individual countries into an effective world economy. Attention is being concentrated initially on developing a world trade system linking the national models, but capital flows will also be emphasized.

The project will contribute substantially to basic knowledge about the structure of international trade and the interrelationships between the various national economies and regions.

In the present state of knowledge an econometric model for a particular nation or region may explain imports endogenously, but must accept the volume of world trade as exogenous. Experience has shown that the inability to forecast accurately export demand is one of the major sources of error in forecasting domestic activity in many national models, particularly for economies heavily dependent of foreign trade. Moreover, in a large industrial country with a substantial share in world trade, a national model cannot now be used to estimate the feedback effect on its own exports stemming from the impact of a change in its import demand on activity levels abroad. Later in this paper we report on our initial efforts to provide a consistent forecast of world trade in 1970 incorporating the import forecasts from national and regional models, and on our plans for more ambitious solution procedures utilizing a structural model of the geographic distribution of world trade.

Development of a world trade model, linking the various national models, will lead to many important applications. These include the study of balance-of-payments adjustments, the international transmission of stabilizing and destabilizing forces, and the domestic and international tradeoffs between the various objectives of economic policy. The influence of international aid on the developing countries will be carefully studied as well. All these applications will be enhanced by the eventual integration of international capital flows into the system, although much will be learned at an earlier stage from the trade model alone.

The project involves complete coverage of world trade. The industrial countries are represented either by large-scale structural models developed at the various model-building centers or by rudimentary reduced form systems constructed at the Coordinating Center or the International Monetary Fund. The United Nations Conference on Trade and Development has responsibility for the construction of trade models for the less developed economies on a regional basis.

Although the principal thrust of Project LINK has been the development of trade linkages between national and regional models for the entire world economy, this is viewed as the first step toward an eventual treatment of all linkages, including financial flows. Meanwhile, two studies have begun of full scale balance-of-payments linkages on a bilateral basis. One of these concerns the Canadian and U.S. economies and is being undertaken by John F. Helliwell (University of British Columbia), Harold T. Shapiro (University of Michigan), Gordon R. Sparks (Queen's University), and Ian A. Stewart (Bank of Canada). Although independently conceived and financed, this study is highly complementary to Project LINK, and there is close liaison and cooperation between the two groups. A similar study of the bilateral linkages between the Japanese and U.S. economies has been started by Hidekazu Eguchi and Chikashi Moriguchi of the Project LINK group. These experimental studies of bilateral balance-of-payments relationships should point the way for the ambitious task of extending similar linkages on a multilateral basis.

Finally, we should note that Project LINK is helping to lay the basis for a standardized international data system and variable notation. Even the preparatory work of constructing value, quantity, and price series for each country's imports, classified according to a uniform system, is of substantial importance. This is a data base that does not yet exist although the basic constituents are available, and the project will serve economic research by providing a central, standardized collection of trade statistics ready for econometric analysis. A uniform system of variable notation is also being developed, which should greatly facilitate the comparison and analysis of national models.

Research is already well advanced at the Coordinating Center at the University of Pennsylvania ′to incorporate the national and regional models into a complete system for simultaneous solution of the world model. The computational problems are sizeable, but by no means unmanageable, and there is reason to expect that before many years have passed it will be feasible to access the data bank and national and world models on a time-sharing computer system from anywhere in the world.

II. Approaches to the Construction of Trade Models

National economies are linked to one another through the exchange of goods, services, and capital assets (including international reserve assets). Economic change in any country may, in principle, affect the flows of goods, services, and assets among all countries, as well as the prices at which they are exchanged. A full description of the entire interdependent system of the world economy, including all the adjustment mechanisms that are at work, is still beyond present capabilities of model construction and estimation. At the present stage of the project a number of simplifications are, therefore, introduced by regarding certain variables as exogenously determined. In particular, policies of governments and central banks, including exchange rate policies, are taken to be exogenously determined, even though they may at times be induced by developments in the balance of payments or the domestic economy. Moreover, capital movements will initially be considered exogenous, but it is hoped that this limitation of the model can be removed at a later stage of the project.[4]

Taking account of these limitations, the international model presently envisaged can be described as follows. The regions to be linked may be individual countries or groups of countries. A set of exogenous variables operating in the various regional economies determines developments in the domestic economies of each region to the extent that these developments are described in the various regional models, as well as the quantities and prices of merchandise exports and imports and the receipts and payments for internationally exchanged services. The current account balances of all regions determined in this manner together with exogenously determined capital movements yield, on the assumption of given exchange rate policies, the over-all balance of payments and the change in international reserves of each region of the model. The purpose of this section is to outline the manner in which that part of the model which determines the quantities and prices of internationally traded goods (the "trade model") could be specified.

The Ideal Trade Model

Although limitations of data and resources will make it necessary to start with highly simplified approaches, it may be best to begin this methodological discussion by setting forth the principal features of what might be considered an "ideal" trade model and to compare approaches that might be practical in the near future with these ideal standards.

For the sake of concreteness we may envisage a model of trade among some 30 regions (some of which are individual countries and others geographic areas). Total merchandise trade among these regions would be divided into a limited number of commodity classes; but regardless of whether as few as 4 or as many as 20 such commodity classes are distinguished, this division can never be fine enough to result in a set of homogeneous goods. The first strategic decision, therefore, concerns the question of whether it is more appropriate to approximate reality by treating the commodity classes distinguished in the model as if they were homogeneous goods or whether the exports recorded in a particular commodity class that are produced by different regions should be regarded as different goods.[5] The specification of the trade model is quite different in the two cases.

If the trade flows reported under a particular commodity class were considered to constitute trade in a homogeneous good for which, in the absence of transportation cost or other trade barriers, there could be only one price in the world market, the appropriate specification of the trade model would be as follows: for each region, there would be a demand schedule for each good indicating the dependence of quantities demanded on income, or on some other measure of economic activity in the region, and on the price of the good relative to prices of other goods. Similarly, for each region there would be a supply schedule for each good indicating the relation between quantities of the good supplied and the price of the good as well as other factors influencing the ability or willingness of residents of the region to supply the good in question. Summation of the demand and supply schedules for all regions would yield schedules of world demand for and world supply of each good; the intersection of these schedules would determine the price of the good and its global output and consumption. At this equilibrium price, every region is demanding either a larger or a smaller quantity of the good than it is itself supplying, and it is therefore either an importer or an exporter of the good in question. Its imports or exports would be measured by the difference between the quantities demanded and supplied at the world equilibrium price. In practical applications, this analysis would have to be modified in the traditional manner to allow for the existence of transportation costs, tariffs, or other trade barriers.

This model has a number of awkward features. First, it implies that every region will, in general, either import or export a particular good, but not both. In view of the fact that most countries both import and export commodities falling under each of several broad commodity classes (such as manufactures, raw materials, etc.), the model could be reinterpreted to mean that each region will be either a net importer or a net exporter of a particular good depending on whether its demand for the good exceeds or falls short of its domestic supply at the world price level. But this reinterpretation begs the question of how the gross trade flows, exports and imports, are actually determined. Second, in this model, prices for the same good in different regions can diverge only because of transportation costs and other trade barriers. Independent price movements in different regions would be confined to the sector of nontraded goods—an implication of the model that is at variance with observed price behavior in many commodity classes. Third, there is the practical difficulty that net imports or net exports in a particular commodity class are not only smaller than the corresponding gross trade flows but may be particularly small relative to domestic consumption and production. Estimates of net exports or net imports would have to based on the difference between separate estimates of total demand and supply, and relatively small errors in these estimates would cause large proportionate errors in the estimate of net trade.

The alternative approach is to regard commodities of a particular class produced in different regions as different goods. The justification for this procedure is that, when relatively broad classes of commodities are being considered, the commodity bundles reported under the particular class heading by various exporting regions may contain few, if any, goods that are identical as between regions and that these bundles would, in any case, differ in composition. Even if one were to go to a rather fine commodity classification containing such classes as coffee, cotton, or steel pipe, it would be found that qualitative differences among the products produced by various regions under one of these class headings are so large as to cause an effective separation of markets and the persistence of price differentials.

The trade model appropriate to this approach is somewhat more complex than that which could be constructed on the assumption that each commodity class constitutes a homogeneous good, regardless of the region of production.[6] We will refer to commodity classes as "goods" and to the output of a good produced in a particular region as a "product"; for instance, manufactures may be one of the goods distinguished in the model, while French manufactures, U.S. manufactures, etc., are products.[7] For every region there is a set of demand functions for the products of each region, including the home region. For n regions and m traded goods there are nm products and thus $n^2 m$ demand functions for traded products. In addition, there will be one or several demand functions in each region for the nontraded products of that region. These demand functions would depend on economic activity and various other nonprice factors, as well as on all prices in the system, i.e., the prices of all products entering into trade as well as the prices of nontraded products in the home country. For each region, there is a supply schedule for each product, so that there are nm supply schedules for traded products, as well as one or several additional supply schedules for nontraded products.[8] In other words, it is assumed that, while buyers differentiate between the products of different sellers, the sellers offer their products to all potential purchasers and do not discriminate between residents of different regions.[9]

The n regional demand functions for each of the nm products can be summed to obtain nm world demand schedules for these products. World demand for one of the products of region j and that region's supply of the product determine the quantity sold and its price. The world price level of any good is the weighted average of the prices of the corresponding regional products. It is to be noted that in this approach producers in the home region enter into competition with foreign producers in various other regions on an equal footing. The solution of the model determines at the same time the domestic sales of domestically produced products and the bilateral trade flows from each region to every other region (and thus each region's global exports and imports).

Traditional import demand functions are typically based on a hybrid approach. Imports are considered to be a product that is different from domestic output of similar commodities, so that there can be a differential of prices between imports and home production to which the demand for imports responds. At the same time, all foreign suppliers of the good in question are considered to produce a homogeneous product, so that it is not necessary to distinguish separate demand schedules for the exports of various foreign regions. In some models separate functions are estimated for imports originating in two or three different regions, say, in one or two principal trading partner countries and in the rest of the world. But even where this is done, foreign regions that are to be individually treated are typically selected on the basis of the size of their market shares in the importing region rather than by the criterion of the degree of product homogeneity.[10]

This discussion could best be summarized by pointing out (a) that, at any given level of practicable commodity disaggregation, the most general model is that which treats the outputs of a commodity produced in different regions as different economic goods (called "products"); (b) that the model underlying the traditional import demand function is a special case of the general model, in which, for every region and every commodity class, the elasticity of substitution between the products of any pair of *foreign* regions is assumed to be infinite; and (c) that the model used in the exposition of the theory of international trade is a still more special case of the general model, in which, for every commodity class, the elasticity of substitution between the products of any pair of regions is assumed to be infinite. It is tempting to argue in favor of using the most general model and permitting the parameter estimates, e.g., the size of the estimated elasticities of substitution, to determine whether or not one of the special cases applies. However, practical considerations of model construction and estimation must also be taken into account in choosing the model. We now turn to some of these considerations.

The main problem on the demand side of the model concerns the large number or prices that enter the demand functions for products. Clearly some simplifications must be introduced. Armington has shown that, under relatively weak assumptions, the competitive effects of changes in product prices (i.e., supply prices of various regions) on the demand for a given product can be separated from the effects of changes in the prices of goods (i.e., world price levels for various commodity classes) on the demand for a given good.[11] This means that a region's demand for a product—say, Italy's demand for U.K. machinery—can be expressed in two steps: (1) Italy's demand for machinery depends on Italy's income (total expenditure) and on the world price levels of machinery and other commodity classes; (2) Italy's demand for U.K. machinery depends on Italy's demand for machinery and on the ratios of U.K. export prices of machinery to those of each of the other countries that produce machinery (including Italy itself).

A further simplification can be achieved by making the assumptions that (a) elasticities of substitution in any market between products pertaining to one commodity class are constant and (b) that these elasticities are the same for all pairs of products competing in a particular market.[12] The demand for a product can then be expressed as a constant share of the demand for the good in question, multiplied by a single relative-price term.[13] This formulation leads directly to a market-shares approach of trade model construction: for each region, the demand for every good is estimated by a traditional demand function and the demand for each component product is a constant fraction of the demand for the good modified by a term depending on the ratio of the price of the product to the weighted average price of the good (i.e., of all products of that class).

It should be pointed out that the preceding discussion was confined to the demand side of the model. For instance, we were not referring to realized market shares of various supplying regions but merely to their shares in the *ex ante* demand of the purchasing region at given prices. If prices are assumed to clear the markets—and only under this assumption—*ex post* market shares will be equal to these *ex ante* shares at the equilibrium prices established in the solution of the model. To the extent that markets are not cleared through equilibrating price movements, the influence of nonprice factors affecting the utility of the product to the purchaser, such as delivery lags, will cause realized market shares to diverge from those that would be expected on the basis of actual (nonequilibrium) prices. Moreover, observed prices would in principle have to be corrected so as to reflect changes over time in the price equivalent of costs or benefits to the purchaser arising from the purchase of particular products, such as those related to tariff preferences, preferential credit terms, or the quality of service. Such corrections are necessary only if these costs or benefits, expressed as percentages of the observed prices, have changed during the period studied; otherwise they may simply be absorbed into the set of qualitative differences among products that cause the substitution elasticities between pairs of products to be less than infinite.

No great conceptual problems arise in the construction of the supply side of the trade model, although the problems of estimation of supply functions in each regional model may be formidable.

The supply function for each product should reflect the production possibilities that exist in the economy, i.e., the increase in supply of product A relative to product B if A's price rises relative to that of B, as well as the over-all elasticity of output of the economy with respect to the over-all price level. The supply, x_{ik}, of commodities of class k by region i could be expressed as:

$$(2.1) \quad x_{ik} = c_{ik} \, P_{i.1}^{\varepsilon_{i1}} \, P_{i.2}^{\varepsilon_{i2}} \cdots P_{i.k}^{\varepsilon_{ik}} \cdots P_{i.m}^{\varepsilon_{im}} \, S_{ik,1}^{\varepsilon_{i,m+1}} \cdots S_{ik,s}^{\varepsilon_{i,m+s}}$$

Where the variables $P_{i.h}$ are prices of the m products produced by region i (which are identical for all destinations, $P_{iqh}=P_{irh}$ for all purchasing regions q and r), $S_{ik,h}$ are any other supply influences operating in region i with respect to commodity class k, the constants e_{ih} are elasticities and c_{ik} is a constant term. The own-price elasticity of supply, e_{ik}, will ordinarily be positive and the cross-elasticities of supply will be negative. If region i's total output were completely inelastic with respect to the general price level, the sum of the own-price elasticity and the cross-elasticities of product k would most likely be zero, since a proportional rise in all prices would leave the output of product k, as well as the outputs of other products, unaffected. In the general case, however, the sum of these price elasticities may exceed zero by an amount that would reflect the extent to which unused capacity could permit general price increases to be associated with rising output in the economy as a whole.[14]

Two extensions of the supply model may be worth considering. First, the over-all elasticity of output with respect to the general price level, which is reflected in the excess of the supply elasticities in equation (2.1) above zero, should be made to depend on the cyclical situation of the economy. Second, by making assumptions corresponding to those used to simplify the demand side of the model it may be possible to express supply functions in terms of the over-all supply of products (i.e., all goods and services) in the economy and the ratio of the product price in question to the general price level, as well as any special supply factors operating only in the sector producing the product.

One question remains to be discussed under the heading of model construction. The model described in this subsection is based on the notion that the domestic economy of a region is treated just like any foreign region as far as the demand functions for products are concerned. National models would, therefore, have to be adapted so as to furnish demand functions for home products, or at any rate demand functions for goods regardless of origin, according to the commodity classification adopted for the trade model and corresponding demand functions for nontraded goods. National model builders may consider this requirement impractical. National models are constructed on Keynesian lines, and the Walrasian features of a trade model do not fit well into the traditional structure of a national model.

For these reasons it may be necessary, at least initially, to operate the trade model and the regional models linked by it in a less than fully integrated manner. Each regional model would contain, for every commodity class distinguished in the trade model, an import demand function and an export supply function. The import demand functions could be constructed on the lines that would be appropriate if there were only two regions, the home economy and the rest of the world. In addition to variables reflecting expenditure on the good in question (whether produced at home or abroad), they could thus, in principle, contain two price ratios: the price of the good relative to the price level of other goods and import prices relative to the prices of competing products at home. Since the effect of domestic capacity utilization on imports is not, then, indirectly covered through domestic supply equations, these effects may have to be introduced directly into the import functions, albeit at the cost of making somewhat of a hodgepodge of demand and supply factors.

The export supply functions could be estimated in the form of export price equations. Since exports are ordinarily only a small part of total domestic output, these equations would have to depend closely on domestic prices in general and on prices in the industries producing for export; in addition, they should of course contain the volume of exports as argument except where the price elasticity of supply of exports is infinite.

The trade model could then be solved in the manner described earlier for the entire model. The demand for regional products would be derived from the demands for imports through an analysis in terms of market shares modified by relative product (export) prices. Simultaneously, world demand for each regional product and its supply price equation determine product (export) prices and quantities for every region.

III. Consistency Approaches

The overriding constraint on the construction and solution of a multinational model system with international trade is that:

World exports = World imports

$$\text{or (3.1)} \quad \sum_{i=1}^{n} x_i = \sum_{i=1}^{n} m_i \quad , \quad n \text{ countries.}$$

In a more refined system with many types of traded goods and services, this constraint must hold for each commodity, summed over all countries.

Other constraints would be

World demand $\leq$ World supply, by commodity. Also, there should be some geographical balance. All supplies should not necessarily emanate from one or too few countries nor should demand be unreasonably concentrated in the solution to the system.

If each country formulates its economic plan or budget for an agreed upon unit of time, say, one year, there is no assurance that all the planned figures will be consistent, i.e. the world supplies of a commodity or service may not correspond with the world demand for that some commodity or service. By successive juggling of accounts, on a somewhat arbitrary or adhoc basis, a consistent solution could always be sought and probably found. International economic bodies presumably follow this procedure in negotiating consistent solutions in direct confrontation and negotiation.

Mini-LINK: The LINK project has, however, worked out a standard procedure for finding a consistent solution in which global imports equal global trade.

The first step in LINK procedures has been the construction of an algorithm for finding a level of world imports that is capable of being sustained by the internal activity levels of each country. In this calculation, price effects are first ignored.

Each country's model has the property that export volume (or the variables determining export volume) are exogenous variables that help to determine the dependent variables of each model. The i-th variable for the j-th country may, in principle, be expressed as a function of all the predetermined variables of j-th model.

$$(3.2) \qquad y_{ijt} = f_{ij} (z_{1jt}, \ldots, z_{mjt}, x_{jt}) \qquad \text{estimated reduced form}$$

$$(3.3) \qquad x_{jt} = g_j (T_{wt}) \qquad \text{export function}$$

The first set of equations are estimates of derived (restricted) reduced forms for the i-th variable in the j-th country. They are solved explicitly as functions of exports, which, in turn, are functions of world trade, in the first instance. If the system is linear, the reduced forms can be derived by direct calculation. If the system is nonlinear it will generally be possible to compute numerical values for y_{ijt} from given values of $z_{1jt}, \ldots, z_{mjt}, x_{jt}$. It will not in general be possible to write f_{ij} in closed mathematical form.

Each model builder has been asked to solve his country's model for y_{ijt} given best estimates of values for $z_{1jt}, \ldots, z_{mjt}, T_{wt}$. A range of possible values of T_{wt} is assigned to all LINK participants. They use these values of T_{wt}, together with a fixed set of all other predetermined variables. For each different input value of T_{wt} given the constancy of other input values and parameters a solution is obtained. In the first LINK exercise, the different country models were solved 4 times, once for each of different assigned values to T_{wt}. These assignments are made uniform for each country. In a 1969 LINK Model, the 4 values for T_{wt} in 1970 are \$200, \$225, \$250, \$275 billion (US). These solutions, for t=1970, will be written as

$$\overset{1}{y_{ij,70}}, \quad \overset{2}{y_{ij, 70}}, \quad \overset{3}{y_{ij,70}}, \quad \overset{4}{y_{ij,70}}$$

One of the y_{ijt} represents imports. This solution is

$$\overset{1}{m_{j,70}}, \quad \overset{2}{m_{j,70}}, \quad \overset{3}{m_{j,70}}, \quad \overset{4}{m_{j,70}}.$$

From each country's solution for $m_{j,70}$, we can form the world totals

$$\overset{1}{\underset{j}{\Sigma} m_{j,70}}, \quad \overset{2}{\underset{j}{\Sigma} m_{j,70}}, \quad \overset{3}{\underset{j}{\Sigma} m_{j,70}}, \quad \overset{4}{\underset{j}{\Sigma} m_{j,70}}.$$

Denote these by $\quad 1 \qquad 2 \qquad 3 \qquad 4$
$$m_{70}, \quad m_{70}, \quad m_{70}, \quad m_{70}.$$

The consistency we seek is $m_{70} = T_{w,\,70}$,

but we do not know that the solution when summed over all countries for any of the assumed levels of world trade will satisfy these restraints. In general they will not, but there is one solution that will, and we are trying to find that one. The solution is easy to depict graphically. (See Figure 1: Consistency Solutions) Along the 45° line, world imports equals world trade. If the values of $m_{70}^{(k)}$ are plotted for each corresponding level of $T_{w,\,70}^{(k)}$, we shall derive a curve as in Figure 1. This empirical curve is found by passing a (curved) line through the four computed pairs $[\,m_{70}^{(k)},T_{w,70}^{(k)}\,]$ The

Figure 1: Graph of the MINI-LINK Exercise

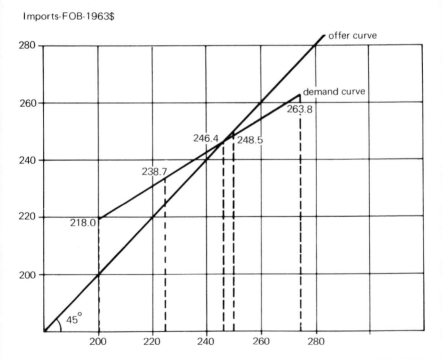

Imports-FOB-1963$

Exports-FOB-1963$

point of intersection between the world import curve and the 45°
line gives the consistency solution. This is a level of world trade that
is consistent with the activity levels and imports estimated from all
the models of different countries in the world. It is a level of world
trade that can be sustained by the activity levels in the countries of
the world.

The point $T_{W,70}$ determined by the intersection of the aggregate demand relationship and the 45° line is regarded as a stable
equilibrium point if displacement to the right generate decreases in
world trade and displacements to the left generate increases in
world trade. This interpretation is consistent with the idea of identifying the 45° line as an aggregate "offer" curve, while the other is
an aggregate demand curve.

The aggregate demand curve is the summation of model solutions
for

Belgium	Free University of Brussels (annual)
Canada	University of Toronto (annual)
France	LINK (preliminary, annual)
Germany	Bonn University (annual)
Italy	LINK (preliminary, annual)
Japan	Japan Economic Research Center (quarterly)
Netherlands	Central Planning Bureau (annual)
Sweden	National Institute of Economic Research (annual)
United Kingdom	London Graduate School of Business Studies (quarterly)
United States	Wharton Econometric Forecasting Associates (quarterly)

All these are indigenous country models, developed, maintained
and regularly used by resident proprietors with the exception of
France and Italy. Some simple interim (GNP) models have been
built by the LINK secretariat for the first consistency exercises. A
model being developed under the direction of G. Basevi, of the
University of Bologna will soon replace the temporary version for
Italy.

For the developing nations, simple one-equation models relating
imports directly to world trade have been estimated by UNCTAD.
These will be replaced eventually by more complete models for the
developing countries. The regional blocs are

Latin American Free Trade Association

Central American Common Market

Rest of Developing America

North Africa minus Libya

West Africa
Central Africa
East Africa
Libya and Middle East oil producers
UAR and Middle East non oil producers
South Asia
East Asia

A final bloc covering the rest of the developed countries is given only superficial treatment by assuming that their imports form a constant fraction of world trade. Equations for this bloc will eventually be prepared for the LINK system by the research staff of the IMF. In 1969, total world trade measured in 1963 US dollars came to $225.80 billion. This figure excludes the Socialist countries which will eventually be included in LINK. The import trade of the residual group (other developed countries) amounted to only $56.56 billion in 1963; so most of world trade is "explained" by fitted model relationships.

The projected value of world trade for 1970, found as the consistency or equilibrium solution of this system is $246.39 billion representing an increase of approximately 8 per cent.

Some problems of measurement: Each country is constructed in local currency units, with proper account taken of price deflation. The consistency solution among countries is carried out in uniform currency units—US dollars of 1963. Other units problems also arise. Some models have trade equations for goods and some for both goods and services. All results are in FOB prices, while imports are entered at CIF in most domestic social accounting systems. We therefore have three units conversions to take into account

1. Imports of goods must be "marked up" to goods and services in some cases.

2. Imports must be reduced from CIF to FOB valuations.

3. Imports must be converted from local currency units to 1963 US dollars, in billions.

Midi-LINK: The calculations demonstrated and carried out by the graphical method can also be done numerically. It was convenient and fast to have each model builder solve his own equation system four times for different fixed assumptions about world trade, all other exogenous inputs unchanged, in order to make up the graph in Figure 1. If all the models were programmed simultaneously for solution on one computer, as they now have been with two exceptions at the LINK secretariat (Wharton-EFA), solutions for

$m_{j,70}^{(1)}$ can be obtained.

The result is compared with $T_{w,70}^{(1)}$, and if $\sum_j m_{j,70}^{(1)} \neq T_{w,70}^{(1)}$, we form

$$(3.4) \qquad T_{w,70}^{(2)} = \sum_j m_{j,70}^{(1)}$$

and compute $m_{j,70}^{(2)}$ Comparison is again made, and the world trade input is changed if an inequality holds. This process is continued iteratively until an equilibrium solution is found. The quarterly models are solved for four successive periods and averaged to get annual values that can be used with the results from the annual models. In this case, a world trade exogenous input for a year must be arbitrarily subdivided into quarterly inputs.

Maxi-LINK, price consistency: If total world imports, estimated from the models and single-equation regressions, do not equal the world trade value assumed for a solution, an adjustment process is initiated, which involves changes in the level of world trade. Since most of the import functions depend, or ought to depend on prices, as well as activity levels, we should consider an extension of the adjustment process to cover both price and trade volume changes. Other endogenous variables in the import equations for separate countries will adjust as part of the solution of the models for the domestic economies. This would cover inventory adjustment and domestic price adjustment but would not cover import or world price adjustment since these variables are exogenous in each model. Yet if world supply and demand are not in consistency balance, trade prices would be expected to change in directions that would help to restore the balance.

The export prices of each country are endogenous variables. They depend on domestic costs and possibly demand pressures. The variation of export prices for a given country in relation to the world price index affects exports, which in turn affect imports. It should also be noted that export prices averaged over all countries make up the world price index.

$$(3.5) \qquad P_{w,70} = \sum_{i=1}^{n} \frac{x_{i,70}}{T_{w,70}} P_{xi,70}$$

where the weights are shares of world trade accounted for by the exports of each country. Also, import prices depend on the world price index. Each country's (exogenous) import price was assumed to change in the same proportion as the adjustment in the world index

$$(3.6) \quad P_{mi,70} = P_{mi,69} \, (1 + \Delta p_{w,70})$$

Two initial assumptions must be made, one for world trade volume and one for the world price index. From the first solution vector, there are values of export prices, export volume and import volume for each country, $P_{xi,70}^{(1)}$, $x_{i,70}^{(1)}$ and $m_{i,70}^{(1)}$ From these values a new world price index and a new world trade volume are jointly computed for input in the next solution round. Import prices for each country adjust proportionally to the change in $P_{w,70}$ from the zero-th to the first iteration.

A new solution is obtained using new import prices and $T_{w,70}^{(1)}$. These iterations cease when both $P_{w,70}^{(r)}$ and $T_{w,70}^{(r)}$ change by negligable amounts from their values on the (r-1)-st iteration.

The 1970 solution of the individual country models with simultaneous adjustment of world prices and world trade volume settles down to an equilibrium with a 3.59 percent rise in the world price index and an eight percent rise in the volume of world trade ($T_{w,70}$ = 244.70). This solution is not obtained graphically. It is based on numerical solutions (iteratively) of each country model, with the exceptions of Sweden and The Netherlands, where suitable solution programs have not yet been developed and the 4-points solutions for different assumed levels of world trade are used together with the full models of the other industrial economies that are given explicit treatment in midi-LINK.

IV. Structural Approaches

The approaches discussed in this section distinguish themselves from the consistency approaches discribed in Section III by the manner in which they deal with the determination of exports. Under the consistency approach, both import and export functions

36

of each regional model are retained; each trade flow is, therefore, estimated twice, once as imports of region i and once as exports of region j, and the consistency method consists of finding a solution at which world imports and world trade are equal. World trade is not necessarily equal to the sum of exports as separately estimated from the export equations of each model, however. In the approaches discussed first in this section, the export functions of each regional model are suppressed and exports calculated from estimates of regional imports and of exporters' shares in each regional market. At a later point, the regional export functions are reintroduced, but in a manner which includes the geographic distribution of trade as a determinant of each region's exports.

As was mentioned in Section II, a model in which the exports of each region are determined in this manner is, on certain simplifying assumptions, consistent with traditional demand analysis.

The Matrix of Market Shares

The matrix of market shares could be computed either from export data or from import data. In principle, the two alternative sources should give similar results provided that proper allowance is made for the difference in valuation (f.o.b. for exports, c.i.f. for imports). In practice, however, a comparison of bilateral trade flows as reported by importers and exporters shows substantial discrepancies and indicates the generally rather poor quality of trade data classified by origin and destination. The matrices discussed in this section are calculated from export data.

Let X_{ij} be exports from region i to region j, $X_{.j} (\equiv \sum_i X_{ij})$ exports of all regions to region j (i.e., the global imports of region j), $X_{i.} (\equiv \sum_j X_{ij})$ global exports of region i to all destinations, and $X_{..} (\equiv \sum_i \sum_j X_{ij})$ total world exports. The world trade matrix, with column sums in the lower margin and row sums in the right margin, is then:

	Market Region				
Exporting Region	X_{11}	X_{12}	....	X_{1n}	$X_{1.}$
	X_{21}	X_{22}	....	X_{2n}	$X_{2.}$
	....	....	....	....	
	X_{n1}	X_{n2}		X_{nm}	$X_{n.}$
	$X_{.1}$	$X_{.2}$		$X_{.n}$	$X_{..}$

The value of X_{ii} will be zero if region i is a single country but will contain the value of "intra-trade" if it consists of several countries.

The matrix of market shares, a_{ij}, is obtained by dividing each column by its column sum, $a_{ij}=X_{ij}/X_{.j}$. When the market shares are modified, for instance by letting them vary in correspondence to a relative price term, the modification must be carried out under the constraint: $\sum_i \alpha_{ij} = 1$.

Available data permit the calculation of the shares matrix for any regional grouping of countries, for instance, that given in Section III, only for trade in all commodities in value terms. In further work on the project, it is intended to distinguish four commodity classes (food, materials, fuels, and manufactures). For these classes, shares matrices will be constructed for a regional grouping consisting of the 25 developed countries listed under this heading in the trade tables of the IMF publication *International Financial Statistics (IFS)* and for the rest of the world derived as a residual. A substantial amount of data processing will be required to fill out the commodity trade matrices so as to cover the geographic regions of developing countries listed in Section III.

In this section we examine methods of using the IMF export shares matrix to incorporate information on the geographic distribution of trade into the world model solution, and to guarantee that total exports as well as total imports equal world trade.[15] We first examine the case in which exports and prices are exogenous to each country model, before turning to the complications introduced by endogenous price and export functions. Similarly, we describe the model in linear form before discussing the solution problems raised by nonlinearities.

In our first model, then, each of the n countries or regions is assumed to have a structural import demand function of the form

$$(4.1) \quad m_i = \sum_{p=1}^{r} a_{ip} y_{ip} + \sum_{q=1}^{s} b_{iq} z_{iq}, \qquad i=1, \ldots, n$$

where m_i is the c.i.f. value in U.S. dollars of imports into country i, and the y_{ip} and z_{iq} are respectively the r current endogenous and s predetermined variables in the model for country i.

In this notation, the y_{ip} and z_{iq} include all endogenous and predetermined variables in the complete country model, but many of the coefficients a_{ip} and b_{iq} will, of course, be zero. In particular, if z_{il} is the exogenous export variable, it may well be absent from the structural import function, and indeed, there may be no exogenous variables of any kind in the import function. As for the endogenous variables, they will probably include domestic activity variables and a ratio of import prices to domestic prices. For the present, it is assumed that both domestic and import prices are exogenous to each country model.

In the complete solution for each country model, the level of imports depends on the values of all the predetermined variables in the model, including exogenous exports. This dependency is shown explicitly by the reduced form equation for imports:

$$(4.2) \quad m_i = \beta_{i1} x_i + \sum_{q=2}^{s} \beta_{iq} z_{iq}, \qquad i=1, \ldots, n$$

where the β's are the reduced form impact multiplier coefficients and the export variable z_{il} has been renamed x_i for convenience. Thus for fixed values of the predetermined domestic variables, the reduced forms provide n equations relating the m_i and x_i to be included in the world trade model.

Although exports may be exogenous to a country model, they are endogenous to the trade model. Thus the export function for country i in the trade model is

$$(4.3) \quad x_i = \sum_{j=1}^{n} \delta_{ij} \alpha_{ij} m_j = \sum_{j=1}^{n} \alpha^*_{ij} m_j, \qquad i=1, \ldots, n$$

where A_{ij} is the market share of exporting country i to market j, α_{ij} is a multiplicative factor to convert the c.i.f. valuation of imports to the f.o.b. valuation of exports, and $\alpha* = \sum_{ij} \delta_{ij} \alpha_{ij}$ is the adjusted market share. The α_{ii} may either be zero, for single countries, or the share of intra-trade in the total trade of a region consisting of two or more countries.

The 2n import and export equations may be expressed in vector notation as

(4.4) $m = Bx + z$

(4.5) $x = A*m$,

where m and x are the import and export vectors, B is the diagonal matrix of the export coefficients β_{i1}, A* is the n x n matrix of adjusted market shares $\alpha*_{ij}$, and z is a vector of constants representing the weighted sums of the domestic predetermined variables $(= \sum_{q=2}^{s} \beta_{iq} z_{iq})$ for the n countries.

Upon substitution of (4.5) into (4.4) and employing the identity matrix I, the solution for imports is obtained as

(4.6) $m = (I - BA*)^{-1}z$, which in turn leads to

(4.7) $x = A*(I - BA*)^{-1}z$.

What are the properties of this solution? First, it satisfies the world trade constraint that the sum of all imports must equal the sum of all exports after adjustment for c.i.f./f.o.b. valuation differences. Thus, unlike the Mini-LINK and Midi-LINK consistency approaches with unconstrained country export functions, the shares approach guarantees that exports as well as imports will sum to the value of world trade.

Second, the solution also satisfies all the individual country models. For the given domestic predetermined variables for country i, consistency is guaranteed between the endogenous value of imports m_i and the exogenous value of exports x_i. Moreover, upon substitution of the x_i calculated from the trade model into the reduced form equations for the other endogenous variables, a complete set of country forecasts for domestic variables can be derived, and these will also be consistent with the calculated trade flows.

Third, in forecasting the exports of each country, the method makes systematic use of information about the geographic distribution of world trade, as summarized in the shares matrix, and it does this is a way which also yields consistent solutions for the individual country models.

Fourth, insofar as imports are concerned, the solution yields a supportable level of world trade, in the sense that each country can absorb the calculated imports, given the consistent solution values for income and other endogenous variables appearing in its structural import demand function.

Fifth, in the linear case, the complete solution can be reached in one step, given the reduced forms for the country models, the A* matrix, and the forecasts of domestic predetermined variables for all countries, provided that no policy or technical restraints are violated in the solution. If such constraints *are* violated—for example, if the forecasted trade balance is outside a tolerable range in one or more countries—the exogenous policy variables or parameters for those countries can be adjusted to yield new reduced form equations and a new world solution to be tested for consistency with the policy constraints.

The linear example has served to clarify the nature of the system. In view of the fact that most of the models for the industrialized countries included in Project LINK are nonlinear, however, an iterative technique is required to obtain the solution. Let $x^{(r)}$ and $m^{(r)}$ stand for the export and import vectors obtained on the rth iteration. Given a preliminary forecast for $x^{(1)}$ and similar forecasts for all other exogenous variables, each country model can be solved in turn to yield the first round import vector $m^{(1)}$. This vector can then be combined with the export share matrix to obtain a new export vector $x^{(2)}$, which can be used in turn to generate $m^{(2)}$ from the country models, and the process can be continued until the solution converges, assuming that a solution exists.

Notice that the procedure is flexible with respect to the complexity of the national and regional models to be linked through the trade model. It is quite possible to have different functional forms and explanatory variables in the structural import functions of the models. The degree of commodity disaggregation of the import functions may also differ among the country models, provided only that the import estimates are aggregated to a common level—in the present case, to total imports—before being combined with the share matrix to estimate a new x vector. Similarly, for some or all models the import demand functions can be specified in real terms, provided the import estimates are converted to current values before they are passed through the share matrix. Finally, a similar flexibility is permissible in the domestic sectors of the country models, which now vary greatly in complexity and probably will continue to do so for some time to come. All this is not to imply that diversity among the models is to be prized—on the contrary, the efforts of the LINK group are partly directed toward achieving greater comparability on important structural features—but only to stress that diversity does not preclude a consistent solution to the system.

Let us now take a step toward greater realism by relaxing the assumption that prices are exogenous. As noted earlier, the structural import demand functions for the individual country models will usually include as a variable the ratio of import to domestic prices. The domestic price level will be determined endogenously in most country models. Import prices may reasonably be regarded as exogenous to the country models, but they cannot be held constant in the complete systems solutions, since the import price index facing a given country is a weighted average of the (domestically determined) export price levels of other countries.

To handle the problem of endogenous prices, we must work with the reduced form equations for export prices as well as imports. The reduced form equations for imports will now be modified as follows to state explicitly the presence of the exogenous import price index:

$$(4.8) \quad m_i = \beta_{i1} x_i + \beta_{i2} P_i^m + \sum_{q=3}^{s} \beta_{iq} z_{iq}, \quad i=1, \ldots, n,$$

where P_i^m is the import price index facing country i and the other variables are as before. There will be a similar set of reduced form equations for the endogenous export price variables:

$$(4.9) \quad P_i = \gamma_{i1} x_i + \gamma_{i2} P_i^m + \sum_{q=3}^{s} \gamma_{iq} z_{iq}, \quad i=1, \ldots, n$$

where p_i is the export price level and the y_{iq} are the reduced form coefficients for the price equations.[16]

The P_i^m are defined as weighted averages of the export price levels which depend on domestic prices and other variables of the non-i countries:

$$(4.10) \quad P_i^m = \sum_{\substack{j=1 \\ i \neq j}}^{n} \alpha_{ij}' P_j, \quad i = 1, \ldots, n$$

where the α_{ij} are the shares of the non-i countries in the ith country's imports—i.e., the elements of the ith column vector of the export shares matrix. The α_{ii} are automatically equal to zero for single countries, but they should also be set equal to zero for multi-country regions when applying equation (4.10). Equation (4.10) is a generalization of the simple equations used in (3.6).

The model is completed with the export functions (4.3) as before. Thus in vector notation, the complete trade system consists of the following equations:

(4.11) $\quad m = B_1 x + B_2 P^m + z'$

(4.12) $\quad P = \Gamma_1 x + \Gamma_2 P^m + z''$

(4.13) $\quad P^m = A' P$

(4.14) $\quad x = A^* m$

where m, x, P, and P^m are the vectors of imports, exports, export prices and import prices, B_1 and B_2 are diagonal matrices of the β_{i1} and β_{i2} coefficients, Γ_1 and Γ_2 are diagonal matrices of the γ_{i1} and γ_{i2} coefficients, z is the vector of weighted sums of domestic predetermined variables in the import equations, z'' is the corresponding vector for the export price equations, A' is the transpose of the export share matrix A, and A^* is the adjusted share matrix as before.

The four equations (4.11) - (4.14) are sufficient to determine the unknown vectors m, x, P, and P^m, although the algebraic solutions are cumbersome and will not be reproduced here. In actual applications with non-linear country models, it is necessary to use an iterative procedure in any event. This procedure consists basically of specifying initial x and P^m vectors arbitrarily, using those vectors in the country models to solve for first-round m and P vectors, using the latter inturn in combination with the A^* and A' matrices to calculate new x and P^m vectors to be used in a new round of solutions to the country models, and so forth until the solution converges.

The new system represents a substantial advance over the first one, since it allows for the endogenous determination of domestic and import prices as part of the global solution. In actual applications with commodity detail, the number of price indexes and trade flows to be determined will be larger, and shares matrices by commodity classification will be necessary for full implementation of the method, but the principle remains unchanged.

To this point it has been assumed that exports are exogenous to all country models. National models frequently explain exports endogenously, however, as functions of an exogenous world trade or external demand variable, a relative price variable that is partly endogenous, an endogenous pressure of demand variable, and so forth. Is it possible to develop an approach that would treat exports as well as imports endogenously in both the national models and the trade models? Let us first see what such a construction would look like in the case where all country models were linear and prices were exogenous.

The structural import and export functions for country (i) could take the following forms:

$$(4.15) \qquad m_i = \sum_{p=1}^{r} a_{ip}\, y_{ip} + \sum_{q=1}^{s} b_{iq}\, z_{iq}, \qquad i=1,\ \ldots,\ n$$

$$(4.16) \qquad x_i = \sum_{p=1}^{r} g_{ip}\, y_{ip} + h_i \sum_{\substack{j=1 \\ i \neq j}}^{n} \alpha^{\star}_{ij}\, m_j + \sum_{q=2}^{s} h_{iq}\, z_{iq}$$

$$i=1,\ \ldots,\ n$$

The import function is similar to the one used in the first model with prices exogenous. As usual, the y_{ip} denote current endogenous variables and the z_{iq} denote predetermined variables. Many coefficients will be zero in the import function. In the export function, the exogenous external demand variable z_{i1} is shown separately in terms of its definition as a weighted average of the imports of all non-i countries or regions, with weights from the adjusted export shares matrix representing the shares of country i in the various j markets.

The corresponding reduced form equations are as follows:

$$(4.17) \quad m_i = \beta_{i1} \sum_{\substack{j=1 \\ i \neq j}}^{n} \alpha^{\star}_{ij}\, m_j + \sum_{q=2}^{s} \beta_{iq}\, z_{iq}, \qquad i=1,\ \ldots,\ n$$

$$(4.18) \quad x_i = \eta_{i1} \sum_{\substack{j=1 \\ i \neq j}}^{n} \alpha^*_{ij} \, m_j + \sum_{q=2}^{s} \eta_{iq} z_{iq} \; ; \quad i=1, \ldots, n$$

Imports and exports of country i depend on the external demand variable plus domestic predetermined variables in each national model.

The 2n reduced form import and export equations in vector notation are

(4.19) $m = B A^* m + z'$

(4.20) $x = H A^* m + z''$,

where B and H are diagonal matrices respectively of the β_{i1} and η_{i1} coefficients, z' and z'' are vectors of the weighted sums of domestic predetermined variables in the import and export equations, and the other symbols are as defined before. The solution of

(4.19) and (4.20) is as follows:

(4.21) $m = (I - B A^*)^{-1} z'$

(4.22) $x = H A^* (I - B A^*)^{-1} z' + z''$

Thus, the system may easily be solved in the linear case even with exports endogenous in the country models.

(If exports were exogenous in some country models, η_{i1} would be set equal to one and $(\eta_{i2}, \ldots, \eta_{is})$ to zero so that $x_i = \sum_{\substack{j=1 \\ i \neq j}}^{n} \alpha^*_{ij} \, m_j$ for those countries, just as before.)

The strength of this formulation is that it allows the observed historical export share of a given country to modified by endogenous internal developments. The collateral weakness is that the condition that $\Sigma x_i = \Sigma m_i$ after adjustment for valuation differences, is no longer automatically satisfied. One way in which the condition could be enforced if it were violated in the initial solution, would be to vary the domestic exogenous variables. This would be natural in a simulation or forecasting context. (Over the sample period, exogenous variables are given and prices or other market variables would be assumed to adjust so as to enforce balance between total exports and imports.) The procedure of adjusting the exogenous variables or parameters has some undesirable features, however, in that conceivably many different configurations of exogenous variables could satisfy the trade constraint, so that a given solution would be arbitrary, and furthermore, perhaps difficult to discover experimentally unless rules could be developed to guide the policy iterations.

Another approach is possible, however, in which a consistent solution may be found without adjusting the domestic predetermined variables. After solving (4.21) and (4.22), if $\Sigma x_i \neq \Sigma m_i$, the trade matrix itself can be altered to reflect the modifications of the predetermined export shares by endogenous internal developments in the exporting countries, thus allowing market forces to affect the necessary adjustments. The key assumption is that such departures from the predetermined export share of country i in world trade as are occasioned by internal domestic forces, affect all the export markets of country i in the same proportion. The new matrix of export shares can then be derived from the original matrix by a simple correction, as follows:

Let x_{ij} be the elements of the original n x n matrix of export flows. Then $\sum_j x_{ij}$ is total exports of country i, and $\sum_i x_{ij}$ is total imports of country j.

The original export share of country i in market j is:

$$(4.23) \quad \alpha_{ij} = \frac{x_{ij}}{\sum\limits_i x_{ij}}$$

Now let the new matrix of export flows be defined as follows:

$$(4.24) \quad \hat{x}_{ij} = \frac{\sum\limits_j \hat{x}_{ij}}{\sum\limits_j x_{ij}} \cdot x_{ij} ,$$

where $\sum\limits_j \hat{x}_{ij}$ is the estimate of total exports of country i obtained in the first round solution of equations (4.21) and (4.22). For notational convenience, set $b_i = \sum\limits_j \hat{x}_{ij} / \sum\limits_j x_{ij}$, where b_i is the correction factor for the ith row of the matrix of export flows. The elements of the corrected matrix of export shares are then obtained as follows:

$$\hat{\alpha}_{ij} = \frac{\hat{x}_{ij}}{\sum\limits_{i} \hat{x}_{ij}}$$

$$= \frac{b_i \, x_{ij}}{\sum\limits_{i} b_i \, x_{ij}}$$

$$= \frac{b_i \, \alpha_{ij} \sum\limits_{i} x_{ij}}{\sum\limits_{i} b_i \, \alpha_{ij} \sum\limits_{i} x_{ij}} \quad , \quad \text{or}$$

$$(4.25) \quad \hat{\alpha}_{ij} = \frac{b_i \, \alpha_{ij}}{\sum\limits_{i} b_i \, \alpha_{ij}}$$

Once the new α_{ij} are obtained, adjustments for c.i.f./f.o.b. valuation may be applied to derive the new matrix A^*. Upon substituting A^* in equations (4.21) and (4.22) new solution vectors for m and x are derived, and these may be tested to see if $\Sigma x_i = \Sigma m_i$. If not, the shares matrix can be adjusted once more and another iteration performed, and this process can be continued until satisfactory convergence is obtained, providing a solution meeting all constraints does exist and the process is indeed convergent.

Once again, the difficulties of solution are compounded in the realistic case of nonlinear country models. A feasible approach might begin by specifying an initial m vector, say $m^{(o)}$, to provide the weighted external demand variables to solve the country models for the $m^{(1)}$ and $x^{(1)}$ vectors of the first iteration. A consistent solution on the first iteration would require that $m^{(1)} = m^{(0)}$ and also that $\Sigma x_i^{(1)} = \Sigma m_i^{(1)}$

That is to say, not only would the endogenous export total have to equal the endogenous import total, but the total and composition of endogenous imports would have to equal the total and composition of imports used to compute the external demand variables for the country models.[17] If one or both conditions were violated on the initial round, further iterations would be needed.

Some experimentation would probably be necessary to develop an efficient solution algorithm for the model. The solution to the nonlinear equivalent of equation (4.21) could be sought by using the solution vector $m^{(r-1)}$ from the previous round to compute the external demand variables for the next round of country model solutions. The success of the Mini and Midi-LINK experiments gives reason to hope that this algorithm would be convergent, although success is not assured. In this more complicated case where not only $\Sigma\ m_i^r = \Sigma^{r-1} m_i$ is required, but also the element-by-element equivalence of m^r and m^{r-1}. Even assuming convergence so that $m^r = m^{r-1}$, however, it need not follow that $\Sigma\ x^r = \Sigma\ m^r$. If that constraint were violated, one of the foregoing methods would have to be used to provide a new $m^{(o)}$ vector upon which to iterate, and so on.

Having considered models in which either prices or exports are endogenous to the individual countries, it is natural to ask whether both variables can be treated endogenously in the same system. In particular, suppose exports as well as imports depend on an endogenous domestic price index and an exogenous index of foreign prices. The import price index P^m was formulated earlier as equation (4.10). An index of prices competitive to the exports of country i may be defined as follows:

$$(4.26) \quad P_i^x = \sum_{\substack{j=1 \\ i \neq j}}^{n} \lambda_{ij}\ P_j\ , \qquad i = 1,\ \ldots,\ n,$$

where P_j is the domestic price level of country j and where λ_{ij} are defined as:

$$(4.27) \quad \lambda_{ij} = \frac{x_{ij}}{\sum_j x_{ij}}$$

Thus the non-i price levels are weighted by the shares

of the non-i countries in the total exports of country i.

The λ_{ij} are computed from the same export flow matrix

48

as the α_{ij}, with each x_{ij} divided by the correponding row sum rather than the column sum used for the α_{ij}.

In the structural model for country i, the p^m variable will enter the import demand function exogenously, whereas P^x will be an exogenous variable in the export function. Thus the reduced form equations in the linear case will be as follows:

$$(4.28) \quad m_i \quad \beta_{i1} \sum_{\substack{j=i \\ i \neq j}}^{n} \alpha^*_{ij} \quad m_j + \beta_{i2} \, P^m_i + \beta_{i3} \, P^x_i + \sum_{q=4}^{s} \beta_{iq} \, z_{iq}$$

$$(4.29) \quad x_i = \pi_{i1} \sum_{\substack{j=1 \\ i \neq j}}^{n} \alpha^*_{ij} \quad m_j + \eta_{i2} \, P^m_i + \eta_{i3} \, P^x_i + \sum_{q=4}^{s} \eta_{iq} \, z_{iq}$$

$$(4.30) \quad P_i = \gamma_{i1} \sum_{\substack{j=1 \\ i \neq j}}^{n} \alpha^*_{ij} \quad m_j + \gamma_{i2} \, P^m_i + \gamma_{i3} \, P^x_i + \sum_{q=4}^{n} \gamma_{iq} \, z_{iq}$$

the model is completed by the definitional equation (4.10) and (4.26) for P^m and P^x respectively. The complete trade system in vector notation is:

$$(4.31) \quad m = B_1 \, A^* \, m + B_2 \, P^m + B_3 \, P^x + z'$$

$$(4.32) \quad x = H_1 \, A^* \, m + H_2 \, P^m + H_3 \, P^x + z''$$

$$(4.33) \quad P = \Gamma_1 \, A^* \, m + \Gamma_2 \, P^m + \Gamma_3 \, P^x + z'''$$

$$(4.34) \quad P^m = A' \, P$$

$$(4.35) \quad P^x = \Lambda \, P$$

where B_1, B_2 and B_3 are diagonal matrices of the β_{i1}, β_{i2} and β_{i3} coefficients and similar definitions hold for the H_i and Γ_i matrices; z', z'' and z''' are vectors of the weighted sums of domestic predetermined variables in respectively the import, export and

49

domestic price equations, A' is the transpose of the A matrix, and Λ is the matrix of the λ_{ij}.

The model can be solved by substitution of (4.34) and (4.35) into (4.31) and (4.33) to yield two equations to determine m and P. Substitution of P in (4.34) and (4.35) will yield P^m and P^x, and finally, (4.32) can be used to determine x from m, P^m and P^x. As in the earlier model with exports endogenous, however, this solution would not force $\Sigma x_i = \Sigma m_i$, which would be satisfied only by accident. If the condition were not satisfied, it would be necessary to use one of the methods outlined in the previous model to seek a consistent solution. If the method of adjusting the export shares matrix were followed, A* and A' would change from iteration to iteration, but the Λ matrix would not. Finally, in the nonlinear case, it would be necessary (1) to use iterative methods to find vectors for m, x, P, P^m and P^x that were consistent with the country model solutions and the definitional equations for P^m and P^x for given export shares matrices, (2) to adjust the A* and A' matrices if the constraint $\Sigma x_i = \Sigma m_i$ were violated, (3) to iterate to a new solution for m, x, P, P^m and P^x, based on A* and A', (4) again to test whether $\Sigma x_i = \Sigma m_i$, and if not, (5) to continue the iterative procedure until a consistent solution were discovered.

This last model with endogenous prices, imports and exports is the most complete of those employing the share matrix. Before attempting an empirical implementation, however, it would be wise to work with the simple formulations, just in order to gain experience with regard to solution algorithms and the properties of systems of differing degrees of endogenity and hence, complexity. The complete system solution when successfully evaluated will be called Maxi-LINK.

Endogenous Market Shares

Instead of the procedure of using market share parameters to modify export equations, the matrix of market shares itself could be considered endogenous in the model. In accordance with the simplifying assumptions mentioned in Section II, and on the further assumption that prices adjust flexibly so as to clear markets, the shares are directly related to the ratios of export prices of the supplying regions to the weighted average of the export prices of all regions.

Regression equations estimating the dependence of market shares on relative export prices in the trade of major industrial countries in manufactures indicated that the influence· of relative prices on shares is statistically significant but that the proportion of the total variation in shares explained by price variation is relatively small, especially in the short run.[18] It may be desirable, therefore, to introduce additional variables for relative capacity utilization and perhaps other supply determinants into the equations explaining market shares.

The computations for solving the system with endogenous market shares are obviously cumbersome, but the method is no more complex than those proposed above. Starting from a trial solution with initial estimates of imports, export prices, degrees of capacity utilization, and market shares, solutions would be iterated by using the solution vector of exports from the last iteration in the new solution for each region's imports, export prices, and capacity utilization; from the last two of these vectors the new matrix of market shares could be calculated and used for deriving a new solution vector for exports.

Although it is desirable to "explain" shares endogenously as explicit functions of pertinent economic variables it is possible to make some iteration calculations of a purely statistical nature that recognize the non-constancy of elements in the share matrix. The equations for computing exports, replacing specific export functions are:

$X = AM$ or

$$
\begin{pmatrix} x_{1.} \\ x_{2.} \\ \cdot \\ \cdot \\ \cdot \\ x_{n.} \end{pmatrix} = \begin{pmatrix} a_{11} & a_{12} & \cdot & \cdot & \cdot & a_{1n} \\ a_{21} & a_{22} & & & & a_{2n} \\ \cdot & \cdot & & & & \cdot \\ \cdot & \cdot & & & & \cdot \\ \cdot & \cdot & & & & \cdot \\ a_{n1} & a_{n2} & \cdot & \cdot & \cdot & a_{nn} \end{pmatrix} \begin{pmatrix} x_{1} \\ x_{2} \\ \cdot \\ \cdot \\ \cdot \\ x_{.n} \end{pmatrix}
$$

Using the observed values of the import vector for period t, M_t, and using a constant A - matrix such as that for base period O, we can obtain computed values of the export vector

$$\hat{X}_t = A_o M_t$$

If the shares matrix actually were constant, we would find

$$\hat{X}_t = X_t$$

but in fact there will be discrepancies because the matrix does change. Instead of "explaining" the discrepancies, it is possible to make purely statistical corrections of the form

$$(X_{i.})_t = \alpha_{i0} + \alpha_{i1} (\hat{X}_{i.})_t + \alpha_{i2}(X_{i.} - \hat{X}_{i.})_{t-1} + \alpha_{13} t$$

$$i=1, 2, \ldots, n.$$

These trend - autoregressive correction equations correct drifts in the computed export values, but the modification of the strict calculation from the shares matrix prevents an automatic realization of the consistency condition

$$\sum_{i=1}^{n} X_{i.} = \sum_{j=1}^{n} X_{.j} = World\ Trade$$

In a projection of world trade for 1970, extending the results in section III by using a share matrix for the export calculation with the addition of trend-autoregressive correction equations, the consistency condition was not far off

World imports = $247.11 billion (1963 prices),
World exports = +250.55 billion (1963 prices).

In this calculation a 1968 matrix was used, and the correction equations used this matrix together with import-export vectors over the sample period, 1950-1969.

If trade matrices were available in constant prices (1963 dollars), this statistical approach may have proved to be even more satisfactory.

V. Further Problems

Price solutions and a price adjustment process have already explained in sections III and IV. It is now in order to give somewhat more detailed attention to types of prices, especially those of traded goods by commodity classification. The versions of LINK that have already been worked out in practice or in principle have dealt with total imports and total exports as single categories. One of the first extensions will be to carry through the calculations for a uniform set of import classifications

SITC	Description
0,1	food and beverages
2,4	materials
3	fuel

The individual import functions, even more than aggregate functions, will depend on relative prices—specific relative prices comparing imported and domestic goods by the indicated service and commodity lines.

It will be necessary to have share matrices and related price equations for each grouping. For the non-manufactured goods, world prices will be related to the total world supply position including carry over stocks as well as current trade flows. In basic commodities, there will be a world price, determined by conditions of world supply and demand; prices charged to importing countries, which will be direct functions of the world price; and prices received by exporting countries, which will also depend directly on world price. All these relationships need to be specified, estimated, and programmed into Maxi-LINK.

Once the complete system is built, there are a number of policy issues that can be studied with the system. At present, attention has been focused on obtaining solutions and using them as forecasts of broad indexes—total world trade and the world trade deflator. The policies that can ultimately be studied with the model are

(i) Changes in exchange rates. In the conversion from results of trade equations in national models expressed in local currency to results in 1963 U.S. dollars an exchange rate is used for each country. In sample period solutions and in extrapolations actual official exchange rates prevailing are used. These can be changed to represent shifts in trade policy, and different solutions will be obtained for comparison with the "control" solution, in which official rates are used.

(ii) Changes in f.o.b./c.i.f. ratios. Shipping costs and tariff policies are largely responsible for this ratio's being significantly less than unity. Policy solutions with changed f.o.b./c.i.f. ratios can be obtained for comparison with the "Control" solution.

(iii) Unusual trade shipments. Soviet-Chinese grain purchases or similar large transactions that would come about in the world economy as a result of major natural events (Crop failure, e.g.) can be superimposed on the system as disturbance shifts of export or import equations. Comparison of world LINK solutions with and without the equation shifts will show the effects of natural events.

(iv) Transmission simulations. Movements in the industrial economies, say business cycle movements, that affect imports significantly will have effects on the primary producing countries that can be traced through LINK model solutions.

FOOTNOTES

1. The participants in the meeting included R.A. Gordon, Bert G. Hickman, Lawrence R. Klein, and Rudolf R. Rhomberg—representing the Committee on Economic Stability—and R. J. Ball, London Graduate School of Business Studies; Petrus J. Verdoorn, Netherlands Central Planning Bureau; Jean Waelbroeck, Free University of Brussels; and Tsunehiko Watanabe, Kyoto University.

2. Research centers were supported during 1969-1970 at the following places: University of Pennsylvania, USA (and central secretariat); Stanford University, USA; University of Toronto, Canada; Kyoto University, Japan; London Graduate School of Business Studies, UK; Central Planning Bureau, Netherlands; Free University of Brussels, Belgium; Bonn University, West Germany. In addition, LINK research was carried out without project financial support in the following places: International Monetary Fund; United Nations (UNCTAD); Economic Research Institute, Stockholm, Sweden; Louvain, Belgium (Italian model research); Bank of Japan; Bank of Canada. *Items*, SSRC, Vol. 34, December 1970.

3. See *Items*, SSRC, Vol. 33, December, 1969 for a list of participants and papers at the world session held in Hakone, Japan (September 1969) and London, England (September 1970).

4. As was mentioned, a project conducted by John Helliwell and others (op. cit.) aims at a full linkage across the entire balance of payments between Canada and the United States. A similar project is also being carried out by researchers at the Bank of Japan with respect to linkage of models of Japan and the United States (see Moriguchi and Eguchi, op. cit.).

5. See, e.g., E.E. Leamer and R.M. Stern, *Quantitative International Economics* (Boston, Allyn and Bacon, 1970), pp. 11-12.

6. Such a trade model has been developed by Paul S. Armington. See his "A Theory of Demand for Products Distinguished by Place of Production," IMF *Staff Papers*, Vol. XVI, No. 1 (March 1969) and "The Geographic Pattern of Trade and the Effects of Price Changes," IMF *Staff Papers*, Vol. XVI, No. 2 (July 1969), in which an analysis of the demand side of such a model is developed, and his "A Many-Country Model of Equilibrating Adjustments in Prices and Spending," Appendix to "Possible Approaches to a Model of World Trade and Payments," by R.R. Rhomberg, IMF *Staff Papers*, Vol. XVII, No. 1 (March 1970), where the complete model is outlined.

7. This is the terminology used by Armington (see references in the preceding footnote).

8. Thee specification of supply schedules imples that products are assumed to be produced under competitive conditions. Monopoly elements could be introduced, where appropriate, by substituting for these supply schedules the familiar analytical apparatus of monopoly pricing.

9. This assumption—namely, that discriminating monopoly is absent—may not be entirely realistic. However, there are generally no data on differences in prices on exports going to different destinations. The simplifying assumption in the text is therefore introduced even at the stage of discussing the "ideal" model and will undoubtedly have to be retained in any subsequent application.

10. There are exceptions to this. Where total merchandise imports from industrial and primary-producing countries are separately estimated, a crude separation of exporting regions by product homogeneity is in fact achieved (manufactures vs. primary products).

11. Armington, "A Theory of Demand . . .," loc. cit. The assumptions mentioned in the text are (1) that buyers' preferences for products in a particular commodity class are independent of their purchases of products pertaining to another commodity class and (2) that the distribution of the demand for a good over the component products varies only with the relative prices of those products.

12. See Armington, "A Theory of Demand . . .," loc. cit., p. 167. The assumption under (b) in the text is not as easily accepted as the other simplifying assumptions so far introduced. It might be more plausible to consider that the elasticity of substitution between two particular products is the same in all markets than to make the assumption stated in the text. For two countries that mainly export coffee the elasticity of substitution in the commodity class "food" will tend to be high in all markets, and for a coffee-producing country and a wheat-producing country this elasticity of substitution will tend to be low in all markets.

13. The demand, X_{ijk}, in region j for that part of commodity k which is produced in region i would be:

$$X_{ijk} = b_{ijk}^{\sigma_{jk}} \, X_{.jk} \, (P_{ijk}/P_{.jk})^{-\sigma_{jk}},$$

where $X_{.jk}$ is the demand in region j for commodity k as a whole $(X_{.jk} = \sum_r X_{ijk})$, P_{ijk} is the price at which commodity k is sold by region i to region j (and presumably to any other region as well), $P_{.jk}$ is the weighted average price of commodity k in region j, σ_{jk} is the elasticity of substitution between any pair of products pertaining to commodity class k in the market of region j, and b_{ijk} is a constant.

14. The supply function described in this paragraph is adapted from a proposal made by Paul S. Armington in an unpublished paper.

15. The basic approach was developed by Rudolf R. Rhomberg and Grant B. Taplin of the IMF and is described in Rhomberg's "Possible Approaches to a Model of World Trade and Payments," a paper presented at the Project LINK meeting of September 16-20, 1969, in Hakone, Japan, and published in the March 1970 issue of the *International Monetary Fund · Staff Papers*. The development in the present paper includes modifications and extensions of the Rhomberg-Taplin model along lines suggested by Bert G. Hickman in his comment on the Rhomberg paper at the Hakone meetings.

16. The linear forms of equations (4.8) and (4.9) imply that P and P^m enter the structural demand functions of country i as separate variables rather than in relative price ratios. This simplification is for illustrative purposes only, and the assumption is unnecessary in the case of nonlinear country models discussed later in the text.

17. These constraints are much stronger than those adopted in Mini and Midi -LINK, which required only that the sum of endogenous imports equal the world export total, without regard to whether the endogenous export predictions for the individual countries also summed to the world total,

and without requiring that the endogenous export predictions be related even partially to the geographic distribution of trade through a weighted external demand variable.

18. See, e.g., Helen B. Junz and Rudolf R. Rhomberg, "Prices and Export Performance of Industrial Countries, 1953-63," *Staff Papers,* Vol. XII (1965), pp. 224-71, and Mordechai E. Kreinin, "Price Elasticities in International Trade," *The Review of Economics and Statistics*, Vol. XLIX (1967), pp. 510-16.

The OECD Trade Model 1970 Version*

F.J.M. Meyer Zu Schloctern and Akira Yajima
Organization for Economic Cooporation and Development

Introduction

The OECD trade model, originally built in 1967, was designed to be a practical forecasting tool. As such it has been subject to periodic revision and extension aimed at improving its forecasting power. Hence, the 1970 version of the trade model differs in a number of ways from the original and intermediate versions. In this article, the 1970 version of the model is described with special attention given to the difference between it and the original and with a discussion of the reasons for some of the more important changes. Therefore, although this article can be read as an outline of a working model of international trade, it will be of special interest to readers familiar with the original version of the model and to those who are interested in observing the way in which a practical model, like any living organism, evolves.

Naturally, this version still has important shortcomings. By lengthening the observation period it becomes more and more doubtful that an accurate indicator of the business cycle can be obtained by simply taking the ratio of industrial production over its logarithmic trend level. At present a detailed study is being made at the OECD to improve business cycle indicators. The results could not be incorporated in the 1970 version but will be used in a forthcoming version of the trade model.

*Reprinted from *OECD Economic Outlook Occasional Studies*, December 1970 by special permission.

This article is divided into three main parts: a description of the model; a discussion of the model with emphasis on the changes from the original version; and an extension of the model.

The discussion of changes and additions to the original version of the OECD trade model during the last three years is divided into three parts. In Part I the model is set out verbally with attention to a major specification change in the export equations. Part II discusses the change from the use of linear specifications in the original version to log-linear forms in the new version; the change from estimating with quarterly data to estimating with semi-annual data; the problem of the choice of the demand variable in the import functions; the question of the distinction between long-run and short-run demand elasticities in interpreting the coefficients of the demand variables; the method of estimation, and the possibility of simultaneous solution of the model. Part III outlines the preliminary extension of the model to take account of the "feedback" effect of trade on GNP.

I. Description of the Model

The 1970 version of the OECD trade model deals with total commodity imports and exports of the major seven countries (France, Germany, Italy, UK, US, Canada, and Japan), other OECD and non-OECD areas. There is a slight difference here from the original version, as Benelux is now included in "Other OECD" instead of being examined separately.

The basic forms of the equations in the model are similar to the original.

a) The volume of imports is a function of:

i) Demand: industrial production;

ii) Business cycle: the ratio of industrial production to its logarithmic trend level;

iii) Relative prices: the ratio of the import price of manufactures to the GNP deflator.

b) The volume of exports is a function of:

i) Market growth: the weighted sum of imports of market countries;

ii) Business cycle: the weighted average of the business cycle in market countries;

iii) Relative price: export price of the country relative to weighted average of the export prices of competing countries' manufactures.

In addition, several dummy variables have been included where necessary to take into account the effect of strikes and institutional factors. Several variables included in the original version were eliminated through statistical tests. The most important of these was the relative pressure of demand variable in the export equation.

The major specification change in the model is in the export function. Here, the elasticity of the market growth variable, which was restricted to equal 1 in the original version, is unrestricted and estimated along with the other parameters, thus inter alia taking into account the differences in commodity composition of exports for each country. With regard to the choice of explanatory variables, it should be noted that the present version of the model uses the "operational" equations i.e. only those which, as far as possible, do not contain explanatory variables which are difficult to forecast (e.g. inventory changes). Since the model is used as a practical forecasting instrument, attention has been focused on the best forecasting specifications.

Equations of the 1970 version were estimated on 30 half-yearly observations covering 1955-1969. The complete set of estimated equations is given in Appendix I (with weighting schemes, sources and data preparation given in Appendices II and III). The highlights of the estimates, the elasticities of imports and exports with respect to demand and relative price are given in Table 1.

TABLE 1
Estimated elasticities of imports and exports
with respect to industrial production,
relative prices and market growth

	Imports		Exports	
	Industrial production	Relative price	Market growth	Exports price
France	1.33	-1.35	1.03	-1.22
Germany	1.64	-0.34	1.23	-0.99
Italy	1.26	—	1.46	-0.99
UK	1.61	—	0.57	-0.33
US[a]	1.10	-1.88	0.81	-1.00
Canada[a]	0.87	-1.49	0.89	-0.94
Japan	0.82	-0.78	1.97	-1.25
Other OECD	1.40	—	1.12	—

[a] For the US and Canada, GNP instead of industrial production. (see Appendix I).

II. Discussion of the Model

1: Use of log-linear equations. A major change in the specification of the equations from that of the 1967 version is that the equations are now log-linear.

The log-linear equations are taken since:

—The export predictions of 1967 and 1968 by the previous versions of the model revealed systematic under-estimates, particularly in cases of fast growing countries,

—Relative price variables for most countries became more significant. Sometimes they became significant where they were not in the previous linear versions.

It should be noticed, however, that the introduction of the log specification causes some mathematical discrepancies in the present export functions. In case of linear relationships used in the 1967 version, exports of country (i) to market (j),

$$X_{ij} = f\,(M_{.j},\ P_{xij}\ldots)$$

where X_{ij} = exports of i to j

$M_{.j}$ = total imports of j

P_{xij} = relative competitiveness variable (of i on j's market)

could be aggregated with respect to j to obtain

$$X_i = a_i + b_i S_i + c_i P_{xi}\ldots$$

where P_{xi} = relative export competitiveness of i in the world

S_i = total imports of i's markets weighted by their share in i's exports in 1963.

The present version assumes a multiplicative relation

$$X_{ij} = A_i\, M_{.j}^{bi}\, P_{xij}^{ci}\ \ldots$$

whose aggregation over markets should not take the form of arithmetic but geometric means of the indices. Thus the estimated equation

$$\log X_i = a_i + b_i \log S_i + c_i \log P_{xi} + \ldots$$

includes an inaccurate implicit approximation because variables are calculated by the linear weighting schemes (see Appendix II) for the sake of simplicity of calculations.

2. Half-yearly model. The original quarterly equations were changed into half-yearly ones for several practical reasons:

—A better correspondence to the forecasting routine,

—Some potentially favourable effects of the aggregation over time (e.g. increased reliability of data),

—The possible use of seasonably unadjusted series (only one seasonal dummy variable is needed compared with three in a quarterly model).

The possibility that the introduction of longer time lags in price and business cycle variables could improve the quarterly was examined.[2] The lags in quarterly import functions do not seem to exceed two or three quarters, while longer lags up to four quarters are likely to exist in export functions. In the half-yearly equations, most of the lags could be eliminated. For the export equations a simple half-yearly lag has been introduced where necessary.

3. *Choice of demand variable of import functions.* The main demand variable of the import function has been industrial production in all the versions between 1967 and 1970 inclusively. There were at least two (one theoretical, one practical) problems concerning this variable:

—Industrial production cannot fully reflect importation of finished goods which are delivered directly to final consumers or investors;

—Industrial production is not a major item in the forecasting routine of the OECD.

On the other hand, if GNP is used as a demand variable, it is not clear enough whether it is possible to:

—Separate the effect of changes in the pattern of GNP, e.g. a change in the share of the services sector;

—Catch the effect of changes in the technical or input structure of production.

A possible solution of these difficulties seemed to be to introduce major items of GNP as separate demand variables or a weighted sum of major items, weighted by delivery of imported goods calculated on an input-output table.

Several regressions along these lines were tested for major countries but rejected because the net statistical gains were sometimes marginal, and sometimes negative. GNP is used only for the US and Canada, and industrial production is used for other countries in the present version.

4. *Interpretation of demand elasticities.* It should be noticed that the interpretation of demand variables of the import and export equation may not be as straightforward as appears at first sight.

Suppose an import function includes variables Z_1 and Z_S which stand for long-run developments of demand and short-run cyclical variations. Respectively, the coefficients b and c of

$$\log M = a + b \log Z_L + c \log Z_S$$

will show long run and short-run elasticities of imports with respect to Z's. When the actual demand variable Z is introduced in place of Z_L, incorporating both long-run trend and cyclical fluctuations, the estimated coefficient of Z_S will become equal to (c - b).[2] This is approximately true in the case of import functions. The effect of the industrial production may be interpreted as a pure demand effect (if total supply from the foreign suppliers is assumed infinite and if institutional factors are ignored for the moment). Thus one could expect a country importing a relatively large volume of goods which are not sensitive to business cycles (for instance, foodstuffs) to have a short-run elasticity smaller than the long-run elasticity (a negative coefficient for the business cycle variable, B_C). The UK provides an example of such a country, with a relatively high proportion of its imports consisting of foodstuffs.

For countries where the effect of business cycles are asymmetrical, only positive values of B_C, i.e. B_C+, can be introduced as indicators of pressure of demand. Hence the economic implication of the business cycle variables is clearer and more straightforward for countries which have a significantly positive sign for the coefficient of B_C+ variable.

In the case of export function the situation is more difficult. Even if one could accept the export-function business cycle variable, WB_C, as the best proxy of cyclical world demand, the estimated coefficient of the market growth variable, S, would be rather difficult to interpret. The coefficient could reflect a composite effect of demand development, the supply ceiling and many other factors.

This was one of the reasons why the authors of the 1967 version of the model put the market variable, S, on the left hand side of the export equation with its coefficient constrained to unity

$$(X-S) = f (RPx\ WBc, \ldots)$$

Indeed, "if all factors had been fully taken into account the growth of exports is likely to be approximately proportional to the market."[4] In practice, however, it is not easy to find good variables to take care of "all factors," and the preference has been to keep the variable S as a mixture of demand/supply and other factors rather than to separate S and to introduce trend variables as proxies of supply, etc.

At present the coefficient of S is estimated from the regression, supposing that the differences in commodity composition between countries may not guarantee the uniform elasticity in the long run and that a "dynamic" exporting country could increase its market share more easily in an expanding market than in a stagnating market. Also, it was difficult to measure the impact of such institutional factors as tariff reductions in the EEC and EFTA area. Perhaps this short term model is not the best tool to measure such medium term effects. The distinction between the first and second stages of the EEC which was dealt with by introducing separate time trends in the original version has been omitted in the present version because the trends seem to catch all the possible effects of other variables missing.

5. *Method of estimation and solution of the model.* Many theoretical and statistical problems appear in the stages of estimating individual equations and solving the system as a whole, due to the simultaneity of income and imports of one country, the simultaneity of income, imports and exports between countries, redundancy due to the constraint of total imports equal to total exports, amplification of serial correlation, and so on. A good example of the nature of the problems faced in this system is provided by the S variable in the export function. This is a weighted sum of imports, and is subject to forecasting error due to estimation error in the import functions. This gave another reason for the authors of the original version to put the S variable on the left hand side of the export equation, to avoid the least-squares bias.

In the present version all the equations are still estimated by direct least-squares and the discrepancy between calculated total imports and total exports is distributed proportionately over the export side. The first problem would be dealt with later by the use of some simultaneous estimation technique such as three least-squares; the second is related to an important point concerning consistency in the world trade model. A considerable volume of study on the consistency problem has been published recently.[5] The extent to which one should be rigorous about these points in practice depends on the degree of comprehensiveness of the model one wishes to use. The issue should be discussed further, in the process of making export price an endogenous variable of the OECD trade model.

III. Extension of the Model

In this section an extension of the model is described which traces the "feedback" effect of trade on GNP. This is done using a numerical example which will also help in understanding how and to what extent a change in the domestic activity of one country influences the international trade flows and the balance of payments of other countries.

The standard version of the OECD trade model treats the GNP or the industrial production index of each country as an exogenous variable. When the model is used for forecasting, the forecasts of GNP or industrial production and other appropriate variables are fed into the model and forecasts of imports and exports are obtained. If, however, the forecasts of the latter are very different from the values tacitly assumed in the initial prediction of GNP or industrial production, then it is desirable to re-examine these initial estimates. The gap between the initial implicitly assumed values and the subsequent forecasts must be taken into account. In the standard OECD trade model the causal chain is cut at this point; the impact is "one-way" and the feedback of trade flows on income could not be traced automatically by the model.

The way in which the feedback process might be endogenized will be illustrated by a numerical example. This example has been worked through to produce, finally, Table 3. The question which the exercise sets out to answer is:

What would have happened to OECD trade in 1968 if, in 1964-1968, everything followed its actual course of development except the GNP of the United States which is assumed to have grown by some 3.5 per cent a year instead of the actual average, 5.1 per cent?[6]

It would be more realistic to assume a lower price increase accompanying the slower growth in the United States over a five year period. But this effect is not taken into account here for the sake of simplicity.

Consider first a "one-way" sequence of changes in trade resulting from a change in GNP. The observed volume index of United States GNP in 1968 was 128.3 (1963=100), the hypothetical figure taken is 118.5. The discrepancy of 9.8 index points implies a difference in GNP of 58.6 billion dollars at 1963 prices.

The change of United States imports resulting from this change in GNP is then calculated, using the import function. The result is that the imports of the United States are reduced by $3.0 billion (18 index points) and this causes decreases in exports of other countries through the export functions of the model. The US improves its trade balance by $3 billion, while Canada and Japan, among seven major countries, experience worsening trade balances, by $0.4 and $1.3 billion respectively, reflecting their high degree of US dependence. In Japan's case, this also reflects its high calculated elasticity of exports (Table 1, column 3). A decrease of $0.4 billion in imports of Non-OECD would result, due to the decline in imports of OECD countries from the Non-OECD area in the previous period, since imports of the Non-OECD area are determined partly by its exports in the previous period.

Since imports are related to the industrial production, not to GNP in the model a linear relation between these two aggregate indicators was estimated to convert the change in the GNP into a change in the industrial production index for other countries.

In the exercise illustrated above, the model was solved period by period from 1964 I to 1968 II. The exercise calculated did in fact continue the sequence of changes beyond the changes in exports described above. Decreases in exports of non-US countries will decrease their GNP through the export multiplier process, and therefore, their imports; and decreases in imports of non-US countries will in turn decrease exports (and thus GNP) of the US as well as other countries. Finally, the calculated growth rate of the US will become different from the assumed 3.5%, and growth rates of other countries will become different from their actual rates.

In working through these effects it is assumed, for the sake of simplicity, that changes in imports and exports of the US have no influence on the US GNP; this approximation is not very unrealistic since shares of imports and exports in GNP of the US were only around 5 per cent in 1963. The multiplier, a, which links changes in exports and GNP through the relation

$$\Delta \ GNP \ = \ \alpha \Delta X$$

could be calculated from existing country models[7] (Table 2).

However, it must be kept in mind that the value of the multiplier depends on the formulation of the model used, and consequently, a

TABLE 2
Export multipliers

		In index form[a]
France	1.0	.143
Germany	1.3	.259
Italy	1.5	.235
UK	1.5	.332
US	2.0	.108
Canada	1.5	.314
Japan	1.3	.130
Other OECD	1.0	.350

a) Since the model uses GNP and export indices, the multiplier in terms of national currency must be multiplied by the ratio of exports to GNP in the base year.

wide range of values may exist even for one country. The following figures which are subject to a certain degree of arbitrariness were used in the continuation of the exercise. The decision to use these figures seems reasonable as the aim is not to present a policy simulation but simply to illustrate how the "feedback" system works.

The system including the exports-income link can then be solved by an iterative procedure.[8] The results of this exercise are tabulated in Table 3. This shows the total decreases in imports and exports including "indirect" effects induced by "feedback." It is an interesting fact that for the European countries the indirect decrease in exports due to the decrease in GNP (and accordingly imports) of non-US countries is far from negligible, indeed it is often bigger than the direct decrease, whereas the indirect decrease in exports is negligibly small for Canada and Japan. In the 'other OECD' area the decrease in imports due to the decrease in GNP is more than offset by the decrease in exports; and the total effect on world trade is calculated as 1.54 times the initial direct effect.

However, the final answer to the originally postulated question depends so much on the values of multipliers used in the calculation that no decisive conclusion should be directly drawn from the results. In order to extend the model into something that is more useful for policy analysis, the two short cuts (the GNP-Ip relation and the export multiplier) for each country would have to be replaced with a full country model which has an explicit and consistent income and price determination mechanism. Then an international trade model in the fullest sense would be obtained.

Table 3
Effects of a Decrease in Imports of the US on World Trade, 1968
Billions of 1963 US dollars

I. Direct decrease in:	Imports	Exports
France	—	0.14 (1.2)
Germany	—	0.26 (1.1)
Italy	—	0.20 (1.9)
UK	—	0.16 (1.1)
US	2.98 (11.0)	—
Canada	—	0.44 (5.0)
Japan	—	1.24 (9.8)
Other OECD	—	0.28 (1.1)
Non-OECD	0.42 (1.0)	0.67 (1.6)
Total	3.40 (1.9)	3.40 (1.9)

II. Total decrease in:	Imports	Exports	Balance
France	0.07 (0.6)	0.33 (2.8)	-0.26
Germany	0.14 (0.7)	0.59 (2.5)	-0.45
Italy	0.26 (3.1)	0.33 (3.1)	-0.07
UK	0.11 (0.7)	0.29 (2.0)	-0.18
US	2.98 (11.0)	0.52 (1.9)	2.46
Canada	0.43 (4.5)	0.48 (5.5)	-0.05
Japan	0.16 (1.6)	1.32 (10.4)	-1.16
Other OECD	0.50 (1.6)	0.44 (1.8)	0.06
Non-OECD	0.58 (1.4)	0.93 (2.2)	-0.35
Total	5.23 (3.0)	5.23 (3.0)	

N.B. Figures in ( ) are percentage decreases from the normal levels of imports and exports. The normal levels were calculated by the model with actual GNP of the US and were slightly different from actual levels of imports and exports (owing to the estimation error of the trade equations).

FOOTNOTES

1. Previous versions are: F.G. Adams, H. Eguchi and F.J.M. Meyer zu Schloctern, *An Econometric Analysis of International Trade*, 1969, "OECD Economic Studies Series." Observation period 1955-1965 (original version). H. Eguchi, DES/NI/F(68)7, October 1968 (unpublished OECD document). Observation period 1955-1966.
2. "Almon lags" were tested in the quarterly equations. See H. Eguchi, *op. cit.*
3. For an arithmetic explanation see Adams-Eguchi-Meyer Zu Schlochtern, *op. cit.*, p. 19.
4. *Ibid.*, p. 30.
5. For a detailed discussion of the "consistency" problem, see R. R. Rhomberg, "Possible Approaches to a Model of World Trade and Payments," IMF *Staff Papers*, March 1970; B. Hickman, L.R. Klein and R.R. Rhomberg, "Background, Organization and Preliminary Results of Project LINK," and J. Waelbroeck, "The Methodology of Linkage," pagers presented to the Second World Congress of the Econometric Society, September 1970.
6. The basic calculation was carried out in early 1970, based on the 1969 version of parameters.
7. Some of the models give static (impact) and others dynamic multipliers. See B.G. Hickman, "Dynamic Properties of Macroeconomic Models: An International Comparison," paper presented to the SSRC Conference, April 1967.

   Some round figures near at hand are (export or government multipliers): France 0.9 (Evans, government multiplier), Germany 1.3 (Konig-Timmermann), 4.4 (Krelle-Rahman), Italy 2.0 (Ackley), UK 1.3 (Ball), 1.8 (Ball-Rahman), US 2.0 (Wharton Schol), 2.0 (Rahman), Canada 0.7 (Sawyer), 1.8 (Sawyer-Rahman), Japan 1.3 (EPA-Yajima), 1.0 (EPA). A. Rahman calculated impact multipliers by linearizing the models built by authors whose names appear in the same brackets. See OECD [DES/NI/F(69)8], May 1969 (unpublished).

   Values of $1/(1-c+m)$ (where c is the marginal propensity to consume and m to import), estimated on 1955-58 annual data are as follows: France 1.6, Germany 1.3, Italy 1.5, UK 1.5, Japan 1.5. For other OECD, 1.0 was taken considering its high import leakage.
8. Let M, X, Y, a and m stand for world imports exports, GNP, average export multiplier and average propensity to import respectively, measured in dollars. The feedback iteration process can be written as

$$\Delta M^{(n+1)} = m \Delta Y^{(n+1)} = ma \Delta X^{(n)}$$

$$\Delta M^{(n+1)} = \Delta X^{(n+1)} \to 0$$

Assume a = 1.5. Then m is obtained from $(ma)^t = 1.54$, $m \simeq 0.24$

and this is consistent with the actual ratio of increase in total imports to increase in total GNP of the OECD countries between 1964 and 1968.

CANADA (1)

	I_p	P_m/P_y	$B_c^{\ddagger}$	const.
	0.870	-1.491	1.011	2.845
	(34.2)	(-7.2)	(3.6)	
	$R^2=0.980$		$S=0.033$	DW=1.14

CANADA (2)

	GNP	P_m/P_y	$B_c^{\ddagger}$	const.
	1.086	-1.304	1.262	-0.169
	(38.4)	(-7.1)	(5.0)	
	$R^2=0.984$		$S=0.029$	DW=1.38

OTHER OECD

	I_p	const.	
	1.397	-1.833	
	(137.7)		
	$R^2=0.998$	$S=0.015$	DW=1.87

NON-OECD

	X_{NO-1}	N_c	R_{-1}	const.
	0.527	0.310	0.313	-0.634
	(6.6)	(2.9)	(5.8)	
	$R^2=0.984$		$S=0.027$	DW=1.50

EXPORTS

FRANCE

	S	R_{px}	WB_c	D	const.
	1.032	-1.216	0.882	-0.091	1.388
	(35.3)	(-4.2)	(2.2)	(-1.5)	
R^2=0.986		S=0.042		DW=1.28	

D: strike dummy (1968-I = 0.5, II = -0.5)

GERMANY

	S	R_{px-2}	WB_c	T_{55-58}	const.
	1.234	-0.985	-0.522	0.0233	5.681
	(50.3)	(-4.4)	(-1.7)	(6.2)	
R^2=0.998		S=0.021		DW=2.43	

T_{55-58}: dummy trend (1955-I=1.0, II=2.0,...1958-II=8.0; others = 8.0)

ITALY

	S	R_{px}	T_{55-61}	D_1	D_2	const.
	1.462	-0.993	0.018	0.043	-0.145	2.447
	(24.7)	(-3.4)	(6.0)	(1.2)	(-3.7)	
R^2=0.997		S=0.034		DW=1.21		

T_{55-61}: dummy trend (1955-I=-14.0; II=-13.0, . . . 1961-II=-1.0; others = 0)

D_1: US dock strike dummy (1965-I=1.0; others = 0)

D_2: general strike dummy (1969-II=1.0; others = 0)

UNITED KINGDOM

	S	R_{px}	WB_c	D	const.
	0.573	-0.327	0.324	-0.184	1.975
	(34.3)	(-2.5)	(1.7)	(-5.0)	

$R^2=0.986$ $S=0.019$ $DW=1.97$

D: seamen's and docks, strike dummy (1966-I=0.3, 1967-II=0.5; others = 0)

JAPAN

	S	R_{px}	WB_c	D_1	D_2	const.
	1.973	-1.248	0.454	-0.218	0.143	-0.842
	(26.5)	(-7.1)	(1.7)	(-1.9)	(3.4)	

$R^2=0.996$ $S=0.041$ $DW=1.70$

D_1: Japan dock strike dummy (1965-II = 0.5; others = 0)
D_2: "Vietnam shock" dummy (1965-I, II = 1.0; others = 0)

UNITED STATES

	S	R_{px}	D_1	D_2	const.
	0.814	-1.004	-0.067	0.212	5.466
	(26.0)	(-4.1)	(-1.1)	(5.5)	

$R^2=0.979$ $S=0.029$ $DW=2.26$

D_1: dock strike dummy (1965-I = 1.0; others = 0)
D_2: Suez crisis dummy (1956-II = 0.7, 1957-I = 0.5, II = 0.2; others = 0)

	S	R_{px}	WB_c	D_1	D_2	const.
CANADA	0.886 (48.0)	-0.939 (-5.6)	-0.203 (-1.4)	0.082 (1.5)	-0.152 (-5.2)	5.800
	R^2=0.989		S=0.027	DW=2.08		

D_1: US dock strike dummy (1965-I = 1.0; others = 0)
D_2: mining strike dummy (1969-II = 1.0; others = 0)

	S	$(R_{px}-R_{px-1})$	const.		
OTHER OECD	1.115 (86.5)	-0.144 (-0.9)	-0.522		
	R^2=0.996		S=0.022	DW=1.54	

	S	WB_c	const.		
NON-OECD	0.772 (106.2)	-0.141 (-1.1)	1.047		
	R^2=0.997		S=0.014	DW=1.60	

LIST OF SYMBOLS

All variables are in index form (1963 = 100)
Price variables are in US dollars

IMPORTS

M	Import volume index
I_p	Industrial production index, all commodities
GNP	Gross national product, volume index
P_m	Import price index, manufactures
P_m^*	Weighted average of export price index of supply countries
P_y	GNP deflator
BC	The ratio of industrial production over its logarithmic trend level
BC^+	If $BC > 100$ $BC^+ = BC$
	$BC \leqslant 100$ $BC^+ = 100$
LIB	Trade liberalization rate
t_m	Import tariff rate index under the EEC or EFTA agreement
X_{n}	Export index of Non-OECD countries
N_c	Net capital inflow, official and private, to less developed countries, deflated by import unit value index
R	Total reserve of less developed countries, deflated by import value index

EXPORTS

X	Export volume index
S	Weighted sum of imports of market countries
WBC	Weighted average of BC's in market countries
R_{p_X}	Export price of the country relative to weighted average of export prices of competing countries, manufactures

DUMMIES

D	Dummy for strikes or other "unusual" fluctuations
SUR	Import surcharge dummy
T	Dummy trend for shift in structures

APPENDIX II
WEIGHTING SCHEMES

The weighting schemes (based on the 1963 trade matrix) were constructed as follows, denoting j's total imports by $X_{.j}$, i's total exports by $X_{i.}$, and the flow of exports from i to j by X_{ij}. ($\overline{X}$'s denote those in 1963)..

$$S_i = \sum_{j \neq i} \frac{\overline{X}_{ij}}{\overline{X}_i} \cdot \frac{X_{.j}}{\overline{X}_{.j}}$$

Thus S expresses the growth of exports of country i corresponding to growth of imports of countries j provided the i-th share in j-th market remains constant over time.

$$R_{P_{xi}} = \sum_{j \neq i} \frac{\overline{x}_{ij}}{\overline{x}_i} \left[\frac{P_{xi}}{\sum_{\substack{k \neq j, \overline{x}_{.j} - \overline{x}_{9j} - \overline{x}_{ij} \\ i, 9}} \frac{\overline{x}_{kj}}{\cdot P_{xk}} \right]$$

The term in [ ] expresses export price of country i in j-th market relative to a weighted average of export prices of competing countries k in j-th market, excluding i-th and j-th countries and Non-OECD area (9) which has no price index. Thus R_{P_x} expresses an average relative export price of country i in total OECD market.

$$WB_{ci} = \sum_{j \neq i, 9} \frac{\overline{x}_{ij}}{\overline{X}_{i.} - \overline{X}_{i9}} \cdot B_{cj}$$

WB_c expresses a weighted average of business cycle indices of non i-th countries, excluding Non-OECD area which has no B_c variable.

$$P^*_{mj} = \sum_{i \neq j, 9} \frac{\overline{X}_{ij}}{\overline{X}_{.j} - \overline{X}_{9j}} P_{xi}$$

P^*_m expresses a weighted average of export prices of non j-th countries, excluding non-OECD area, in j-th market. Thus given export prices for all countries, one can calculate an import price index for a country which has no published import price series.

APPENDIX III
SOURCES AND PREPARATION OF DATA

Industrial production index and volume index series of imports and exports (1963 = 100) were taken from the Historical Series of *The Main Economic Indicators*. Seasonal factors for value indices are applied to obtain the seasonally adjusted volume series. The following special factors were deducted to obtain the final series.

—Car trade between the US and Canada,
—German imports of weapons,
—Canadian exports to Communist countries,
—UK imports of aircraft from the US,
—Series B, OECD *Foreign Trade Statistics*.

As far as possible import and export prices of manufactures (not unit values) were taken from original country statistics (Germany and Japan). Sources are listed below.

Industrial production
The Main Economic Indicators, for Other OECD, The Statistics Division, OECD.

Volume trade
The Main Economic Indicators; seasonal factor taken from value figures; for Non-OECD, value series were taken from *MEI* and deflators from *Monthly Bulletin of Statistics* and *International Financial Statistics*.

Export unit value, manufactures
UN *Monthly Bulletin of Statistics*, Special Tables; for Other OECD, total export unit value as far as given in *MEI*. For Germany and Japan, same sources as import unit values.

Import unit value, manufactures
France: "Produits manufactures" in *Bulletin Mensuel de Statistiques*.
Germany: *Reihe 1, Preise und Preis Indices fur Aussenhandelsguter,* the series for "Fertigwaren".
Italy: *Commercio con l'Estero,* the series "Beni di Consumo Durevoli" (weight 0.22) and "Beni di Investimento impianti, machine e attrezzature" (weight 0.78).
UK: *Monthly Digest of Statistics,* the series for "manufactures products".
US: *Statistical Reports,* the series for "semi-manufactures" (weight 0.4) and "finished manufactures" (weight 0.6).
Canada: *Foreign Trade Statistics,* the series for "end products" have been taken for the later years. For earlier years a weighted average of several series covering manufactures has been taken.

Japan: *Bank of Japan import and export prices,* the series "metal and related products" (weight 0.6) and "machinery and equipment" (weight 0.4).

GNP deflator
France and Italy, EPC; Germany, *Vierteljahrshefte zur Wirtschaftsforschung;* UK, US, Canada and Japan, *MEI*

Capital flow to Non-OECD
DAC Statistical tables for the Annual Aid Review.

Foreign Exchange reserves of Non-OECD
International Financial Statistics.

Liberalization
OECE, *Douziéme Rapport Economique Annuel,* table 25.

Import tariffs
IMF *Annual Report of Exchange Restrictions.*

The Effects
of the Business Cycle
on Trade Flows
of Industrial Countries*

F. Gerard Adams
University of Pennsylvania

Helen B. Junz
Federal Reserve System

Summary

THE U.S. TRADE SURPLUS, which had run at a healthy $5 billion annual rate in the early 1960's, declined sharply after the middle of the decade until mid-1969, by which time it had eroded to virtually nothing. The magnitude of this decline has necessarily raised questions about its underlying causes and about the future trend of the U.S. trade balance. These questions are aimed at determining whether a fundamental and structural shift has occurred in the U.S. competitive position in world markets or whether the severe deterioration in the trade position is mainly a cyclical phenomenon, associated with the inflationary boom, which characterized the second half of the 1960's. Specifically, this paper addresses itself to the question of the effect of macro-economic conditions, here and abroad, upon trade flows. It is important to recognize and measure this effect not necessarily in order to tailor domestic economic policy to external constraints, but rather to be able to anticipate, and deal with, the balance of payments effects of domestic policy decisions.

A simple application of an updated version of the OECD world trade model[1] was used in order to put quantitative dimensions on

---

*Adapted from The Journal of Finance, Papers and Proceedings of the 29th annual meeting, May 1971.
(Recent international monetary realignments are not included in the computations of this article.)

the effects of business cycle changes on trade flows. The model, which was designed to isolate pressure of demand and price effects from other influences upon trade flows, is a good vehicle for such calculations. Like all such models though, it can indicate only the approximate range of magnitudes involved. Within this limitation, the model has been used to contrast a base solution—which assumes that economic activity and prices moved as they actually did throughout the period —with alternative solutions postulating first, non-inflationary growth for the U.S. economy at or near its potential rate after 1964; second, growth rates for other industrial countries such as to keep their economies fully employed throughout the period, and third, various combinations of growth and price patterns for the United States ranging from low growth with high rates of inflation to high growth rates with low price changes.

The results of these comparisons show that the inflationary boom that gripped the Unites States after 1964 had a very considerable impact upon trade flows. It reduced the U.S. trade surplus markedly and it augmented the surpluses of Japan and, though less substantially, those of European countries, notably Germany and Italy. If the U.S. economy had followed a non-inflationary growth path from 1965 onward—that is if real GNP had grown about in line with the underlying growth rate of productive capacity—the U.S. trade balance in the first half of 1969 would have been almost $3 billion larger than it was in fact.

The question of the size of the underlying full-employment trade surplus for the United States in the early 1970's, of course, cannot be solved in terms of what it might have been if the growth paths in the second half of the 1960's had reflected an ideal high-employment, non-inflationary world. But given the general responsiveness of trade flows to alternative growth paths, it is possible to investigate further the implications of varying macro-economic conditions. Thus, one can ask what might be the effect of a period of relatively low U.S. activity rates combined with relatively high rates of inflation—such as prevailed in the late 1950's and is likely to prevail in 1971—as compared with the steady growth assumption. Simulations based on varying combinations of GNP growth and price change show that exports are rather more responsive to changes in the relative price term and imports to those in activity rates. Both effects build steadily over time. For example, a fall in the rate of growth from 4 per cent to 3 per cent p.a. combined with a rise in the rate of inflation from 2 per cent to 3 per cent p.a. yields an improvement in the trade balance, after 4 years, of $0.7 billion (in 1963 dollars). This improvement is the result of a $0.6 billion export loss and a $1.3 billion decline in imports, primarily associated with the low activity rate.

Conversely, movement from a growth pattern which combines a low rate of real growth with a relatively high rate of inflation (i.e., a 3 per cent growth rate with a 4 per cent price change) to a pattern of faster growth with the same inflation rate (i.e., a 4 per cent growth rate with a 4 per cent inflation rate) would result in a deterioration of the trade balance by about $1 billion in the third year after the change.

This final set of simulations strengthens the conclusions regarding the dependence of trade flows upon general macro-economic conditions, and the consequent importance of demand management policies.

The OECD Trade Model

The vehicle used for testing the relationship between trade flows and macro-economic conditions is an updated version of the OECD world trade model.[2] This model consists of a system of interrelated import and export equations shown in Appendix Table I. Imports are predicted for each country—the "countries" are the seven most important OECD countries, "other OECD" as a group, and "non-OECD" also as a group—primarily on the basis of economic activity, such as industrial production or GNP, pressure of demand, and relative prices. The pressure of demand effect, which reflects the business cycle emphasis of this model, is captured by the ratio of actual industrial production to its semi-log trend value. This serves as a simple, practical measure of business cycle position and avoids dealing with more ambiguous data such as unemployment or inventory change. Imports of non-OECD, principally developing countries, are a function of lagged exports, capital movements and reserves.

Estimated imports then enter into the export equations in the form of a market variable which represents the exports which each country would have if its trade share in world markets remained at its base year (1963) level. Relative prices and business cycle conditions are the other principal factors determining each country's exports. Import prices are linked to export prices, i.e., for each country import prices are derived from the weighted average of the export prices of the supplier countries. Total estimated exports are reconciled with total imports by a proportional adjustment, but this adjustment represents only a small percentage of the total. The model does not include feedbacks from the trade balance to economic activity or prices. Such feedbacks link business cycle developments among different countries and have to be kept in mind, but they are not necessary for the calculations carried on here. Our simulations begin with assumptions about economic conditions—growth, pressure of demand, and prices—in each of the countries and from these the implications for imports, exports and the trade balance are then derived.

OECD Trade Model Simulation of Variations in Rates of Growth and Inflation in Industrial Countries

Simulations with the OECD trade model involved estimation of a base case, using the values of the exogenous variables as they actually occurred, and alternative solutions, substituting different values based on assumptions, first, of moderate non-inflationary growth in the United States and Canada, second, of rapid expansion of activity combined with a higher rate of price increase in other industrial countries, and finally of varying combinations of macro-economic conditions in the United States and Canada. The simulations cover the period 1964 to mid-1969. The equation constants were adjusted to equalize the estimated values and the actual values of imports and exports in each country over the average of the year 1964 in order to provide an appropriate starting point for the simulations.

Simulation Assumptions

In the first instance, the following simulation cases were considered:

Base Case

The base case introduces all exogenous variables at their actual values during the sample period.

Alternative Case I: Moderate non-inflationary growth in the United States and in Canada.

The statistics on economic growth and inflation in the United States show a fairly clear break between 1964 and 1965, when the economy returned to high-employment levels. The point in time when the slack in resource utilization had been more or less fully absorbed differs depending upon the criteria used. It is put rather early in 1965 on basis of capacity utilization and pressure of demand criteria, but towards the end of that year if the unemployment rate is used. But clearly, sometime during 1965, the economy moved into the "narrow band" around full employment and continued rates of growth above trend were combined with an acceleration of the rate of price increase. It was assumed, consequently, that beginning in the first half of 1965, the U.S. economy expands at a rate of 4 per cent p.a.—slightly above the 3.75 per cent of underlying capacity growth estimated by the Council of Economic Advisers for the mid-1960's. The rise in GNP deflator associated with this rise of growth was assumed to be 2 percent p.a. and that of export prices 1.5 per cent p.a., slightly above the rate of the early 1960's. By the first half of 1969 this results in GNP approximately 3¼ per cent and in prices 5½ per cent below actual levels. By mid-1970, the elimination of cyclical troughs and peaks from 1965 onward would have yielded levels of output very close to those that actually occured. Steady growth of real GNP at a 4 per cent annual rate would have resulted in a first halt 1970 GNP level ¾ per cent above actual.

While the present model lacks feedback features, it is clear that economic expansion in Canada is greatly dependent on developments in the United States. Consequently, in addition to the assumption of moderate growth in the United States, it was thought appropriate also to assume slower growth and smaller price increases in Canada. Therefore, it was assumed that Canadian GNP would have expanded at an annual rate of 5 per cent (corresponding to the underlying growth rate as estimated by the Canadian Economic Council) beginning with the first half of 1965 and that the rate of price increase would have been 1.5 per cent p.a., a little below that in the United States. Smoothing out the cyclical variations from 1965 onward, yields an assumed real GNP in the first half of 1969 equal to the actual GNP and a price deflator 7 per cent below actual levels.

Alternative Case II: More rapid expansion and price increase in other industrial countries

In many of the major industrial countries outside the United States and Canada, economic activity expanded at a slower pace after 1964 than in preceding years and a sharp upward surge of activity and prices did not occur until 1968. In fact, Germany experienced a recession in 1966-67 and France, Italy, and Japan, all had under-utilized resources at some time during the period. The

United Kingdom pursued stringent stabilization policies during a major part of the period. In order to test how much this non-concordance of cyclical paths contributed to trade developments, in this simulation it is assumed that growth was such as to maintain the 1964 level of resource utilization and that prices continued to increase at about the same or at a slightly lesser rate than was recorded from the second half of 1963 to the end of 1964. The specific assumptions about economic growth and rates of inflation for the major industrial countries other than the United States and Canada for the period from the end of 1964 to the first half of 1969 are as follows:[3]

	France	Germany	Italy	U.K.	Japan
	Assumptions Alternative Case II				
GNP deflator, % change p.a.	4.0	3.0	4.0	5.0	5.0
Export prices, % change p.a.	4.0	2.5	2.0	3.0	0
	Position in first half 1969[a]				
	Index numbers, 1963=100				
Industrial production,					
actual	140	142	144	122	212
assumed	138	141	147	123	214
GNP deflator,					
actual	124	117	123	104	129
assumed	125	119	129	113	129
Export prices,					
actual	111	109	100	107	103
assumed	124	116	110	102	102

[a]Price changes adjusted for exchange rate changes.

In general, the growth assumptions lead to levels of output and cyclical positions in the first half of 1969 that are rather similar to those which actually prevailed. But price levels are higher because elimination of cyclical troughs resulted on average in higher pressure of demand after 1964 than actually occured. While it is questionable, at least in some cases, whether these relatively high pressures of demand could have been sustained throughout the period, the assumptions underlying this simulation either approximate quite reasonably or understate the cyclical positions actually prevailing in the first half of 1970. For example, the rates of inflation, as measured by the GNP deflator, in the first half of 1970 were as follows: France 5¾ per cent, Germany 7½ per cent, Italy 6¾ per cent, United Kingdom 5½ per cent, Japan 6½ per cent. In all cases, they were significantly above the rates assumed for the simulations. Pressure of demand in France, Germany, and Japan was higher than in 1964 and in the United Kingdom and Italy it was about the same. In further work it might be interesting to test additional alternatives which would attempt to approximate a more realistic growth path for each of these countries. This would involve postulating different and changing values for the economic growth and price variables of each country. The more global assumptions chosen for the present study suffice here, because it addresses the *general* question of the effect on trade flows of alternative rates and combinations of economic activity in major industrial countries.

Alternative Case III: Moderate non-inflationary growth in Canada as well as in the United States and more rapid expansion and price increase in other industrial countries

This is a combination of Alternative Cases I and II.

Simulation Results of Non-Inflationary Growth for the United States

Taking the United States first, the simulation shows that slower economic expansion combined with a very moderate rate of price increase would have resulted in substantially lower imports and somewhat increased exports.[4] If activity rates were changed only in the United States, the U.S. trade balance in the first half of 1969 would have been $4.1 billion higher than it actually was. In case I, it is assumed that lower activity rates in the United States should be combined with slower growth in Canada also. Constraining the expansion of the Canadian market results by the first half of 1969 in a reduction in the export improvement for the United States of almost $1 billion; the better Canadian price performance results in somewhat higher U.S. imports from Canada and the improvement in the U.S. trade balance, in this case, is $2.8 billion.

The impact of more rapid expansion in the other industrial countries (case II) on U.S. imports occurs through the relative price term. While in this case U.S. imports would have been lower than estimated in the base case for the entire period 1965 through 1968, the import estimate for the first half of 1969 obtained by simulation II corresponds to the result of the base case. U.S. exports, on the other hand, would have been substantially higher throughout the entire period.

Finally, the two assumptions—slower growth in North America and faster growth elsewhere—are put together in simulation III and

TABLE 1
Effect on U.S. Trade of Moderate Non-Inflationary Growth
in the U.S. and Canada (Case I)
(billions of 1963 and current $, seasonally adjusted, annual rates)

	Exports	Imports	Trade Balance	Trade Balance (current dollars)
		(1963 dollars)		
1965 I	- .0	- .3	+ .3	+ .3
II	0	-1.0	+1.0	+1.0
1966 I	- .2	-1.6	+1.4	+1.5
II	+ .3	-1.6	+1.9	+2.0
1967 I	+ .1	-1.2	+1.2	+1.3
II	+ .6	-1.2	+1.7	+1.9
1968 I	+ .6	-1.6	+2.1	+2.3
II	+ .6	-1.9	+2.5	+2.7
1969 I	+ .8	-1.8	+2.6	+2.8

Totals may not add due to rounding.

the results show that the two effects are cumulative (see Table 2). If the U.S. and Canada grow more slowly and other countries more rapidly, the impact on U.S. imports is to produce a smooth path (a reflection of the smooth path of activity and prices assumed in the simulations) substantially below the results of simulation I (non-inflationary growth in North America). By the first half of 1969, however, when other industrial countries were approaching similar cyclical positions in the simulations as in actuality, U.S. imports in simulation III begin to approximate those obtained in simulation I. The impact on U.S. exports of more rapid economic expansion and higher rates of inflation in industrial countries other than Canada is pronounced. The balance of trade impact of simulation III rises to between $4½ and $6 billion (1963 dollars) from the second half of 1967. In the first half of 1969 it amounts to $4.6 billion in 1963 dollars and $5.1 billion in current dollars.

Simulation Results for Other Countries

With regard to Canada, where activity and prices in the simulations are assumed to move parallel to those in the United States, the balance of trade impact is similar to that for the United States, though it is, of course, smaller in absolute magnitude. Thus, improvements in the Canadian trade balance of up to $1.2 billion (1963 dollars) and $1.5 billion (1963 dollars) per annum, result from simulations I and III, respectively. This is remarkably close to the improvement actually registered in the first half of 1970 when the cyclical constellation was quite similar to that assumed in simulation III, though the U.S. rate of inflation was rather higher and pressure of demand both in Canada and in the United States rather lower than assumed.

The impact on other countries of the postulated economic developments in the United States and Canada (simulation I) varies (see Table 3). The effect is most pronounced on the exports of Japan and the Japanese trade balance deteriorates by up to $1½ billion (1963 dollars) per annum. For all other countries the effect is much smaller ranging from a maximal annual loss of $¾ billion for Germany to $0.2 billion for the United Kingdom (both 1963 dollars). These results would support the conclusion that the exchange rate adjustments which took place in 1967 and 1969 reflected adjustments to structural imbalances that were independent of U.S. cyclical developments in 1965-1969.

Since Simulations II and III assume steady high rates of growth and rather higher price increases in the industrial countries other than the United States and Canada, it is not surprising that the main

TABLE 2

Effect on Trade Flows of Steady High Employment Rates of Growth in Other Industrial Countries as Well as in the U.S. and Canada (Case III)

(billions of 1963 $, seasonally adjusted, annual rates)

A. Exports

Change from actual

	1965 I	II	1966 I	II	1967 I	II	1968 I	II	1969 I
U.S.	+ .3	+ .7	+ .6	+1.1	+1.2	+1.9	+2.2	+2.4	+2.2
Canada	+ .0	- .1	- .2	- .1	0	+ .0	+ .3	+ .2	+ .4*
France	+ .0	- .2	- .1	- .2	+ .1	+ .4	--.9	-1.2	-1.3
Germany	+ .4	+ .3	+ .1	- .2	- .1	- .2	- .2	- .9	-1.4
Italy	- .1	- .3	- .4	- .4	- .2	- .5	- .6	-1.6	-1.6
U.K.	+ .1	+ .2	+ .1	+ .1	+ .2	+ .2	- .1	- .3	- .4
Japan	- .2	- .3	- .7	- .7	- .6	- .5	- .4	- .7	- .7
Other OECD	+ .2	+ .3	+ .2	+ .6	+1.3	+1.3	+1.3	+ .2	- .6
Non-OECD	+ .4	+ .2	- .0	- .0	+ .7	+ .4	+ .5	- .6	- .8

B. Imports

	1965 I	II	1966 I	II	1967 I	II	1968 I	II	1969 I
U.S.	- .4	-1.4	-2.2	-2.3	-2.2	-2.8	-3.1	-3.5	-2.4
Canada	- .1	- .4	- .5	- .6	- .6	- .5	- .8	- .9	-1.1
France	+1.0	+ .8	+ .9	+ .8	+1.4	+1.5	+2.3	- .2	-1.1
Germany	- .3	+ .2	+ .1	+1.3	+2.5	+2.2	+1.9	+ .7	- .4
Italy	+ .5	+ .3	+ .2	+ .0	- .1	+ .1	+ .5	+ .6	+ .4
U.K.	- .1	+ .1	- .0	+ .5	+1.0	+1.0	+ .7	+ .5	- .0
Japan	+ .6	+1.0	+ .9	+ .5	+ .7	+ .4	+ .6	+ .3	+ .7
Other OECD	0								0
Non-OECD	- .0	+ .2	+ .1	- .1	- .1	+ .3	+ .1	+ .1	- .5

TABLE 3

Effect on Trade Balances of Non-Inflationary Growth in North America (Case I)

(billions of 1963 $, seasonally adjusted, annual rate)

									Change from actual
	1965 I	II	1966 I	II	1967 I	II	1968 I	II	1969 I
U.S.	+ .3	+1.0	+1.4	+1.9	+1.2	+1.7	+2.1	+2.5	+2.6
Canada	+ .1	+ .2	+ .3	+ .5	+ .6	+ .5	+ .8	+ .9	+1.2
France	- .0	- .1	- .1	- .3	- .2	- .3	- .4	- .5	- .6
Germany	- .0	- .1	- .2	- .3	- .3	- .3	- .5	- .5	- .7
Italy	- .0	- .1	- .2	- .2	- .2	- .2	.3	- .4	- .4
U.K.	- .0	- .1	- .1	- .2	- .1	- .1	- .2	- .2	- .2
Japan	- .2	- .3	- .7	- .8	- .8	- .9	-1.1	-1.4	-1.6
Other OECD	- .0	- .1	- .2	- .3	- .2	- .2	- .2	- .2	- .2
Non-OECD	- .1	- .4	- .3	- .4	0	- .2	- .3	- .3	- .2

Totals may not add due to rounding.

trade balance impact is concentrated on the imports of these countries. It is interesting to note, however, that the assumptions used are such as to smooth out the path of imports so that the level of imports reached by the first half of 1969 under the simulation II and III assumptions is not very different from that in the base case. Since utilization of resources in Italy has been rather lower than in other industrial countries in recent years, the simulation assumptions make a more consistently significant difference in this case than in others. In general, recent developments seem to bear out the overall reasonableness of the simulation results.

The combination of slower expansion in the United States and Canada and more rapid expansion in Europe and Japan results in substantial balance of trade deterioration spread among the major continental European countries (see Table 3). Toward the end of the period, the change, as already noted, is largest for Italy. The German trade balance from mid-1968 to mid-1969 is less favorable by an annual rate of between $1 and $1½ billion (1963 dollars). However, the highest impact, a deterioration of $2-2½ billion (1963 dollars, p.a.), is registered in 1967 and in the first half of 1968 when economic activity in Germany fell well below potential. The negative impact on France, which ran at around $1 billion (1963 dollars, p.a.) for most of the period, is also greatest during the first half of 1968 ($3¼ billion), when there was a significant amount of slack in the economy. Subsequently, when actual inflationary pressures began to approximate those assumed in simulation III, the simulation impact dwindles to almost nothing. Perhaps one of the more interesting effects is that the elimination of the 1967-68 slowdown in European economic activity improves the trade balance of Japan (compare simulation III with simulation I) despite the assumption of somewhat higher rates of growth and inflation in Japan itself.

Effects of Alternative Growth and Price Change Combinations

While it is clear that the pace of economic activity and the associated rates of price change have important effects upon trade flows, it is also clear that the estimated results of what could have been achieved under ideal type circumstances are not very realistic. Combinations of growth and inflation rates other than the "ideal" 4 and 2 per cent p.a., respectively, certainly would have been possible and, in fact, are probably more relevant now.

In order to evaluate the implications for trade flows of varying growth/price patterns, an additional set of simulations was carried out assuming alternative combinations of growth and price changes ranging from relatively low growth rates with fast price rises to higher growth rates with low inflation rates.

Assumptions for Alternative Growth/Price Change Simulations

The alternative simulations were run using the period from end-1964 to mid-1969 as a basis. It was assumed that outside the United States and Canada, economic activity and prices moved along the steady, high-activity path postulated for the earlier simulation II. Canadian activity and price changes were assumed to parallel those in the United States. The growth/price alternatives considered for the United States were: *

GNP	GNP deflator
(percent p.a,)	
4	4
4	3
4	2
3	2
3	3
3	4

*Corresponding but not identical assumptions were made for Canada.

TABLE 4
Effect of Variations in Rates of Growth and Inflation on U.S. Trade
Differences from steady high employment growth rates
GNP: 4% p.a. deflator: 2% p.a.
(billions of 1963 $, seasonally adjusted, annual rates)

GNP/Deflator	1965 I	II	1966 I	II	1967 I	II	1968 I	II	1969 I
			Trade Balance						
4%/4%	- .1	- .2	- .4	- .6	- .9	-1.1	-1.4	-1.7	-2.0
4%/3%	- .0	- .1	- .2	- .2	- .3	- .4	- .5	- .6	- .8
4%/2%	0	0	0	0	0	0	0	0	0
3%/2%	+ .1	+ .3	+ .4	+ .6	+ .7	+ .9	+1.1	+1.3	+1.5
3%/3%	+ .1	+ .2	+ .2	+ .3	+ .4	+ .5	+ .6	+ .7	+ .7
3%/4%	- .0	- .0	- .0	- .1	- .2	- .2	- .3	- .4	- .5

Results of Growth/Price Change Simulations

The results of these simulations for the United States are summarized in Table 4. The simulation period covers four and a half years—the period from the first half of 1965 through the first half of 1969—and it is important to note that the effect of alternative growth and price assumptions builds up over time.

Table 4 shows that substantially different balance of trade patterns result under different growth/price combinations. The approximate impact is measured by comparing deviations in the estimated trade results from those obtained by assuming a growth pattern of 4 per cent real growth in GNP p.a. combined with an annual rate of inflation of 2 per cent. The results allow some conclusions to be drawn regarding the different impact of price changes as compared with changes in activity rates. However, this distinction cannot be drawn too sharply because first, the elasticities derived from the model are subject to all the qualifications with which such estimates necessarily are hedged, and second, because of the interaction between the two variables over any length of time.

Looking first at the price effects, with this limitation in mind, it seems that exports are affected rather more by the relative price term than imports. Second, the level as well as the change in the rate of inflation is important. Thus, a change in the rate of inflation from 3 to 4 per cent has a larger effect than a change from 2 to 3 per cent. For example, the trade balance under a 3/3 growth price assumption would have been $¾ billion less by the first half of 1969 than under the 3/2 assumption, but $1¼ billion more than under the 3/4 growth path (1963 dollars, annual rates). And almost the entire acceleration in the change is accounted for by the change in exports.

Conversely, changes in the rate of activity affect imports more strongly than exports. Part of the lesser export reaction results from the fact that activity rates in Canada are assumed to change in tandem with those in the United States. Because Canada is an important market for U.S. exports, lower rates of growth in Canada, which reduce Canadian import demand, largely offset U.S. export gains elsewhere. But abstracting from this effect, the import reaction to activity changes still is considerably larger than that of exports. The difference in imports between a 4/2 and a 3/2 growth path builds by the end of the period to $1.7 billion (1963 dollars), while the difference in exports is negligible.

Putting together a combination of relatively low growth with a higher rate of inflation, that is a 3/3 growth path, as compared with a 4/2 growth pattern, yields an improvement in the trade balance of $0.7 billion (1963 dollars) by the end of the period. This improvement results from a $1.3 billion (1963 dollars) improvement in imports and a $0.6 billion (1963 dollars) deterioration in exports. Moving from the 3/4 growth path to a 4/4 pattern brings about a deterioration in the trade balance of $1.5 billion (1963 dollars), because an improvement in exports of $0.2 billion partly offsets a deterioration in the import bill of $1.8 billion (1963 dollars). Perhaps more relevant for current trends is that a movement from a 3/4 pattern to one of 4/3, which is not an unlikely assumption for 1971-72, involves a very small deterioration in the trade balance in the second half year after the change.

Conclusion

The calculations made in this study present an approximate measure of the impact of various types of alternative economic conditions on trade. The study indicates that the past few years of inflationary pressures in the United States have had substantial effects on the trade balance. Quantification of these effects shows that if demand management policies had succeeded in achieving a steady non-inflationary growth pafh for the United States economy from 1965 onward, the U.S. trade balance would have been almost $3 billion (current dollars, annual rate) higher in the first half of 1969 than it actually was. If other industrial countries at the same time had maintained continuous high employment of resources throughout the period, the first half 1969 trade surplus might have been $5 billion (current dollars, annual rate) higher.

But asking what might have happened under more ideal circumstances can be useful only insofar as it demonstrates that the difference would have been very great indeed. The results of this study cannot indicate the magnitude of the underlying strength—or otherwise—of the U.S. trade position in the 1970's. The lesson to be drawn is that macro-economic conditions can and do have large effects upon trade flows. Different combinations of growth and inflation rates have very different effects on trade flows as do different rates of capacity utilization even when combined with identical rates of growth. Thus, insofar as economic policy instruments shape domestic macro-economic conditions, they affect international trade flows in very specific and important ways. It is important to recognize this fact and to quantify it, as far as possible, not necessarily in order to tailor domestic policy to external constraints, but rather to be able to anticipate, and deal with, the balance of payments effects of domestic policy decisions.

FOOTNOTES

1. F.G. Adams, H. Eguchi, and F. Meyer-zu-Schlochtern, *An Econometric Analysis of International Trade*, OECD, Paris, 1969.
2. The original model is described in F.G. Adams, H. Eguchi, and F. Meyer-zu-Schlochtern, *op. cit.* An updated version developed by A. Yajima and F. Meyer-zu-Schlochtern, was used for this work. We wish to thank them for providing the card deck and for other assistance in adapting the model for our purpose.
3. In this simulation it was assumed that there is no feedback so that activity in the United States and Canada was taken at its actual level.
4. As noted, comparisons should be made between the base case and the alternatives. This is particularly important for the 1967 period, because the U.S. equation did not catch the temporary slowdown of U.S. imports at that time.

Management Science Models for Multicurrency Cash Management

Alan C. Shapiro
University of Pennsylvania

Introduction

One of the significant economic risks which confronts firms engaged in international business is the exchange loss due to foreign currency devaluations and revaluations. While the international monetary system is currently in a state of flux, it appears likely that there will once again be fixed exchange rates although with bands wider than the present 1%.

A key decision problem thus faced by the treasurers of most multinational corporations is how to manage the firm's liquid assets and liabilities in various currencies so as to minimize its exchange rate losses adjusted for the cost of this management.

The available literature, with two exceptions (see Ferber [3] and Lietaer [5]), is mostly verbal and does not provide explicit decision rules. This paper attempts to fill the gap by formulating the problem of determining when the danger of exchange loss outweighs the hedging (or protection) costs.

Foreign exchange problems vary from company to company but presumably all attempt to maximize expected income denominated in a base currency (dollars for an American firm) with due consideration for risk factors. Instead of postulating a particular corporate loss function, risk is handled by various constraints on maximum loss.

Where forward markets exist, the most widely used means of protection against exchange risks arising from parity changes is the purchase or sale of forward contracts. To be more specific, from now on we will only talk about the exchange risks arising from the devaluation of a foreign currency. The following hedging procedures for devaluations are reversed for upward revaluations since revaluations present the exact opposite problems. The businessman who has accounts receivable, denominated in a soft currency (one liable to be devalued), can sell these expected receipts forward in a bank. This forward contract calls for delivery at a future date of a specified amount of foreign currency against dollar payment, with the exhange rate fixed at the time the contract is entered into. By the time the contract matures, the spot (or present) rate for the currency may be above or below the agreed upon rate but this has no effect on the contract.

In order to sell a soft currency forward there must be someone willing to buy it. However, since the currency's stability is suspect, the buyer will normally be willing to buy this currency only if it is being sold at a discount. This discount can be considered to be an insurance premium to the seller (or a risk premium to the buyer). The size of this premium reflects the buyer's expectations regarding the future spot rate of this currency as well as on the extent of government intervention in the forward market. Governments often support their currencies foıward in order to relieve speculative pressure on the spot market.

A key feature of the forward market is that it is possible to cover periods t to t+t in the future, without covering any intervening periods, by buying the suspect currency forward for t-1 periods and selling it forward for t+t. For example, depending on the structure of forward rates and the probabilities of devaluation in the future a firm might decide to only be covered for months 4 through 6.

Banks do not usually charge a commission on their foreign exchange transactions, but instead make their profit on the small spread between their buying and selling rates. Competition keeps this spread minimal. The banks' profits arise from their large volume of transactions. The hedging problem studied here assumes that a firm has known but varying amounts of exposure in each of a finite number of future periods. If forward contract prices didn't change over time, one could just compare the expected extent of a devaluation in any particular period t with that period's hedging cost and thus decide whether or not to hedge. However, these costs do change over time. In addition, a devaluation may occur before t thus obviating the need to hedge for period t.

If a firm thinks that present structure of forward rates is out of line with the risks involved, it could wait till a later time period to enter into a forward contract in the expectation that a future forward rate structure will be more attractive. The optimal hedging policy must therefore be determined by means of multi-period sequential decision strategy.

Model Formulation

The way in which any problem is formulated makes a big difference in the ease with which it can be solved. The hedging problem can be viewed as one of determining how to protect a certain exposure over time, i.e., at the beginning of each period we decide for which future periods to hedge. A model describing this decision process would be enormously complex. At any stage, it would be necessary to keep track of all the periods which have already been hedged for and those which are still uncovered. In order to determine which periods to cover now, the movement of all future forward prices must be considered along with the chances of a devaluation in each period.

Another way of looking at the problem leads to a formulation which is much simpler and far more amenable to solution. With this view in mind, we make a separate decision problem for each period that we wish to consider covering. Thus, a T-period problem can be decomposed into T separate binary decision problems. Suppose we are interested in determining when to hedge for the t-th period in the future. At the beginning of each period, given that devaluation has not yet occurred, we receive a hedging price for the t-th period. We then decide either to hedge now or wait for the next period price. There is always the chance that if we delay hedging this period we may be able to get a more favorable rate in the future. Conversely, 'future rates may not be more favorable and a devaluation may occur in the meantime. These decisions are made sequentially using the method of dynamic programming. This method is founded on the principle of optimality which says that "an optimal set of decisions has the property that whatever the first decision is, the remaining decisions must be optimal with respect to the outcome which results from the first decision." [1, p. 83] In the first period, we only know the present rate and not what the future forward rates will be. However, we assume that we do know the probability distributions of these future prices. In computing the cost of our present decisions, we must consider that our future decisions will be optimal on the basis of the particular values that these stochastic variables will take on.

We can go through this process at most t times. If we do not hedge at any of the t decision points and a devaluation has not yet occurred, we will then accept the risk of a devaluation in this particular period ourselves. Since we are only protecting against a t-th period devaluation, an earlier devaluation does not cost us anything in period t. The loss is ascribed to the period in which the devaluation occurred. If we are using a T-period horizon, we will initially solve T separate problems and put these solutions together to determine which periods to cover now and which to leave uncovered, at least until next period.

The T-period problem can be decomposed into T separate problems if there are no external economies resulting from hedging for more than one period at a time. According to a trader for one of the major New York banks engaged in foreign exchange transactions, the cost of hedging for an odd date is relatively more expensive but not significantly so. Forward contracts for any maturities besides 30, 60, 90, 180 days or one year are assumed to be odd.

In actual practice, a horizon of about 18 months would be used. This particular time period was chosen because, to quote one treasurer interviewed, "After this period of time, prices and other conditions have usually adjusted sufficiently so that the profit margin is no longer threatened." The lengths of these periods can be increasing over time to take account of our greater uncertainty as we go further out in the future. The only constraint on these lengths is that they must correspond with the lengths of forward contracts available in order to be able to hedge completely for any period at the beginning of either that period or a previous one. This constraint is not very restrictive since contracts can be made for most odd dates of less than one year (see above).

The loss function is assumed to be sufficiently linear to permit the use of expected cost as a criterion. This assumption is valid whenever the exposure during any one period is sufficiently small as to have a minimal effect on the profit and loss statement. The use of a separate account for devaluation losses could provide sufficient motivation to look only at expected cost. In addition risk can be handled by using expected costs plus additional constraints on maximum loss. These constraints are developed mathematically in Section 4.

In the following models, we concentrate on hedging for the t-th period in the future, $t = 1, \ldots, T$.

Parameters

t - the period we are protecting

$\bar{\pi}_j$ - the conditional probability of no devaluation in the j-th period given that a devaluation has not yet occurred by period j

$\bar{K}_t$ - the expected extent of a t-th period devaluation given that no devaluation has occured by period t

P_j- the cost of hedging for period t if it is done at the beginning of the j-th period

z_j - the particular value of the error term indicating the unknown change in the cost of hedging from period j to j+1 $(E(z) = 0)$

f(z) - the stationary probability density function for z

μ_j- the price trend from period j to j+1

Price Movements

Initially, we are assuming an absolute random walk and a maximum of one devaluation during the horizon. This random walk hypothesis is that $P_{j+1} = P_j + \mu_j + z_j$ where $z \approx f$ with mean zero. This hypothesis assumes that price determination is Markovian, i.e., next period's price is only dependent on this period's price.

An alternative stochastic model is the mean reversion process. In this process

$$P_{j+1} = P_j + \mu_j - z_{j-1} + z_j$$

where the z_j's are independently distributed random variables. In this process, the occurrence of z_j has no implication for the expected value of prices in the future, since the mean of the process reverts back to the initial value plus the trend. A model such as this could describe a fairly thin market which is sensitive to large purchases. Wide swings in price could occur but there would be a tendency to revert back to a "normal" price.

Under either of these two models, negative prices are possible. This problem is avoided by using the geometric random walk. This stochastic process is described by

$$P_{j+1} = P_j(1 + \mu_j + z_j)$$

where the z_j's are independently distributed random variables and $1 + \mu_j + z_j \geq 0$

These future forward rates only hold true if a devaluation has not already taken place. If a devaluation has occurred, the decision problem is over unless a second devaluation is assumed possible.

The trend in prices of a forward contract for a particular period is allowed to be either positive, negative, or some combination over time. If the only additional information expected to be gained over time is whether or not a devaluation has yet occurred, then prices should have a positive trend. The price right now for protecting the t-th period reflects the probability and extent of a devaluation in the t-th period. If a devaluation does not occur in the first period, then the conditional probability of a t-th period devaluation will increase. Since the hedging price is determined by the risk perceived by the market participants, the new price must now be greater, on average, than it was in the first period.

It is possible, though, to foresee circumstances in which the trend in prices could be negative. A smaller trade deficit than expected will decrease the a priori possibility of a parity change in succeeding periods. Similarly, the exchange crisis may be seen as over if a devaluation does not occur by a particular time. Any event which will decrease the possibility of a devaluation in the future should lower the cost of forward cover.

The Basic Hedging Model

Let $K_j(p)$ be the expected cost, at the beginning of period j, of following an optimal hedging policy when $p_j = p$. $K_j(p)$ must balance off the cost of hedging right now against the chance of receiving a more favorable rate next period. Then the problem can be formulated as:

$$K_j(p) = \min\{p, \ \bar{\Pi}_j \ E[K_{j+1}(p+\mu_j+z_j)] + (1 - \Pi_j)0\}; \quad j=1,\ldots, t-1$$

$$= \min\{p, \bar{K}_t\} \ ; \ j=t$$

where $\bar{k}_t$ is the expected extent of a devaluation in period t given that no devaluation has yet occurred.

$E[K_{j+1}]$ is multiplied by $\bar{\pi}_j$ because the expected cost of an optimal policy from period j+1 on is only incurred if a devaluation does not occur in period j. If a devaluation does occur in the j-th period, then the future costs of protecting period t are zero, since there is no longer any risk of a t-th period devaluation. This of course assumes that a maximum of only one devaluation will occur within the planning horizon. From now on, the term $(1 - \bar{\pi}_j)0$ will be dropped.

There is no discounting in this or any of the other forward exchange hedging models because no costs are incurred until period

t. There are normally no margin requirements on a forward contract and no money changes hands till the period hedged for arrives. Similarly, the loss from a t-th period devaluation accrues only to that period.

As shown by Breiman [2], this can be formulated as a linear programming problem if we assume that the distribution of z_j is discrete. The L.P. formulation can facilitate the problem's solution; nevertheless, the dynamic programming forumlation is the most natural approach. Using this approach several qualitative results can be derived which simplify computation effort in both the linear and dynamic programming models. The proof of the following statements can be found in [8].

Optimal Policy

The structure of the optimal policy can be simply described. In each period j there is a critical number c_j such that if $p_j < c_j$ it is optimal to hedge immediately; otherwise we would wait till the following period. There are several conclusions about c_j which can be drawn (see [8] for proofs).

Conclusion 1: c_j is a nondecreasing function of μ_j. This means that as the greater the expected price rise wext period, the more we are willing to pay to hedge in this period.

Conclusion 2: c_j is a nondecreasing function of $\bar{\pi}_j$. This means that as the chance, $1-\bar{\pi}_j$, of a j-th period devaluation increases, we will pay less to hedge in period j against a t-th period devaluation. This makes sense once we realize that a devaluation in period j would spare us the cost of protecting against a devaluation in period t for t > j.

Conclusion 3: $p < c_j$ only if $\bar{\pi}_j (p + \mu_j) > p$. An interpretation of this condition is that we will only hedge in period j if the expected cost of hedging in period j+1, $\bar{\pi}_j (p + \mu_j)$, is greater than the cost, p, of hedging right now. As a corollary to this condition, we will not hedge in any period for which $\mu_j \leq 0$.

Under suitable restrictions, the c_j's are monotonically increasing. More specifically, $c_1 \leq c_2 \leq \ldots \leq c_t$ if $\Pi_j \leq \Pi_{j+1}$ and $\mu_j < \mu_{j+1}$ for j = 1, $\ldots$, t-1. In other words, we are willing to pay a higher price for protecting period t as time passes if the expected hedging cost is increasing and the conditional probability of a devaluation prior to t is declining.[1]

Most of the above statements hold true for the mean reversion process $P_{j+1} = P_j + \mu_j + z_j - z_{j-1}$
as well. The only difference is that now the necessary condition for hedging becomes $\bar{\pi}_j(p + \mu_j - z_{j-1}) > p$ where $p = b + \sum^{j-1} \mu_i + z_{j-1}$. With this process, hedging could take place in period j i= $\mu_j \leq 0$ as long as z_{j-1} is sufficiently negative.

. With the geometric random walk, the necessary condition for hedging is $\bar{\pi}_j \, p(1+\mu_j) > p$. Also hedging will not take place in any period j for which $\mu_j \leq 0$. Using the same methods previously employed, it is easy to show that the c_j's are monotonically nondecreasing if $\bar{\pi}_j(1 + \mu_j) \leq \bar{\pi}_{j+1}(1+ \mu_{j+1})$.

Optimal Hedging With Recourse to Unhedging

The model we have been dealing with so far assumes that once a firm hedges it will hold the forward contract till maturity. However, firms may hedge at a particular point in time only to decide at a later date that prices of forward contracts and devaluation probabilities have changed sufficiently to make it advantageous to unhedge. The following model describes an optimal hedging policy with the possibility of unhedging and rehedging each period considered explicitly. The only constraint is that hedging must occur before unhedging can take place.

In this model, the buying and selling price for forward contracts are assumed equal. This is not quite true but the spread between the two prices is usually close enough to zero to ignore it.

Let $K_j(p,0)$ be the expected cost, at the beginning of period j, of following an optimal hedging policy when $p_j = p$ and period t is not covered. Similarly, let $K_j(p,1)$ be the expected value of following an optimal unhedging policy when $p_j = p$ and period t is hedged. Then,

$$K_j(p,0) = \min \left\{ \overset{\text{Hedge}}{p - \bar{\pi}_j E[K_{j+1}(p_{j+1},1)/p_j = p]}, \overset{\text{Wait}}{\bar{\pi}_j E[K_{j+1}(p_{j+1},0)/p_j = p]} \right\};$$
$$j=1, \ldots, t-1$$

$$= \min \left\{ p, \bar{K}_t \right\}; \quad j=t$$

and

$$K_j(p,1) = \max \left\{ \overset{\text{Unhedge}}{p - \bar{\pi}_j E[K_{j+1}(p_{j+1},0)/p_j = p]}, \overset{\text{Wait}}{\bar{\pi}_j E[K_{j+1}(p_{j+1},1)/p_j = p]} \right\};$$
$$j=1,\ldots,t-1$$

$$= \max \left\{ p, \bar{K}_t \right\}$$

Both $K_j(p,0)$ and $K_j(p,1)$ have $\bar{\pi}_j \, E[K_{j+1}]$ terms on the left hand side of their functional equations. These terms arise as follows: if we hedged in period j then the cost to us is p. However, the option of unhedging adds value to our optimal policy. The value of holding this contract in period j+1 is $K_{j+1}(p_{j+1},1)$ if a devaluation does not occur in period j and 0 otherwise. Then by taking expected values, we see that the cost of purchasing a contract now is the price, p, that we pay minus $\bar{\pi}_j E[K_{j+1}(p_{j+1},1)/p_j = p]$, the expected benefit that we receive from having the option to unhedge. Similar reasoning explains the $-\bar{\pi}_j E[K_{j+1}(p,0)/p_j = p]$ in $K_j(p,1)$.

The optimal policy is extraordinarily simple, particularly when compared to the complex functional equations. The policy is:

If

$\bar{\pi}_j \, E[p_{j+1} \mid p_j = p] > p$, remained hedged if you are already hedged j hedge if you are unhedged. For $\bar{\pi}_j E[p_{j+1} \mid p_j] < p$, unhedge if you are hedged; remain unhedged if not. If $\bar{\pi}_j E[p_{j+1} \mid p_j = p]$, remain as you are. Thus, the former necessary condition for hedging in j is now a sufficient condition as well.

Optimal Financing Policy

The hedging problem, though, cannot be separated from the optimal financing pattern since any financing decision affects the firm's exposure to parity changes.

Companies always have the problem of how to finance inventories, accounts receivable, and other current assets. Suppose that a company has the option of borrowing either dollars or the local currency. By the time the dollars must be repaid, the local currency may have devalued necessitating an increase in the local currency required to repay the dollar loan. If instead borrowing were done locally, there would be a decrease in exposure. Depending on the relative interest rates in the two countries (local interest rates are often much higher) and the possibility and extent of a devaluation, companies may choose to finance their foreign operations locally.

Many companies also have some flexibility as to the timing of their hard currency remittances and timing of their payments for hard currency imports. A company which suspects that a devaluation is approaching can borrow the local currency and sell it spot for dollars. It can then remit these dollars or else keep them in a special dollar account in a local bank until such time as a dollar payable comes due. Where government regulations permit, this excess liquidity can be loaned to affiliates in other countries.

Rutenberg [7] pioneered the concept of using mathematical programming techniques to maneuver liquid assets on a world wide basis so as to take "advantage of being multinational." His paper concentrated on how best to channel excess funds from those subsidiaries which are net generators to those forecast to be net users. The various constraints, costs, and tax implications of four ways of transferring funds are analyzed in some detail: adjusting transfer prices, charging fees and royalties, making intersubsidiary loans, and remitting dividends. However, the model does not explicitly deal with financing sources external to the firm.

This section focuses on the multi-subsidiary financing decision in the light of risks arising from devaluation and revaluation-prone currencies. It extends Rutenberg's model by treating a subsidiary's excess funds as variables to be determined in the context of all available financing options including external sources as well as intersubsidiary loans.

The financing problem is formulated using a network model with $(n+1)T$ nodes where the horizon is broken into T periods which could be of uneven length. In any real application of this model, the initial periods would be of fairly short length, with the lengths of the succeeding periods increasing.[2] The basic idea behind this is that a firm has fairly good information about the near future but becomes increasingly uncertain about later periods.

In each time period, there are $n+1$ nodes representing the parent corporation and its n subsidiaries with the i'th affiliate assumed to require a minimum cash balance, $c_i(t)$, in each period t. These minimum balances are assumed to be determined outside of this model but the dual variables associated with the cash balance constraints can be used to evaluate the marginal costs of increasing or decreasing these minimum balances. The financing requirements may be positive or negative depending on whether the particular affiliate is a net user or generator of funds in that period.

Some of the external financing options are common to all subsidiaries and others are unique to particular subsidiaries. Access to the local capital markets, at least for the lower cost loans, is often limited to those who have "legitimate" business interests within that particular country. Companies which have built up contacts and expertise in dealing with various national and international capital markets can be expected to make more use of this knowledge in the future as the liquidity squeeze, brought on in large part by the O.F.D.I. regulations, increases.

There are assumed to be m_i available financial markets within the ith country. Three of the more common means of local borrowing include overdrafts, discounting of receivables, and short-term loans.

There is usually a clearly defined hierarchy of borrowing within each country i in the sense that any given option k, its cost, $r_{ik}(t,s)$, for a loan from t to t+s, relative to that of the other options can generally be determined a priori. Some options may be used, even though cheaper ones are available, in order to keep these sources open in the case of a future liquidity shortage. This feature can be entered as minimum borrowing constraints on these options.

In addition, there are generally limits on loans available from any one source. These limits can be entered as borrowing constraints.

The basic decisions involving each subsidiary in time period t then are the determination of which local borrowing options to use as well as the term of the borrowing. Given the anticipated future movements of interest rates, it may be best to meet future financing needs by borrowing now and investing the loan in a short-term asset till it is needed.

The purpose of this model is to make short-term decisions in order to minimize the after tax cost of the multinational firm's financial plan adjusted for interest earned.

It assumes that cash requirements and other relevant parameters such as interest rates are deterministic. According to Van Horne [9,p.435], "For many firms near-term cash flows are highly predictable. To overlook their predictability and treat all cash flows as random is likely to result in cash management policies that are less than optimal." Orgler [6,p.22] agrees that "the uncertainty element is less important in making cash management decisions than in deriving long-range financial plans such as capital budgets." In addition, most executives interviewed felt they could predict short-term interest rates with near certainty.

The model would be re-run every period, incorporating new information on parameter values, and thus should not compound any mistakes based on the use of mean value estimates. Parametric analysis can be used to determine the sensitivity of the solution to changing parameter values. Since only the first period decisions are actually implemented, the model's solution should not be too far from the optimal one provided that parameter estimates are not too inaccurate.

Additional constraints can be added to make this model conform more closely to reality. The maximum amount of loans available from a particular source might be a function of the previous levels of borrowing. An example of such a constraint which could be added to the model is that the amount of money borrowed in period t cannot be more than 10% greater than the amount borrowed in t-1 with the upper limits on total borrowings outstanding previously mentioned.

Past history could also affect the maximum amount of money that a subsidiary could transfer out of its host country in any one period. This might be reflected in a constraint that the amount of money sent out of the country in period t cannot exceed the amount sent out in t-1 by more than 5% with an absolute upper limit on transfers.

As was mentioned before, though, any financing decision affects the total exposure of the firm to parity charges. If we let $E_i(t)$ represent the multinational corporation's expected t-th period exposure in currency i before the model is run, its new exposure, $e_i(t)$, can be found by aggregating the financing decisions of the parent and all of its subsidiaries. Of course, $e_i(t)$ depends on the value, $f_i(t)$ of forward contract hedging in currency i carried out for period t.

Borrowing for hedging purposes has been greatly facilitated by the development of the world's first truly international capital market, the Euromoney market. Most multinational companies have established stand-by Eurocurrency facilities, usually through the London branches of the major New York banks. The determination of which currency or currencies to borrow as well as the term of the loan depends on the relative interest rates along with the possible extent of devaluations or revaluations of the different currencies.

Foreign Exchange Risk

This section will discuss some ways of coping with the risk aversion evidenced by most corporate officials interviewed. Management is often willing to pay a large premium in order to avoid a large foreign exchange loss in any one period. Creating an accounting reserve for exchange losses is one technique which would avoid the appearance of sizable losses, on the income statement, in any one year. Its basic function is to cushion the impact of exchange losses and thus lessen management's incentive to pay uneconomically high premiums for exchange risk protection. This concept is discussed further in [4].

Whether or not a reserve fund is set up, top management might still be hesitant as to whether stockholders and security analysts will accept a sizable exchange loss with equanimity. To reduce this possibility, a firm could establish constraints on the maximum exchange loss it would accept in any one period. Let $d_{M_i}(t)$ be the maximum possible extent of a devaluation in country i in period t. With $e_i(t)$ as the exposure in currency i during t, a restriction on the maximum devaluation loss would appear as

$$\sum_i d_{Mi}(t)\ e_i\ (t) \le F(t) \quad t=1, \ldots, T$$

However, even though a loss this size is possible, it may not be very probable.

We can use either of two possible approaches to take account of the probabilities associated with the various possible losses. One would be to constrain the maximum expected loss. If $\pi_{ik}(t)$ is the probability of currency i devaluing by the faction d_k in period t, constraining maximum expected loss in all currencies by $G(t)$ in any one period t, would appear as

$$\sum_i \sum_k \pi_{ik}(t)\ d_k e_i(t) \le G(t); \quad t=1,\ldots,T$$

The other method would directly consider the various probabilities by using a chance-constrained programming approach. This approach would be useful if a company feels that while it is highly desirable to constrain losses below a certain point, there is a limit to what it is willing to pay to achieve this goal. In other words, the firm might decide to accept a small probability of losses greater than it would really like in order to make a substantial savings in hedging costs. This constraint would say that the probability of losing more than K dollars in any one period should be less than or equal to α . For losses in any one currency, this constraint is expressed as $e_i(t) \le D(t)$

where $D(t)$ is found by the following procedure: Rank the d_k's by decreasing size, i.e., $d_1 \ge d_2 \ge d_m$; then find the value of j for which $\sum_{k=1}^{j} \pi_{tk} \le \alpha$; the value of $D(t)$ will then be $\frac{K}{d_j}$. It can be seen that, with this limit on exposure, the probability of losing more than K will be less than or equal to α. In general, it will not be possible to find closed form limits on the $e_i(t)$'s when we try to probabilitistically constrain the losses on several currencies together. However, we can have several constraints — $K_1,...,K_n$ — with associated risk levels — $\alpha_1,...,\alpha_\ell$ — for any particular currency. The $D(t)$ for any arbitrary loss and risk level pair, K_i, α_i, can be found by using the procedure described above.

These constraints can cost a firm a sizable amount of money. The dual variables associated with them will reflect the value to the firm of making marginal changes in the size of these maximum allowable losses. By running the chance-constrained problem parametrically, a firm can determine its expected savings from increasing α. Given this information, the company can decide on a reasonable level for α.

The expected loss from one dollar's worth of exposed assets in currency i in period t, $L_i(t)$, is derived from the appropriate optimal hedging through forward contracts model developed previously. The hedging models consider the optimal timing of the purchase of a forward contract. It is possible for the optimal policy to be to leave the assets exposed because the cost of hedging outweighed the potential losses from a devaluation. This is the relevant cost to use because we are concerned with the cost of managing exposed assets.

Thus far, we have assumed that the criterion function is in the form of an expected after tax cost which we are attempting to minimize subject to some constraints on the size of the foreign exchange loss. These constraints, however, may not adequately represent management's risk aversion which views losses in a nonlinear manner.

There are several ways of dealing with this problem. One is to take the approach of Lietaer [5] and use a quadratic or some other continuous nonlinear loss function. A more fruitful approach, both computationally and descriptively is to establish a preference ordering in the form of a piecewise continuous linear function. Its theoretical justification is that as the magnitude of potential loss increases, managers tend to be willing to pay a higher proportion of the expected loss as insurance. This fraction will generally be more than 1. As the expected loss rises, this fraction would increase in discrete steps. The more steps there are, the better is the approximation to management's true preferences. The fewer linear segments used, though, the fewer variables needed for the linear program.

Summary

These models make no pretense to being substitutes for managerial experience and judgment. They are designed to be used interactively, to reflect the knowledge and various tastes and expectations of management in order to determine which actions are most suitable under certain conditions. Their computational simplicity allows optimal policies to be found for many different assumptions and conditions.

FOOTNOTES

1. Since $\bar{\pi}_j$, the conditional probability of no devaluation in period j is increasing, the conditional probability of a j-th period devaluation must be declining.

2. See Orgler [6] for a good discussion of unequal time period models.

REFERENCES

1. Bellman, Richard, *Dynamic Programming*, Princeton, New Jersey: Princeton University Press, 1957.
2. Breiman, Leo, "Stopping Rule Problems," Chapter 10 in *Applied Combinatorial Mathematics*, (E. Beckenback, ed.) New York: John Wiley and Sons, Inc. 1964.
3. Ferber, Robert C., "Optimal Hedging Against Devaluation", Paper delivered at T.I.M.S. XVIth International Meeting.
4. King, Alfred M., "Budgeting Foreign Exchange Losses," *Management Accounting*, Vol. 51, No. 4 (October 1969), pp. 39-41, 46.
5. Lietaer, Bernard A., "Managing Risks in Foreign Exchange," *Harvard Business Review*, Vol. 48, No. 2 (March-April 1970), pp. 127-138.
6. Orgler, Yair E., *Cash Management: Methods and Models*, Belmont, California: Wadsworth Pub. Co., 1969.
7. Rutenberg, David P., "Manuevering Liquid Assets in a Multi-national Company: Formulation and Deterministic Solution Procedures," *Management Science*, Vol. 16, No. 10 (June 1970), pp. B-671-684.
8. Shapiro, Alan, "Management Science Models for Multicurrency Cash Management," Ph.D. thesis, Graduate School of Industrial Administration, Carnegie-Mellon University, 1971.
9. Van Horne, James, *Financial Management and Policy*, Englewood Cliffs, New Jersey: Prentice-Hall Inc., 1971.

Maneuvering Liquid Assets in a Multinational Company: Formulation and Deterministic Solution Procedures*

David P. Rutenberg
Carnegie-Mellon University

Introduction

Over a finite horizon each national subsidiary of a multi-national company can be forecast to be a net source or sink of funds. Each of these subsidiaries in each year is considered to be the node of a network; funds flow along the directed arcs connecting the nodes. Liquid assets carried by the subsidiaries on the arcs between time periods earn interest minus adjustments for expected devaluations. In each time period a flow of funds between each pair of subsidiaries can be achieved by manipulating transfer prices and managerial fees, by making short term intersubsidiary loans, and by paying dividends up the intersubsidiary ownership tree. The costs and constraints on these flows are outlined with particular attention given to the IRC Subpart F regulations of the U.S. 1962 Revenue Act, and to the 1968 regulations of the Office of Foreign Direct Investment. It is shown to be extremely important that subsidiary dollar accounts count toward the compensating balance requirements of a U.S. bank, and it is also shown that there are benefits to a global tax consolidation under Subpart F. The problem can be solved as a generalized network (weighted distribution problem). This avoids the need to guess at the average discount rate if it is to be solved as an ordinary network.

*Reprinted from *Management Science*, Vol. 16, No. 10, June, 1970 by special permission.

The Revenue Act of 1962 changed the rules under which U.S. corporations could use tax havens. Before 1962 there were no U.S. taxes imposed directly on the earnings of subsidiaries incorporated abroad; only when these subsidiaries remitted dividends to their U.S. parent were taxes levied on these dividends. So it became quite common for U.S. based international companies to create a headquarters and a two-tier legal structure. On the top was the U.S. parent. In the first tier was a holding company, incorporated in a low tax nation which levied no taxes on dividends received from abroad. And in the second tier were all the national subsidiaries, legally owned by the first tier holding company. The holding company was used as a low (tax) cost reservoir and conduit for sending funds between national subsidiaries.

By the 1962 Act, the U.S.A. became the only nation in the world to tax profits of subsidiaries abroad before these profits are repatriated as dividends. Certain relief provisions, or loopholes, were created in the Act (supposedly to stave off concerted lobbying by corporations most affected). Nevertheless, not much cunning use has been made of these provisions. For example, a U.S. company need pay no tax on a subsidiary incorporated in Bermuda for the purpose of manufacturing in Ireland, and selling the products to the world. This lack of use is partly because the Act has not been subject to any judicial interpretation to clean up areas of ambiguity; it is also because there have been too many opportunities and problems requiring immediate resolution by capable management.

Seven years have now passed. Capable international managers are more numerous so some have time for tactical planning. The benefits of analyzing the world wide movement of liquid assets depend upon the cost of capital. Not only has there been a long run increase in interest rates over the last few years, but there was a jump in the opportunity cost of capital in foreign subsidiaries of U.S. corporations with the January 1, 1968 promulgation of capital controls administered by the Office of Foreign Direct Investment (OFDI). In a like manner, other nations erect emergency currency controls, and then dismantle them slowly.

Companies differ in the guidelines they impose on subsidiaries for handling liquid assets, but three patterns predominate each corresponding to the archetype [12] of headquarter-subsidiary relationships. Some companies used to insist that the entire profits of each subsidiary be repatriated to the headquarters as dividends each year; this assured control though at a high cost in taxes. Some companies view each subsidiary as totally independent (which it legally is), and do not interfere in the management of liquid assets; this policy has the fewest bad behavioral consequences though the result is that the company's worldwide liquid asset inventory is quite high. Between these two extreme policies is a third, the subject of this paper, in which liquid assets are sent to subsidiaries when needed by manipulating transfer prices, managerial fees and royalties, dividends, and intersubsidiary loans so as to minimize taxes paid to the world minus interest received. Clearly, such headquarters intervention is destructive to incentive systems built upon profit centers. Whether maneuvering is worth the effort can be determined only by building a model; the difference between current costs and model optimal costs provides a benchmark against which to judge the behavioral costs of headquarters intervention.

If maneuvering liquid assets is deemed prudent, one main use should be in reacting to anticipated devaluations, currency controls and other such risks and opportunities. Only a deterministic model is presented in this paper. Yet many cases can be run so as to explore a strategy for dealing with an anticipated risk. To formally plan for optimal flexibility in the face of risk had better wait until there is data and experience with a deterministic model. Using stochastic programming with recourse [16] one can plan for flexibility so long as updated information can be inputted at only one instant of time (though conceptually more stages can be added). In reality information is arriving continuously to change expectations about future events. The maximum principle and canonical equations of Pontryagin have been extended to stochastic control systems by Kushner and Schweppe [9], and though they provide a conceptual scheme for the control of continuously changing expectations work on computational procedures has barely started and appears extremely complicated.

2. The Model

The subject of this study is the optimal use of tax havens, bilateral tax treaties, non-uniform treatments of income received from abroad, and national differences in income tax rates, import duties and border taxes. This is a partial analysis for tactical planning because it takes as given the planned operations of each national subsidiary, and hence whether in each year the subsidiary is to be a net source or recipient of funds.

There are N subsidiaries around the world, and the analysis will be done over T years. Each subsidiary in each year causes a net outflow of funds $b_i(t)$ from the pool of liquid assets in subsidiary i in year t (a net inflow would be represented as a negative $b_i(t)$). For example, if subsidiary i intends to construct a new plant in four years' time, then for the next three years it will likely be a net source of funds $(b_i(t)<0)$ but on the fourth year (construction year) it will be a net sink for funds $(b_i(4)>0)$. Pro forma balance sheets and income forecasts have to be made for any kind of financial planning, so we assume that the net availability or requirements for funds are known. The transactions demand for cash in each subsidiary should also be estimated, for changes in this inventory affect the net availability for funds. Also associated with each subsidiary in each year is its profit π_i, its subpart F income (as defined in the U.S. Internal Revenue Code), and the effective rate of foreign income tax. Liquid funds can be held by a subsidiary from one year to the next. This holding is represented as a flow through the arc connecting a subsidiary in one year to the same subsidiary in the succeeding year. If there is a significant term structure to the best interest rates obtainable by a subsidiary, then two year arcs can be added to take advantage of the higher interest rates obtainable on longer term loans. However, to simplify exposition we shall use only one year arcs. A peculiar feature of U.S. banks must also be depicted: if any part of the company has obtained a loan from a U.S. bank, then the company will be required to keep on deposit in branches of that bank no less than a specified "compensating balance." If each subsidiary maintains a dollar account in the U.S. bank, then the sum of these accounts can be used to satisfy the compensating balance requirement (even though the individual accounts are members of different OFDI class nations). Thus an aggregated compensating balance is an effective way to make intersubsidiary loans. The compensating balance requirement is depicted by the bunched parallel y arcs in Figure 1; the sum of flow through these arcs must be greater than or equal to the compensating balance requirement.

In Figure 1, operations in country i drain the system of $b_i(t)$ and $b_i(t + 1)$ in years t and $t + 1$ respectively, whereas in country j the local subsidiary is forecast to be a net generator of funds $b_j(t)<0$ in year t, but a net user of funds $b_j(t + 1)>0$ in year $t + 1$. A feasible solution is one which gets funds to the subsidiaries that need them. For a given pattern of intersubsidiary ownerships, there are at least four ways to transmit liquid assets from one national subsidiary to another. These control variables are:

$p_{ij}(t)$ Adjust the transfer prices on shipments between subsidiaries i and j.

$f_{ij}(t)$ Charge legal and managerial fees and royalties on technical knowledge supplied to subsidiary i by subsidiary j.

$l_{ij}(t), l_{ji}(t + 1)$

Make new intersubsidiary loans, and repay old ones with interest. Delayed invoicing is a loan.

$d_{ij}(t)$

Remit dividends from subsidiary i to its legal stockholder subsidiary j.

There are N subsidiaries, and the analysis is done over time periods $0, \ldots, T$. The state of the system is specified by the amount of liquid assets held by each subsidiary:

$x_i(t,t+1)$ Amount of liquid assets employed in their most profitable manner by subsidiary i in the one year period from t to $t+1$.

$y_i(t,t+1)$ *Amount of cash held by subsidiary i* (usually in a dollar account in a U.S. bank) that can satisfy compensating balance requirements.

In order to simplify modeling, it will be assumed that fund flow is averaged over the year, and only this average flow will be depicted. Of course, the time periods can be made as short as desired to more accurately depict reality. In each year N compensating balances must be specified, as must $N-1$ dividend flows, $N(N - 1)$ transfer price flows, and $N(N - 1)$ loan flows. The number of managerial fee flows will be either $N(N - 1)$ or $N-1$ depending on whether or not fees and royalties have to follow the ownership pattern. Thus at most $T(3N^2 -N-1)$ flows will have to be calculated.

Figure 1: A Network Representing Flows Between Subsidiaries i, j, and k.

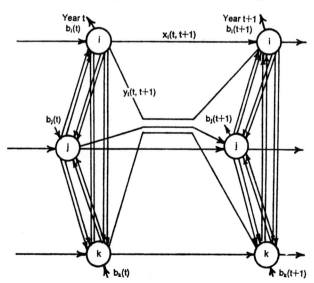

3. Costs and Bounds on Flow Through the Arcs

There is a cost flow through an arc, say the arc $p_{ij}(t)$ from i to j in year t depicting manipulated transfer prices. This cost depends on the pair of nations i and j, and can be expected to vary with time. Hence it would be formally correct to let the cost function be $P_{ij}(t) [p_{ij}(t)]$. This notation would be very cumbersome, however, $aP[p_{ij}(t)]$ will be used instead; it must be understood that P is a function of i,j and t. The four methods of transferring funds between nations will be discussed first.

3.1. Adjusted Transfer Prices $P[p_{ij}(t)]$

Suppose subsidiary i manufactures subassemblies which are shipped to subsidiary j. If the transfer price is lower than "normal" then there occurs a net flow of funds from i to j. If the transfer price is set higher than "normal," then the flow of funds is from j to i.

There is a direct cost to flow through a p_{ij} arc. A lower transfer price reduces the revenue appearing in subsidiary i, and this usually reduces income tax and value added tax in country i. Any *ad valorum* export duty on subassemblies imposed by country i or import duty imposed by country j will be reduced by the lower transfer price (so long as the invoices are believed). A lower transfer price will increase profits and value added appearing in country j. Hence the direct cost of sending funds through arc p_{ij} is:

Marginal rate of income and value added tax of subsidiary in country j, minus marginal rate of income and value added tax of subsidiary in country i minus *ad valorum* tariff on exports by country i and on imports by country j.

There are two internal indirect costs to flow through a p_{ij} arc. If each subsidiary is a semi-autonomous profit center, then there will be a bilateral monopoly relationship between i and j. An imposed transfer price will work so long as producing to demand remains in the self interest of subsidiary i. One indirect cost lies in the required efforts to persuade i to produce. Another indirect cost lies in the profits foregone by subsidiary j as it tailors its promotional efforts to its cost of goods, partly the manipulated transfer price. Clearly these costs of acrimony over negotiated and imposed transfer prices are greatly reduced if unit sales and production quotas are set centrally. The external indirect costs arise from government inquiries. If the price is too low both governments will intervene. The tax authorities of country i will see tax revenues foregone (in

114

USA, I.R.S., Section 482: see the recent case of Eli Lilly [5]). The import tariff commission of country j will see dumping. If the transfer price is too high, income tax will be foregone to country j. These external indirect costs have to be paid in bribes, time and effort at investigatory hearings, additional advertising to counter ill-will, and actual settlements. Section 482 of the U.S. Revenue Code confers great power to the Secretary of the Treasury. Its full text is:

> In any case of two or more organizations, trades or, business (whether or not incorporated, whether or not organized in the United States, and whether or not affiliated) owned or controlled directly or indirectly by the same interests, the Secretary or his delegate may distribute, apportion, or allocate gross income, deductions, credits, or allowances between or among such organizations, trades, or businesses, if he determines that such distribution, apportionment, or allocation is necessary in order to prevent evasion of taxes or clearly to reflect the income of any such organizations, trades, or businesses.

In light of such regulatory power by the U.S. government, and similar power by most other governments, it appears to be current industrial practice to abide by standard transfer prices on standard items. However, the continual introduction of new products requires that new transfer prices by established, and this is done with an eye to the considerations of this paper. Nonstandard items such as rejects, returned goods, and contaminated scrap can have any transfer price between zero and the standard price of a good item, and can easily be manipulated. One final technique used in practice is to invoice the goods through a chain of subsidiaries, each of which adds its commission.

3.2. Fees and Royalties $F[f_{ij}(t-1),f_{ij}(t)]$

Managerial advice, allocated headquarters overhead, and royalties on patents and trademarks are very elusive and difficult to price. Hence they appear to be very suitable conduits through which to move funds.

There is a direct cost. If these fees and royalties are a tax deductible business expense in country i, then a tax saving occurs. However, this need not be so, and there may be a witholding tax. If fees and royalties received from abroad are taxable as income in country j, then there is a tax cost.

There will likely be an indirect cost to any increase in fees and royalties. A treasury official in country i, struggling for foreign exchange, will be more likely to intervene the larger the increase. Hence the cost is a nonlinear (quadratic perhaps) function of $[(f_{ij}(t)-f_{ij}(t-1)]$. Many governments have become very severe about allocating foreign exchange for fees and royalties [18].

3.3. Intersubsidiary Loans $L_{ij}[l_{ij}(t)]$

The most prevalent form of intersubsidiary loan is a speed-up or delay in invoicing shipments between a pair of subsidiaries because normal terms of payment differ between regions of the world. In addition, actual shipping schedules can be accelerated in one direction and decelerated in the other so that one subsidiary carries inventory for both. Outright loans may also be possible. The danger in any intersubsidiary loan is that it will be deemed to constitute a dividend by the governments of the countries involved (especially the U.S. government). Hence, ritualistically, loans are made for 364-½ days and are then repaid with interest; a new loan is regranted immediately if desired.

There are direct costs. Let the interest rate on the loan be r (presumably reasonable to both governments). The loan $l_{ij}(t)$ departed from country i and arrived (presumably intact) at country j. At the end of the year $(1 + r)l_{ij}(t)$ must be repaid. If interest is a business expense in country j then the income tax payment will be reduced. Hence the net outflow from subsidiary j is $(1 +r-rT_j)l_{ij}(t)$, where T_j is the marginal rate of taxation in country j, (including witholding). If there is no witholding tax on interest leaving country j, then $(1 + r)l_{ij}(t)$ will be repaid to subsidiary i. If interest received from abroad is taxable income in country i, then the inflow to subsidiary i (net of tax) will be $1 + r - rT_i)l_{ij}(t)$. A constraint that the loan must be repaid (with interest) must be added to the formulation.

3.4. Dividends $D[d_{ij}(t)]$

There are N wholly owned subsidiaries. The intersubsidiary ownership pattern is fixed, hence the $N - 1$ dividend arcs are known. The problem is to estimate the cost function $D[d_{ij}(t)]$ for each arc. The cost function (if nonlinear) and restrictions on dividend flow depend upon the tax base. It is presumed that aspects of the tax base internal to each country have been optimized, so that in this formulation we need consider only intersubsidiary allocations of the tax base, such as manipulations to transfer prices and fees, and the receipt of interest on intersubsidiary loans.

First we shall sketch a few foreign taxes on dividends, starting with the uncomplicated tax laws of Liechtenstein. Though they will not be examined here, local taxes imposed by states, countries and cantons are substantial enough that they should be included in the cost functions. Brief mention will be made of tax treaties between pairs of nations; their intimate details should be studied, especially when a company operates with a foreign corporate charter in a nation.

Secondly, we shall examine in detail the U.S. laws that pertain to dividends received from abroad. Due to the U.S. Revenue Act of 1962, all cost functions (even on dividends which do not flow to the U.S.A.) must be somewhat augmented. Due to the 1968 Office of Foreign Direct Investment, minimum bounds are imposed on certain groups of dividends.

3.41. $D[d_{ij}(t)]$ *When j is not USA.* Liechtenstein: Corporations pay income tax (Ertragssteuer). Dividends paid by resident corporations pay a 3 percent coupon tax. This is never refunded, or permitted to be credited as a cost of doing business. There is no tax on dividends received. No tax treaties are currently in force which change these provisions.

Belgium: Corporations pay income tax (impot des societes) at the rate of 30 percent, but income going into retained earnings above 5,000,000 Belgian francs is taxed at the rate of 35 percent (model this as a 5 percent incentive for paying dividends until retained earnings drop to 5,000,000 Belgian francs). Dividends paid by a resident corporation are subject to a 18.2 percent withholding tax, which is never refunded nor permitted to be credited as a cost of doing business (deduct this from the incentive for paying dividends). Of dividends received into Belgium (after any withholding taxes by the government of the sending country) the tax imposed by the Belgian government is 18.7 percent (15 percent Belgian withholding tax plus 30 percent Belgian income tax on 15 percent of the 85 percent that survived Belgian withholding tax). By tax treaty, dividends received from an Italian corporation are exempt from Belgian withholding tax.

Germany: Income tax (Korperschaftsteuer) and business tax (Gewerbesteuer) are imposed on corporations doing business in Germany. A 25 percent withholding tax is made on dividends paid. Profits not distributed to shareholders are taxed at 51 percent, but profits distributed to shareholders are taxed at only 15 percent. Dividends received by a German corporation are given a credit against company income tax, but not business tax. The effective tax rate depends, as before, on whether or not these profits from abroad will be distributed to shareholders.

3.42. U.S. Controls on di, USA. While planning a base company in the popular tax haven countries of Surinam, Panama, Liechtenstein, Switzerland, Bermuda and the Barbados, usually the most applicable laws are the U.S. Revenue Act of 1962, the U.S. Foreign Investors Tax Act of 1966, and the U.S. Foreign Direct Investment Program administered by the Office of Foreign Direct Investments (OFDI). The combination of these three laws is so complicated, that it would not be trivial for a company to prepare a computer simulation for its tax position. Interestingly, however, (assuming all subsidiaries are 100% owned, and that subsidiaries in less developed countries are not legal parents to subsidiaries in advanced countries) U.S. law ignores patterns of legal intersubsidiary ownership so that subsidiaries can be regrouped annually at the discretion of the company. "Where there are many such foreign corporations and branches, this [regrouping] will provide ample opportunity for the exercise of ingenuity, alone or in connection with an electronic brain." [13, p.15,203]

The OFDI regulations impose *lower* bounds on four sums of dividends. The four sums are defined by the geographical schedules.

U.S.A. and Canada

A Underdeveloped, from Aden to Zambia

B Developed, from Abu Dhabi to United Kingdom

C Most of Europe plus South and South-West Africa, from Andorra to Switzerland

Let π_i be the annual profits (net transfer of capital plus reinvested earnings) in subsidiary i; this will be negative for subsidiaries which lost money. For a small company the applicable OFDI regulations (Section 503 allowables) impose four constraints on dividends, limiting the retained earnings to $200,000.

$$\Sigma_{i,j}\, d_{ij} + \Sigma_{i,j}\, p_{ij} - \Sigma_{i,j}\, p_{ji} + \Sigma_{i,j}\, f_{ij} - \Sigma_{i,j}\, f_{ji}$$

$$+ \Sigma_{i,j}\, l_{ij}\, r_{ij} - \Sigma_{i,j}\, l_{ij}\, r_{ji} \geq \Sigma_i\, \pi_i - 2000,000$$

For $i \in A,\ j \in A$

The other three constraints are for $i \in B, j \notin B$, for $i \in C, j \notin C$, and a worldwide formula $i \notin$ U.S. or Canada, $j \in$ U.S., Canada. These Section 503 allowables, if not used in any year, may not be carried forward for use in later years.

If the company so chooses, and it probably will unless it is a small company that is new abroad, it can replace the set of four equations (Section 503) with $200,000 annual limits by three

118

equations (Section 504). One cannot have the benefit of both Sections. In the Section 504 allowables there is no single worldwide constraint. In the three geographical schedule constraints:

In A, $200,000 is replaced by 110% of average direct investment (net capital plus reinvested earnings) of company aggregated over all A countries during 1965 and 1966.

In B, $200,000 is replaced by 65% of average 1965, 1966 direct investment in all B subsidiaries.

In C, $200,000 is replaced by the smallest of (1) 35% of average 1965, 1966 direct investment in all C countries (2) average reinvested earnings in 1964, 1965, 1966 of all C subsidiaries. Use 0 if either (1) or (2) is negative.

3.43. U.S. Revenue Act of 1962. In attempting to calculate $D[d_{i,USA}(t)]$ it is convenient to catorgorize three sources of dividends, (a) less developed countries, (b) foreign subsidiaries which have been organized into Western Hemisphere Trade Corporations, China Trade Act Corporations, and special corporations which can operate only in Puerto Rico or U.S. possessions, (c) all other countries.

Subsidiaries in less developed countries (the list is not quite identical with Schedule A countries of the OFDI regulations) are exempt from U.S. taxation on their retained earnings, and are subject to a low tax on dividends received into the U.S.A. The low tax results from the fact that U.S. tax *credit* is granted on the base of before-foreign-tax-income, whereas U.S. tax is calculated on the dividend received, which is net of foreign taxes. If the subsidiary pays its *entire* earnings as dividends d_{iUSA}, then the total tax rate will be

$$D[d_{i,USA}(1969)] = [T_{USA} - T_i T_{USA} + T_i^2] d_{i,USA}.$$

If T_{USA} = 48 percent, then a 5.76% saving is the most that can be achieved by paying dividends from a subsidiary in a less developed country that has a 24 percent tax rate.

The incentive to use Western Hemisphere Trade Corporations, China Trade Act Corporations, and Section 931 Corporations operating in Puerto Rico and other U.S. possessions. was greatly increased by the Revenue Act of 1962. For a company which has already planned its physical operations, these special U.S. laws operate much as tax treaties: they reduce $D[d_{i,USA}(1969)]$.

Most subsidiaries are not in less developed countries, nor are they qualified as Western Hemisphere Trade Corporations. Their U.S. parent is therefore liable to U.S. tax on the Subpart F income of such subsidiaries, even if it is retained abroad. Subpart F income consists of nonmanufacturing income (rents, royalties, licensing fees, dividends), income from services performed for related persons outside the nation, and income from the sale of property to related persons outside the nation.

Subpart F income is precisely defined in Internal Revenue Code Sections 951 (a) (1) (A) (i) and 952. Legal counsel competent in this portion of the code should be

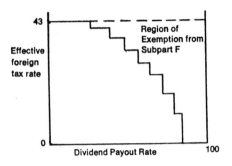

FIGURE 2. Graph of IRC Section 963(b)(3)

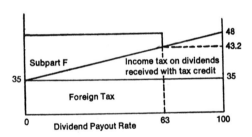

FIGURE 3. Total Taxes as a Function of Dividend Payout Rate

consulted, for carefully reading the definitions of these is like trying to debug someone else's computer program that was written compactly with layers of nested DO loops. Nevertheless, a Subpart F income figure is required. Manipulations to transfer prices and fees will be magnified by a factor of 2.5 in their influence on Subpart F income because of the "70-30" rule of Section 954 (b) (2) (B), but only within these 70-30 limits.

The 1962 Revenue Act offers significant tax relief under the "minimum distribution provisions" of Section 963. Section 963 (b)

(3) provides a table, associating with each effective foreign tax rate a required percentage minimum distribution of earnings and profits.

To avoid misunderstanding Figure 2 it would be helpful to examine the total tax to be paid as a function of the subsidiary dividend payout rate. For example, consider a subsidiary with an effective foreign tax rate of 35 percent. From Figure 2 (or IRC 963 (b) (3), this effective foreign tax rate calls for a minimum distribution of earnings and profits of 63 percent. The U.S. government grants a tax credit for taxes paid abroad, so that the total tax does not exceed the U.S. rate of income tax of 48 percent (ignoring the current surtax).

Unless a minimum distribution is made, the *entire* Subpart F income of the subsidiary is taxed. Figure 3 implies that for dividends in excess of the minimum distribution the per unit cost is the slope of the total tax line. The figure applies to each year; if liquidity must be built up in a subsidiary, a sensible strategy would be to alternate minimum distribution years with zero dividend years. Unfortunately this may run afoul of the OFDI minimum repatriation regulations, referred to in the previous section. In fact, most U.S. corporations are findng that the OFDI regulations are so stringent that the dividends they must pay exceed the Subpart F minimum distributions. The network model of this paper can be applied ignoring Subpart F taxation, then re-run constraining insufficient flows to equal or exceed their minimum distribution. Alternatively, a minimum distribution can be applied to a chain of subsidiaries (a different consolidation to that required by OFDI A, B, and C country schedules) that the *sum* of dividend flows exceed a prescribed minimum. Such a consolidation is permitted by the U.S. Internal Revenue Code:

963 (c) (2) AMOUNTS TO WHICH SECTION APPLIES—CHAIN OF CONTROLLED FOREIGN CORPORATIONS

Subsection (a) (2) shall apply to amounts which (but for the provisions of this section) would be included in the gross income of the United States shareholder under section 951(a) (1) (A) (i)—
(A) by reason of its ownership, within the meaning of section 958 (A) (1) (A) of stock of a controlled foreign corporation, and
(B) to the extent that the United States shareholder so elects, by reason of its ownership,within the meaning of section 958 (a) (2), of stock of any other controlled foreign corporation (an account of its ownership of the stock described in subparagraph (A) or of stock described in the subparagraph), but only if there is taken into account the earnings and profits of each foreign corporation, whether or not a controlled foreign corporation, by reason of which

the United States shareholder owns, within the meaning of section 958 (a) (2), stock of such controlled foreign corporation.

For a given pattern of intersubsidiary ownership there are numerous possible chains of subsidiaries. If a corporation has such generous OFDI constraints that it is liable for Subpart F taxation unless it increases dividends, it might consider searching for optimal chains of subsidiaries. Though this subject will not be explored in detail in this paper, the company could organize chains whose average effective foreign tax rate is *just* above each of the breaks in IRC 963 (b) (c), so that the tax saving is greatest. Unfortunately, for most companies the OFDI regulations preclude such considerations, and furthermore IRC 964 (a) (a safety net provision) deems that no chain or group may pay less than 90 percent of the U.S. tax rate.

3.5 $X[x_i(t, t+1)]$ Liquid Assets Held in Country i

Section 203 (c) of the OFDI regulations stipulates that a direct investor whose total liquid foreign balances exceeds $25,000 is required "to reduce the amount of liquid foreign balances (other than direct investment liquid foreign balances) held by such direct investor to an amount not in excess of the average end-of-month amounts of the same so held by such direct investor (whether or not a direct investor at that time) during 1965 and 1966". That is to say

$$\sum_{x=1}^{N} x_i \leq a$$

where a is greater of $25,000 and average during 1965 and 1966.

If a company wants to hold liquid assets abroad totalling more than a, then it must confine them to less liquid or less desirable assets such as those specified in Section 203 (a) (2). Then $X[x_i(t, t-1)]$ is the effective interest rate earned by a less desirable asset such as OFDI Section 203 (c) (ii)

bank deposits, negotiable instruments, non-negotiable instruments, commercial paper and securities with a period of more than 1 year remaining to maturity when acquired by the direct investor and which are not redeemable in full at the option of the direct investor within a period of 1 year after such acquisition

If the multi-national company has raised money abroad then the "direct investment liquid foreign balances" are exempt. Then marginal changes to liquid balances in country i would presumably be held in the unrestricted foreign raised funds, for which $X[x_i(t, t-1)]$ is higher.

3.6 $Y[y_i(t, t + 1)]$ Cash Held in the U.S. Dollar Account of the Subsidiary

Foreign banks commonly grant loans on an overdraft basis, so that the borrowing company pays interest only on the amount of the granted loan which it has in use, much as a U.S. bank grants a line of credit. Nevertheless, when a U.S. bank actually grants a loan the borrowing company pays interest on the entire amount of the granted loan (whether or not withdrawn from the bank) and furthermore must keep specified compensating balances on deposit in the bank. As the company has to keep transaction and precautionary cash, the compensating balance requirement is not as onerous as it would be in a deterministic world, though it should be reflected in a slight upwards adjustment in U.S. interest rates to make them comparable with foreign "overdraft" interest rates.

U.S. dollar accounts held in the bank by the many corporate subsidiaries around the world are generally considered to count towards the compensating balance requirement:

$$\sum_{i=1}^{N} y_i(t, t + 1) \geq R_{t, t+1}$$

Loan officers generally refer only to the average balance through the preceding period, and would generally be unaware of the variance of the daily balance through the period. Furthermore, the fact that attention is focused on the sum of subsidiary balances permits the company to arrange a costless partial movement of funds between subsidiaries as the composition of the compensating balances is changed. Unless interest can be obtained for compensating balances $Y[y_i(t, t + 1)] = 0$.

Example

Most confusion appears to arise over dividend taxation, so this will be illustrated. Let the parent company in Liechtenstein own a subsidiary in Germany, which has a subsidiary of its own in Belgium.

Let us work up the ownership tree. The Belgian subsidiary declares a divident of 100 to its German parent. The Belgian government withholds 18.20, so that 81.80 arrives in Germany. The German business tax (Gewerbesteuer), based on the *entire* dividend of 100, is 13.50 percent, so income net of business tax is 86.50.

Company income tax (Korperschaftsteuer) is 51 percent of income net of business tax, so is 0.51 x 86.50 = 44.11 (this rate assumes income will be retained within the firm; income destined for dividends is taxed at only 15 percent). Only at this point is credit granted for the Belgian withholding tax, so that German company income tax due is 44.11 - 18.20 = 25.91. The Belgian withholding tax was 18.20, the German business tax was 13.50, and the German company income tax is 25.91; their total is 57.61. That is to say, only 42.39 percent of the dividend gets through from the Belgain subsidiary to its German parent. That is to say $D[dd_{BG}(1970)] = 0.5761$.

The German company now declares a dividend of 100 units to its parent in Liechtenstein. In Germany, the company income tax is 51 percent for retained earnings, but is only 15 percent for earnings paid out as dividends. The simplest way to model this is that the company income tax is 51 percent on all earnings, but that the German government gives the German company an income tax rebate of 36 percent of dividends paid out. Thus 100 - 36 = 64 units leave the German company. However, the German government imposes a 25 percent (of 100) withholding tax on dividends leaving Germany, so that 75 units arrive in the Liechtensteinian subsidiary. Thus 17.18 percent of the dividend gets through from the German subsidiary to its parent in Liechtenstein. That is to say $D[d_{GL}(1970)] = -0.1718$. Naturally a contraint must be added that total dividends do not exceed earnings!

4. *Solution Procedure as a Generalized Network*

Refer back to Figure 1 which presents the problem of maneuvering liquid assets in a multi-national company as a network problem. The costs on each arc are actually reductions in liquidity (even government chafing has to be paid for with legal fees and "political contributions"). Consider flow through one of the ij arcs. If liquidity at source node i is reduced by p_{ij} units, liquidity at node j will be increased by less than p_{ij} units; only s,p_{ij} $P[p_{ij}(t)]$ units will get through to subsidiary j. The factor of attenuation on the arc $p_{ij}(t)$ is $1 - P[p_{ij}(t)]/p_{ij}(t)$.

If deductions from liquidity are handled automatically by factors of attenuation, then the objective of the problem becomes to maximize the sum of liquid assets remaining after period T (this could be a weighted sum if one can guess desirable countries in which to hold assets). Naturally, all requirements for funds must be satisfied. The problem is a generalized network (also called weighted distribution, or machine loading problem). Dantzig [2, Ch. 21] presents an excellent discussion of the generalized network problem, as does Eisemann [4]. The nonlinear aspects of the indirect costs can be charged as costs [11].

Computational procedures for the generalized network problem assume that all nodes could be connected, and that there are no constraints on arc flows other than node material balance equations. It appears sensible to decompose the problem. There are T subproblems, each an annual p, l, f, d maneuver around N nodes. The master problem consists of the material balance equations on the x and y arcs, the intertemporal constraints that loans must be repaid with interest, and that a cost of government chafing be imposed on any *change* in the f flow of fees.

5. Solution as an Ordinary Network

There are the fewest conceptual problems if one solves the problem as a generalized network sketched in §4 above. However, another approach would be to solve the problem as an ordinary network in which the costs are costs on flow through arcs. After all, the problem has $T(3N^2 - N - 1)$ arcs, and an ordinary network is quicker to solve than a generalized network.

Two conceptual problems arise if an ordinary network is used. Firstly, at what interest rate should future costs be discounted to get their present value? The interest rates in each country are different. Secondly, costs on all arcs flowing into a node must be deducted from the availability of funds of the subsidiary in that year. To do so is to presuppose the optimal flows. Both of these problems *might* be surmounted by an iterative procedure. Run the problem and study the flows that occur. Represent taxes by deducting liquidity from nodes with inflows. Discount all the costs according to the route of flows. Then rerun the problem.

6. Systems within Systems

Maneuvering liquid assets reallocates revenue from high tax rate nations to the multi-national company and low tax rate nations. If this were all this model did, it would represent a somewhat dubious contribution to mankind's knowledge. Fortunately the model can be run to evaluate effects of people's ideas by simulating parts of a larger reality. Four areas of current interest to international managers will be mentioned:

1. Short Term Loan Negotiations, Both Local and Multi National

The model presented in this paper is a linear program, and, therefore, has dual variables associated with each constraint. If the problem is formulated as a weighted distribution problem, the dual variable associated with the constraint that funds be available in a subsidiary in a certain year represent the value of taking a small loan and keeping it until the end of period T. All T of these dual variables for a given subsidiary can be translated into a term structure of interest rates from which the year to year value of additional money can be calculated. This data provides a very clear guideline for making short and medium term loans in that nation [1].

Some banks are themselves multi national. In one nation the bank may ration credit because of a high demand for loans within the permitted interest rate. In another part of the world the bank may be short of deposits as it strives to expand. In exchange for depositing money in one part of the bank, the multi-national company can achieve loan priority in another part of the bank. The rationale behind this is that most currencies are blocked and it may be easier for a company to move money than a foreign bank. The worthwhileness of such induced swap transactions can be evaluated with this model.

2. Raising Long Term Capital

Long term capital can be raised in most nations of the world, usually after negotiations with the host government and promises that local investments will result. To support such negotiations worldwide manufacturing models must be supplemented by worldwide financial models such as this on which to simulate the consequences of different financing schemes. Similarly one can evaluate the benefits of mergers intended to qualify as a Western Hemisphere Trade Corporation, or to buy OFDI exemptions.

3. Restructuring the Pattern of Legal Ownership

If the company has N subsidiaries, there are $(N - 1)^2$ different patterns of intersubsidiary ownership possible even if each subsidiary is restrained to have just one legal parent. In theory one could use the theory of optimal spanning trees [3] to iterate to a worldwide tax minimizing legal structure a pattern of dividend conduits. If one removes the restriction that a subsidiary have one legal parent (but require that the percentage of ownership by each legal parent be constant once reorganization has occurred) then the problem is computationally much simpler and is much more difficult for tax authorities to unsnarl. Unfortunately, the tax data required for cases of partial ownership is appreciably more complicated and vague than for cases of complete ownership. In practice the model presented in this paper, by taking some drudgery out of creativity, should stimulate new patterns of intersubsidiary ownership. A subcalculation, about which tax lawyers are well informed, is the benefit of operating in nation i with a corporate charter granted in nation j.

4. *Inserting High Profit Products*

The Swiss pharmaceutical companies prefer to produce their high profit products in the nations where they incur their largest cash drains to research and dividends. This practice, a vivid example of Vernon's product cycle theory [15], reduces the need to flow funds between nations, though at a high production and transportation cost. Ideally, one would like to simulate the effect of inserting a high profit product into any subsidiary technically sophisticated enough to manufacture it.

In a multi-national company there are many opportunities for maneuvers that take advantage of the fact of being multi national. Most of these do not appear to be used for fear of causing confusion and computational chaos. Hopefully, mathematical models provide a rational framework within which analysis can take place, and it is with this hope that the article was written.

REFERENCES

1. Calman, Robert F., *Linear Programming and Cash Management: CASH ALPHA*, Cambridge; The MIT Press, 1968.
2. Dantzig, George B., *Linear Programming and Extensions*, Princeton; Princeton University Press, 1963.
3. Edmonds, Jack, "Optimum Branching," *Journal of Research, National Bureau of Standards B*, Vol. 71B, No. 4 (October–December 1967), pp. 233-240.
4. Eisemann, Kurt, "The Generalized Stepping Stone Method for the Machine Loading Problem," *Management Science*, Vol. 11, No. 1. (September 1964), pp. 154-176.
5.. *Eli Lilly & Company v. The United States*, 372 F. 2d 990, 178 Court of Claims, [No. 293-61, Decided February 17, 1967], pp. 666–733.

6. Hellawell, Robert, "United States Income Taxation and Less Developed Countries: A Critical Appraisal," *Columbia Law Review*, Vol. 66, No. 8. (December 1966), pp. 1393-1427.

7. *Information Guide for U.S. Corporations Doing Business Abroad*, New York; Price Waterhouse & Co., July, 1967.

8. *Information Guide for U.S. Direct Investors*, New York; Price Waterhouse & Co., November, 1968.

9. Kushner, Harold J. and F.C. Schweppe, "A Maximum Principle for Stochastic Control Systems," *Journal of Mathematical Analysis and Applications*, Vol. 8 (March 1964), pp. 287-302.

10. Lichtman, Paul B., "Taxation of Intercorporated Dividends Received in Europe," *European Taxation*, (August 1964), pp. 135-156.

11. Rutenberg, David, "Generalized Networks, Generalized Upper Bounding, and Decomposition of the Convex Simplex Method," *Management Science*, Vol. 16, No. 5 (January 1970).

12. ——, "Organizational Archetypes of a Multi-National Company," *Management Science*, Vol. 16, No. 6 (February 1970).

13. Seghers, Paul D., "How to do Business Abroad at Least Tax Cost,'" *Transaction Tax Guide*, Englewood Cliffs; Prentice-Hall, 1964.

14. Shulman, James, "When the Price is Wrong—By Design," *Columbia Journal of World Business*, (May-June 1967), pp. 69-76.

15. Vernon, Raymond, "International Investment and International Trade in the Product Cycle," *Quarterly Journal of Economics* (May 1966).

16. Walkup, D.W. and R.J.B. Wets, "Stochastic Programs with Recourse," *SIAM Journal of Applied Mathematics*, Vol. 15, No. 5 (September 1967), pp. 1299-1314.

17. Wentz, Roy A., "Corporate Transfers of Intangibles Abroad," *The Tax Executive* (April 1967), pp. 142-159.

18. Zenoff, David B., "Remitting Funds from Foreign Affiliates," *Financial Executive* (March 1968).

19. —— and J. Zwick, *International Financial Management*, New York, Prentice-Hall, 1969.

Factors Affecting Resource Transfer Through Direct Investment*

Robert R. Miller and Dale R. Weigel
Iowa University

I. *Introduction*

Resource and technical transfer by an international enterprise usually involves direct investment by firms in other countries. For this reason, the forces motivating such investment have received increasing attention in recent years. This study subjects some direct investment theories to empirical testing, using fairly elaborate investment data on a single contry, Brazil. Of particular interest in this study is the work of Aharoni [1], Aliber [2], Hymer [10], and Vernon [12]. These theories are discussed in more detail in Section II. The specific hypotheses tested and the methodology used are described in Section III; Section IV discusses data and measurement specification; Section V outlines results of the study.

II. *Theories of Direct Investment*

The research in this study is most closely related to several recent theories advanced to explain foreign direct investment flows. Yair Aharoni's theory derives from work on the behavioral theory of the firm by Cyert and March [7]. Of particular interest in this study is Aharoni's idea of search patterns undertaken by international firms prior to making foreign investment decisions. This study suggests

*Adapted from the *Journal of International Business Studies*, Vol. 3, No. 2, Fall 1972 by special permission.

that firms are limited in the number of investment opportunities considered at any given time. In his terminology, an "initiating force" usually is required for particular projects to come to the attention of decision-makers, followed by a complex review process. This stimulus can take many forms, but the present study concentrates on two: (1) the threat of loss of a foreign market by tariff changes, and (2) prior investment by competing firms. Both are conditional on the market being relatively important to the investor. The existence of an "initiating force" is a most important element of Aharoni's theory, because the review process is strictly limited to investment opportunities within the firm's identified set of alternatives.

After potential investment projects come to the attention of corporate decision-makers, profitability considerations become more important. According to Stephen Hymer [10], foreign investment is undertaken mostly by certain types of mono-politically competitive companies. These firms will not invest unless through some monopoly advantage they can (1) earn higher profits abroad than at home, and (2) make higher profits than host country firms in the same industry. This monopoly advantage can take numerous forms, including technology and patents, easier access to capital markets, lower cost sources of raw materials, and even superior management.

Raymond Vernon's product cycle theory [12] provides further insight into the direct investment process. This theory, which might be considered a subset of Hymer's monopoly hypotheses, suggests that overseas investment is an outgrowth of the stages of development and marketing of new products. Comparatively heavy research and development expenditures in the United States, combined with unique characteristics of our domestic markets, foster the relatively early appearance of new and differentiated products. Later exports of the products are followed by direct investment, as firms discover cost advantages of manufacturing overseas. Empirical research by Vernon and others [9], by Keesing [11], and by Baldwin [3], have demonstrated that R and D expenditures are related to trade and investment flows.

Robert Aliber's [2] thesis is that the pattern of direct foreign investment can be explained by the fact that "source-country" firms capitalize a stream of expected earnings from a foreign direct investment at a discount rate lower than firms in the host country. As a result, equivalent earnings streams are valued higher by the foreign investor and, in cases where investment occurs, sufficiently higher to overcome the extra costs of doing business abroad. Moreover, as capital intensity increases in the production process, so also does the advantage accruing to the foreign investor. In Aliber's view, therefore, investment is more likely in industries characterized by comparatively high capital intensity. Clearly, this hypothesis runs counter to another, more traditional economic rationale for investment, which states that firms invest in less developed countries to take advantage of lower labor costs. In this view, relatively labor intensive companies might be expected to invest overseas.

III. *Hypotheses and Methodology*

This study employs a two-stage linear discriminant model to examine the following general hypotheses: foreign direct investment is contingent upon "search" activity being undertaken by firms and, after the search is initiated, upon expected economic profitability. That is, the model conforms to the decision process outlined by Aharoni in that it posits an initiating force stimulating investment search activity. In the first stage of the analysis, variables believed to motivate search are used to discriminate between investment and non-investment industries. The second stage employs economic variables to separate the remaining non-investing industries from the investors.

The two-stage discriminant procedure was selected for several reasons. Most importantly, the hypothesis suggests that *both* search and profitability are necessary conditions for investment. To represent this decision process in a single estimating equation would require multiplying two sets of variables together. Multiplication, however, introduces significant collinearity among the independent variables. This problem is avoided by analyzing the investment decision sequentially using, first, search and then economic variables.

The fact that discriminant analysis is employed at each stage rather than, say, a linear regression technique is due to the particular nature of the investment data. The data indicate the industry pattern of investment, and our interest here is simply to determine whether or not investment occurred in an industry. The dependent variable of a linear regression, therefore, would be zero or one, i.e., one when investment was made and zero otherwise. Use of such a dependent variable introduces heteroscedasticity in the error term of a regression equation. Discriminant analysis, on the other hand, is a multivariate statistical procedure designed to determine which variables best classify a set of data into two or more mutually exclusive and exhaustive categories, and it is therefore more appropriate.

In the first stage of the analysis, the discriminant function's independent variables are intended to determine whether or not a motivation existed for industries to search for investment opportunities. The particular variables which are hypothesized to induce search are (1) the relative size of the market (x_1), (2) previous investment in the industry (x_2), (3) a change to a higher tariff barrier (x_3), and (4) a change in tariff combined with relative importance of the market (x_4). The general hypothesis tested in the first stage can be summarized as follows: firms which invest must first be motivated to investigate possible opportunities, and this motivation is a function of one or more of the four variables listed above. That is, search activity will be initiated only if the market is important in some measurable sense, which might be related to export sales or to the fact that firms have past investments to oversee. Likewise, firms react to an existing market being threatened by some event, in this case an upward shift in tariffs, and are more likely to search if, in addition to the tariff, the market is important.

Several alternative, but related, search hypotheses were tested. Most importantly, the following discriminant functions were estimated:

$$1) \quad z_1 = a_0 + a_1 X_1 + a_2 X_2$$

$$2) \quad z_2 = b_0 + b_1 X_1 + b_2 X_2 + b_3 X_3$$

$$3) \quad z_3 = c_0 + c_1 X_2 + c_2 X_4$$

The difference between these forms mainly consisted of interchanging x_1 and x_4 in equations 1 and 3, and the inclusion of x_3 in equation 2. These variations were employed to determine the ability of each independent variable (and especially variables including tariff changes) to discriminate between investing and non-investing industries. It should be pointed out that the particular search variables used here are by no means intended to be exhaustive, and Aharoni's work suggest that many other stimuli in fact exist. The intention here, however, is to concentrate on a relatively few important and comparatively easily measured variables in the hope that their power to discriminate would at least demonstrate the importance of the "initiating force" concept in the investment decision process.

The second stage discriminant procedure employs investment data from only industries engaging in search activity, as determined in the first stage. This analysis, therefore, concentrates on various economic variables derived from the investment theories of Hymer,

Vernon, and Aliber. Hymer, for example, asserts that foreign investment is undertaken by firms having one or more monopolistic advantages, while Vernon believes that one of the major advantages is product innovational activity. In this study, we use two measures of monopolistic advantage: (1) the degree of vertical integration characterizing an industry (Y_1), and (2) the relative intensity of research and development (R&D) activities in the industry (Y_2). In addition, increased profitability in a market might stem from changes in the tariff rate. This variable is utilized in two ways: (1) the absolute tariff level (Y_3), and (2) the tariff multiplied by the importance of the existing market (Y_4). In addition, relative market size (Y_5) is included as a variable which, by itself, affects profitability.

Aliber's notions on the effect of capital intensity on investment are more difficult to deal with on an empirical level than are other economic variables. Aliber suggests that U.S. firms have an advantage over foreign-based firms, particularly in less developed countries, because of lower cost sources of capital. Therefore, U.S. foreign investors are likely to be more capital intensive in their production processes. Traditional economic theory, on the other hand, would conclude that a prime motivation for foreign investment by American firms would be to take advantage of lower labor costs in the foreign location. Thus, labor-intensive firms would be the major foreign investors. Obviously, the two conclusions are conflicting, and therein lies the problem in running empirical tests of the theory.

This study attempts to separate Aliber's hypothesis from the traditional theory by including capital intensity in the discriminant tests in two ways. First, capital intensity is treated as an individual independent variable, (Y_6), similar to vertical integration, (Y_1), and R&D intensity, (Y_2). The variable is considered here as another "monopolistic" advantage, as Aliber would indicate, and investing industries would tend to be more capital intensive. Therefore, the coefficient on Y_6, like the coefficients on Y_1 and Y_2, would be expected to be positive.

Capital intensity is also combined with both vertical integration and R&D intensity to form two other variables, Y_7 and Y_8. These combined variables are intended to demonstrate that industries which have an advantage in either being vertically integrated or heavily involved in R&D activities will invest overseas to lower labor costs. Therefore, such investors tend to have more labor intensive production processes, and the anticipated coefficients would be negative. The expectation of negative coefficients on the composite variable is based, in part, on Vernon's product cycle hypothesis.

which argues that production of newly developed products tends to move from capital-intensive to labor-intensive countries as the market matures.

To summarize, the second stage discriminant analysis incorporates in various combinations eight independent variables:

Y_1 Degree of vertical integration

Y_2 Intensity of R&D activities

Y_3 Change in tariff level

Y_4 Y_3, combined with relative market size (Y_5)

Y_5 Relative market size

Y_6 Capital intensity

Y_7 Y_6, combined with vertical integration

Y_8 Y_6, combined with R&D activity

The discriminant functions tested in the second stage are summarized in table 3 and, in general, were of the following forms:

1) $Z_1 = a_0 + a_1 Y_1 + a_2 Y_2 + a_4 Y_4 + a_6 Y_6$

2) $Z_2 = b_0 + b_1 Y_1 + b_2 Y_2 + b_5 Y_5 + b_6 Y_6$

3) $Z_3 = c_0 + c_2 Y_2 + c_6 Y_6 + c_8 Y_8$

4) $Z_4 = d_0 + d_2 Y_2 + d_5 Y_5 + d_6 Y_6 + d_8 Y_8$

5) $Z_5 = e_0 + e_1 Y_1 + e_2 Y_2 + e_4 Y_4 + e_6 Y_6 + e_7 Y_7 + e_8 Y_8$

Equations 1 and 2 interchanged market size variables and included monopolistic factors. The other equations included both monopolistic advantages and one or more combined variables to achieve a closer approximation of the effect of capital intensity on investment.

IV. *Data*

The hypotheses that have been outlined are tested using data relating to U.S. direct investment in Brazil during the period 1956-61. There are several reasons for focusing on Brazil. First, it is a large country where foreign direct investment has been an important component of total industrial investment. Second, a major changes in tariffs occurred in 1957, and therefore it is possible to investigate the effects of this change on direct investment decisions. Finally, disaggregated investment data are available for the period.

134

A. *Investment Data*

The investment data list all direct investments made in Brazil during 1956-61 under a special regulation, instruction 113 of the Superintendent of Money and Credit, permitting foreign investment in the form of imported equipment; a privilege that was attractive because of Brazil's multiple exchange rate system in force at the time. The automatic privilege of investing in kind was extended only to investors establishing new plants (and sometimes major expansions of existing plants) in industries thought to be particularly desirable for Brazil's development [4, pp. 73-78]. The investment data used in this study, then, covers most, (though probably not all) investment made by firms to establish new plants in Brazil.

The individual investments have been classified according to a 214 industry breakdown. These industries are, in general, equivalent to the four-digit classification of manufacturing industries in the 1957 Standard Industrial Classification. Not all four-digit SIC industries are used, however, and some of the 214 industry groups are combinations of more than one four-digit industry.[1]

Table 1 shows the two-digit industry SIC pattern of U.S. direct investment made in Brazil under instruction 113 during the 1956-61 period. Although it is not completely evident from the table, the underlying data show that there was a basic shift in the composition of investments between 1956-57 and 1960-61. During 1956-57, the majority of investments were made in industries which produce consumer products (i.e., textiles No. 22), food products (No. 20), appliances and radio and television sets (No. 36), drugs and plastics (No. 28), motor vehicles (No. 37), hand tools and hardware (No. 34). In 1958 and later, the pattern of investment began to shift from consumer goods industries to intermediate products and capital goods. Investments in non-electrical machinery and transport equipment increased as a proportion of the total, and investments in electrical machinery shifted from electronic components and appliances to heavy electrical equipment.

It is this shift in the industry composition of investment that is to be explained. Consequently the industry composition of investment during 1958-61 is the dependent variable in the discriminate analysis. That is, the 214 industries are divided into groups according to whether investment did or did not occur during 1958-61. The purpose of the statistical analysis is to determine which independent variables discriminate between these groups.

Of the 214 industries, investment under instruction 113 occurred in 54 industries. In the non-investment group, however, were some

Table 1: Number of Manufacturing Direct Investment in Brazil: Two-Digit SIC Industries

Industry	1956-1957	1958-1959	1960-1961
20 Food products	8	5	3
21 Tobacco	0	0	0
22 Textiles	9	0	0
23 Apparel	0	0	0
24 Lumber, wood	0	0	0
25 Furniture	0	0	0
26 Paper	3	2	3
27 Printing	0	0	0
28 Chemicals	13	8	6
29 Petroleum	2	0	0
30 Rubber	2	3	2
31 Leather	0	0	0
32 Stone, clay, glass	1	1	0
33 Primary metals	7	2	3
34 Fabricated Metals	8	3	5
35 Non-electric machinery	17	15	21
36 Electrical machinery	17	10	12
37 Transport equipment	10	19	23
38 Instruments	6	2	2
39 Miscellaneous	1	0	1
Total	104	70	81

industries in which foreign investment was not permitted under the instruction. The statistical analysis relating to causal factors clearly would be inapplicable to such industries, and accordingly a strong motivation exists to drop them from the analysis. Unfortunately, the identity of industries excluded by the instruction is generally unknown. For this reason, this study incorporates a procedure which removes from the data all four-digit industries contained in a two-digit category in which no investments were made during the entire six-year period. In addition, all specific industries, such as petroleum refining, where foreign investment is prohibited, are exluded from the data. In total, 71 four-digit industries are excluded, leaving 89 industries in the non-investment group.

B. *Causal variables*

The variables affecting search for investment opportunities examined in this study are prior investment, importance of the market, and changes in tariffs. Variables affecting profitability are market size, tariffs, capital intensity of the industry's production processes, the extent of vertical integration in the industry, and the amount of research and development undertaken. Measures employed for these variables, and sources of data are described in the following paragraphs.

136

1. Search variables

a. Prior investment (I_{t-1}). This is a dummy (i.e., zero-one) variable indicating the pattern of U.S. direct investment in Brazil in the period 1956-57. It is obtained from the basic investment data described above.

b. Relative importance of the market. The importance of the Brazilian market to U.S. industries is measured by the ratio of industry exports to Brzail (E_{iB}) to total industry exports (E_i). The ratio has been calculated as of 1955 and 1959 from data in [14] and [15].

c. Tariffs (T_{it}). Brazilian tariff data on over 400 products are available from Professor Paul Clark [6].[2] Clark has adjusted the specific and ad valorem tariffs to reflect the effect of multiple exchange rates. Each of the adjusted tariffs then has been assigned to one of the original 214 industries. More than one product was assigned to some industries in which case the arithmetic average was computed and assigned as the industry tariff. Changes in tariffs were computed over the period 1955-1959.

2. Profit variables

a. Market size. The measure of market size employed here is the ratio of the industry's exports to Brazil from the U.S. (i.e., E_{ib}) to the industry's optimum plant size in the U.S. (P_i). The measure of optimum plant size is average plant size in the U.S. in 1957. Average plant size is the value of the industry's shipments in 1957, divided by the number of establishments. These data have been obtained from the 1957 *Census of Manufactures* [16].

b. Tariffs. The measurement of tariffs was discussed above.

c. Capital intensity. Capital intensity is measured as the ratio of the gross book value to total employment of firms in the four-digit SIC industries comprising the 214 industries utilized in this study. The data for both measures are taken from the 1963 Census of Manufactures [18], since the 1957 *Census* did not contain information about book value.

d. Vertical integration. The measure of vertical integration is constructed from several sources. Michael Gort [8] has developed an index of vertical integration for two-digit SIC industries from data obtained from a sample of 111 firms. His measure is the ratio of employment in auxiliary activities to total employment. Gort's measure of vertical integration is used in the following way to construct a measure for the component four-digit industries.

I_{ij} - vertical integration in four digit industry i, a component of two-digit industry j.

I_j - Gort's measure of integration in two-digit industry j.

VAij - value added in 1957
VSij - value of shipments in 1957

$$I_{ij} = \left(\frac{VA_{ij}/VS_{ij}}{\Sigma VA_{ij}/\Sigma VS_{ij}}\right) I_j$$

A dummy variable indicating vertical integration also was constructed. When the dummy is 1, the industry is said to be integrated. When the dummy is 0, it is not integrated. The decision as to which industries are integrated and which are not was made from a frequency distribution of the calculated vertical integration index. Since the distribution has a single mode, approximately half of the industries are classified as being vertically integrated.

e. Research and development. Considerable difficulty was encountered in finding indications of research and development activities of four-digit industries. The most disaggregate data that could be obtained was employment of engineers and scientists in three-digit industries, as compiled in the 1960 *Census of Population* [17]. The ratio of such employment to total employment was computed for each three-digit industry, and was used as the measure of R&D activity of the component four-digit industries.

A dummy variable indicating R&D activity also was constructed. As in the case of vertical integration, a frequency distribution of the calculated measure of R&D activity was examined to determine which industries should be classified as strong in R&D. Unlike the earlier case, however, the distribution is bi-modal, indicating a natural division into R&D and non-R&D industries. Consequently, 49 industries are classified as being strong in R&D.

V. *Results*

1. Search variables affecting investments.

Table 2 contains discriminant function coefficients obtained when search variables are used to discriminate between 54 investment and 89 non-investment industries. Several positive results emerge from this table. First, both prior investment and the relative importance of the Brazilian market (as measured by industry exports to Brazil divided by total industry exports) provide statistically significant discrimination between investment and non-investment industries when the variables are employed separately. However, the variable measuring importance of the Brazilian market does not significantly improve the discrimination provided by the prior investment variable when the two are employed together. On the other hand, the prior investment variable, when added to the market variable does increase discrimination.

Unlike the market variable, the tariff change variable does not discriminate in any of the forms tested. Change in tariffs is multiplied by the market variable to indicate simultaneously the importance of the market to an industry and threats to the market from changes in tariffs. This composite variable is not statistically significant, while the market variable is significant when used alone. Thus, it appears that use of changes in tariffs not only does not help but in fact reduces discrimination possible with the market variable. This conclusion is reinforced when it is noted that addition of the tariff change variable to market and prior investment variables does not improve discrimination. Moreover, the coefficient of the tariff change variable has a negative sign, indicating that larger increases in tariffs tend to reduce search! This strange result provides further evidence that, in fact, changes in tariffs have had little or no effect on search and, thus, on the pattern of investment.

Table 2
DISCRIMINANT FUNCTION COEFFICIENTS 143 INDUSTRIES

$\left(\dfrac{EB}{E}\right)\Delta T$	$\dfrac{EB}{E}$	I_{t-1}	ΔT	F	D^2
1.	.082*			6.2998*	0.187
2. .030				0.4059	0.012
3.		.019**		43.344**	1.289
4. .030		.019**		21.729**	1.302
5.	.081	.019**		24.581**	1.473
6.	.079	.019**	-.001	16.314**	1.477

*Statistically significant at the 5 percent level of confidence.
**Statistically significant at the 1 percent level of confidence.

The pattern of search activity is significantly affected by prior investment and possibly by the relative importance of the market. Consequently, the fifth discriminant function in Table 1 has been used to identify the industries in which search occurred. Industries where search has not occurred are identified by ranking all industries according to the value of the discriminant function. The group of non-investment industries ranked below the investment industries are the ones in which search did not occur. Actually, a few investment industries are interspersed between several large blocks of non-investment industries at the end of the ranking. The last 55 industries in the ranking, therefore, are classified as those in which search did not occur. This group contains 47 non-investment industries and 8 investment industries.

2. Profit variables affecting investment.

Profit variables described earlier have been used to discriminate between the remaining 46 industries in which investment occurred, and 42 in which it did not. The results of this second stage discriminant analysis are reported in Table 3. A statistically

Table 3: Discriminant Function Coefficients—88 Industries, Profit Variables

	Market size	Market size tariff	Tariff	Capital intensity	Vertical integration	R & D activity	Capital Intensity Times		F	D²
							Vertical integration dummy	R&D dummy		
1.		.003							.349	.016
2.				-.001		-.001			.292	.013
3.						-.002			.059	.003
4.		.003		-.001	-.001	-.002			.199	.037
5.	.003			-.001	-.001				.138	.026
6.								-.005	3.804	.173
7.				.004		.013		-.008 *	2.349	.216
8.						.030*		-.009 *	2.923	.269
9.				.011*		.030*		-.021 *	3.742 *	.523
10.			-.001	.011*		.030*		-.-21 *	2.776 *	.524
11.	.001			.011*		.031*		-.021 *	2.776 *	.524
12.		.004		.011*	-.004		.002	-.022 *	2.046	.594

Table 3 (cont.)

*Statistically significant at the 5 percent level of confidence.

significant discrimination is provided by variables measuring capital intensity, R&D activity, and capital intensity multiplied by the R&D dummy variables (line 9 of Table 3). Coefficients of the first two variables show the effects of capital intensity and R&D activity on investment when the industry is not research intensive. The coefficient of the third variable measures the shift in the effect of capital intensity in R&D industries.

The evidence indicates that investment in positively related to R&D activity in all industries. In those industries where R&D activity is not particularly important, investment is more probable in capital-intensive industries (i.e., the coefficient of the capital intensity variable is positive). But the coefficient of the composite variable is negative and larger in absolute value than the capital intensity coefficient. Consequently, in R&D intensive industries, investment in Brazil is more probable the more labor intensive the production process.

These results provide support for the hypotheses advance by Hymer, Aliber, and Vernon. They indicate, in support of Hymer, that foreign investment tends to occur when the industry has some advantage relative to foreign firms. The particular advantage might be access to capital, as suggested by Aliber. Consequently, in the absence of other advantages, investment is more probable the more capital intensive is production. However, when foreign firms have an advantage relative to host country firms as a result of R&D activity, they invest to exploit cheap labor, as suggested by Vernon.

The other striking result in Table 3 is that tariffs and market size seem to have no effect on the pattern of direct investment. As indicated in lines 10 and 11, addition of either variable to the three variables that have been found to be significant does not improve discrimination. Nor does addition of a composite variable formed by multiplying the market size variable by the tariff improve discrimination. Consequently, it would appear that tariffs and market size have not influenced the decision to invest by firms searching for investment opportunities.

Several reasons can be advanced to explain this seeming unimportance of tariffs. However, the finding is congruent with Bergsman's conclusions about the general process of import substitution in Brazil [4, pp. 102-110]. Bergsman shows that considerable import substitution took place after 1949 in a wide variety of industries where *effective* protection was relatively low (i.e., 30%). Direct investment was important in all of these industries, which include machinery, metallurgy, chemicals, and pharmaceuticals. Bergsman attributes import substitution in these industries, particularly in capital goods, to natural advantages possessed by Brazil, and to the large and growing size of the Brazilian market for these products. That is, investment was profitable even in the absence of substantial protection because the market size was large enough to support efficient production.[3]

The validity of conclusions derived from the second stage is reinforced when the same variables are applied to the total set of industries (134 rather than 143, since economic data could not be obtained in 9 cases). Capital intensity, R&D activity, and a composite variable obtained by multiplying capital intensity by the R&D dummy variable are all statistically significant at the 5 percent level. In addition, market size multiplied by the tariff is significant at the 10 percent level.[4]

In summary, perhaps the most striking finding of this study is the unimportance of tariffs as a factor inducing direct investment. On the positive side it is particularly interesting to note that investment is more probable the more capital intensive the industry's production process, *except* when the industry is heavily engaged in R&D activity. In that case, more labor intensive firms are most likely to invest.

It should be clear by now that foreign direct investment decisions are complex. A start is made here to reveal this complexity. Further progress in this direction will require more sophisticated statistical techniques and better measures of the variables.

FOOTNOTES

1. Manipulations of the four-digit SIC classifications is necessary so that industries may be constructed for which equivalent export data are available.
2. The work cited contains only summaries of the basic data. The detailed data have been obtained privately from Clark.
3. Considering this conclusion, it is surprising that the market size variable does not contribute to discrimination in the second stage. The seeming unimportance of the market size variable, however, may be a result of the statistical procedure used in this study. The variable used to measure market size in the second stage is strongly correlated ($r = .74$ over the 214 industries) with the variable used to measure the relative importance of the Brazilian market in the first stage (exports to Brazil divided by the industry's total exports). The effect of market size, therefore, is taken into account in the first stage discrimination.
4. The two-stage procedure, on the other hand, does not significantly add to the overall discrimination provided by first-stage search variables. In the first stage, 77.5 percent of the 143 industries are classified correctly by the search

variables. In the two-stage procedure, only 73.5 percent of the industries are classified correctly. Thus, second-stage profit variables do a poorer job of discriminating among the 88 industries in which search is presumed to occur than would search variables applied to the same industries.

This finding, of course, does not mean that profit factors really do not affect investment decisions. If a statistical procedure could be devised to investigate the effects of search and profit variables simultaneously, it is entirely possible that the latter would add significantly to the discrimination provided by search variables. The importance of profit factors is demonstrated by their statistical significance when applied to the total set of industries, as noted above. Nevertheless, when considered independently, search variables do a better job of discrimination.

REFERENCES

[1] Aharoni, Yair, *The Foreign Investment Decision Process*, Harvard Graduate School of Business Administration, Boston, 1966.
[2] Aliber, Robert Z., "A Theory of Direct Foreign Investment," in *The International Corporation*, A Symposium, Charles P. Kindleberger (ed.), The M.I.T. Press, Cambridge, 1970, pp. 17-34.
[3] Baldwin, Robert E., "Determinants of the Commodity Structure of U.S. Trade," *American Economic Review*, Vol. LXI, No. 1, March, 1971, pp. 126-146.
[4] Bergsman, Joel, *Brazil: Industrialization and Trade Policies* (New York, Oxford University Press, 1970).
[5] Government of Brazil. Superintendencia da Moeda e do Credito, "Investments in Brazil Under Instruction 113," *Boletim* (1956-62).
[6] Clark, Paul and Richard Weisskoff, "Import Demands and Import Policies in Brazil," Unpublished research report for office of Program and Policy Coordination, Agency for International Development, 1966.
[7] Cyert, R.M., and J.G. March, *A Behavioral Theory of the Firm*, (Englewood Cliffs, N.J.: Prentice-Hall, Inc., 1963).
[8] Gort, Michael, *Diversification and Integration in American Industry* (New York, Princeton University Press, 1962).
[9] Gruber, W., D. Mehta, and R. Vernon, "The Research and Development Factor in International Trade and International Investment of U.S. Industry," *Journal of Political Economy*, February 1967, pp. 20-37.
[10] Hymer, Stephen H., "The International Operations of National Firms: A Study of Direct Investment, Unpublished doctoral dissertation, M.I.T., 1966.
[11] Keesing D.B., "The Impact of Research and Development on U.S. Trade", *Journal of Political Economy*, February 1967, pp. 38 ff.
[12] Vernon, Raymond, "International Investment and International Trade in the Product Cycle," *Quarterly Journal of Economics*, May 1966, pp. 190-207.

[13] Weigel, Dale R., "The Relation Between Government Economic Policy and Direct Investment in Developing Countries," Unpublished doctoral dissertation, Standord University, 1966.

[14] U.S. Bureau of the Census. *Report No. FT 410; United States Exports of Domestic and Foreign Merchandise* (Washington: G.P.O., 1955, 1959).

[15] U.S Bureau of the Census. *U.S. Commodity Exports and Imports as Related to Output, 1961 and 1960* (Washington: G.P.O., 1963).

[16] U.S. Bureau of the Census. *1957 Census of Manufactures* (Washington, G.P.O., 1961).

[17] U.S. Bureau of the Census. *1960 Census of Population* (Washington, G.P.O., 1961).

[18] U.S. Bureau of the Census. *1963 Census of Manufactures* (Washington, G.P.O., 1966).

Comparative Management Models: Structure and Research Potential

S. Benjamin Prasad
Ohio University

The purpose of this essay is twofold: to assess the significance of three comparative management "models" which are well known to the students of world business, and to illustrate the potential value (or lack of it) stemming from survey studies that are truly comparative.

The main value of the comparative approach is eloquently underscored in a statement by Kendell, made more than three decades ago with reference to the value of comparative studies in education: "The chief value of a comparative approach to such (educational) problems lies in an analysis of the causes which have produced them, in a comparison of the differences between the various systems and reasons underlying them, and finally in a study of the solutions attempted."[1] Thus increased understanding of different societies and analysis of the causes which underlie different situations therein, constitute part of the usefulness of cross-national comparative studies. Furthermore, as Bendix (1963) advocated: "To be analytically useful, universal concepts (in sociology) require specifications which will help us bridge the gap between concept and empirical evidence."[2] If we were to substitute the term "management" to sociology in the brackets, it would make equal sense.

An overview of the "developmental dialogue" leads to a fundamental premise: that industrialization and economic development are a function not only of capital inputs but also, more importantly, of the mangerial inputs. It is needless to stress the importance of managerial inputs especially in the developing countries in Africa, Asia, and Latin America. The phrase "comparative management" has various meanings. One can start out by identifying the field of comparative management as the study of the management phenomenon on a comparative basis.

Furthermore, as a discipline it can be thought of as a cross-national subject matter. As a research methodololgy, its role can be defined as detection, identification, classification, measurement, and interpretation of similarities and differences among the phenomena being compared.

The importance of this young discipline lies in recognizing that findings emanating from comparative studies could enhance a better understanding of the management phenomenon elsewhere, which in its turn could lead to "theorizing." The logic of theorizing in an applied discipline such as management is not only to explain and to predict but to engender appropriate managerial action.

From a pragmatic point of view, findings from comparative studies are likely to minimize the impediments to the introduction of advanced management know-how into developing countries, and may provide insights into cross-cultural business behavior.

Comparative Management Models

The three constructs or models[3] referred to in this paper are those originally formulated by Harbison and Myers (1959), Farmer and Richman (1964), and Negandhi-Estafen (1965). Boddewyn (1969), and Prasad (1966, 1971) have attempted to *compare* these three comparative management models. A fairly good understanding of the strengths and weaknesses of these models can be summarily obtained by noting the commentaries of Boddewyn and Prasad.

Boddewyn's Commentary: The triple analysis of Harbison and Myers compares "management in the industrial world" in economic, political, and social terms as a resource, system of authority, and class or elite. It focuses on large-scale industrial organizations operating within the milieu of noneconomic institutions as well as on small and nonindustrial firms...The internal and environmental dimensions analyzed by Harbison and Myers are interrelated and can be schematized, shown in Exhibit 1.

In the first place, the overall perspective of their analysis is dynamic. They focus on the evolution of management toward professionalism and democracy, and on the forces likely to mold its future... Furthermore, their conceptual scheme for comparative management studies is oriented to the problem of industrialization. This interest obviously slants their analysis, which may have to be

EXHIBIT 1. HARBISON AND MYERS' COMPARATIVE CONSTRUCT

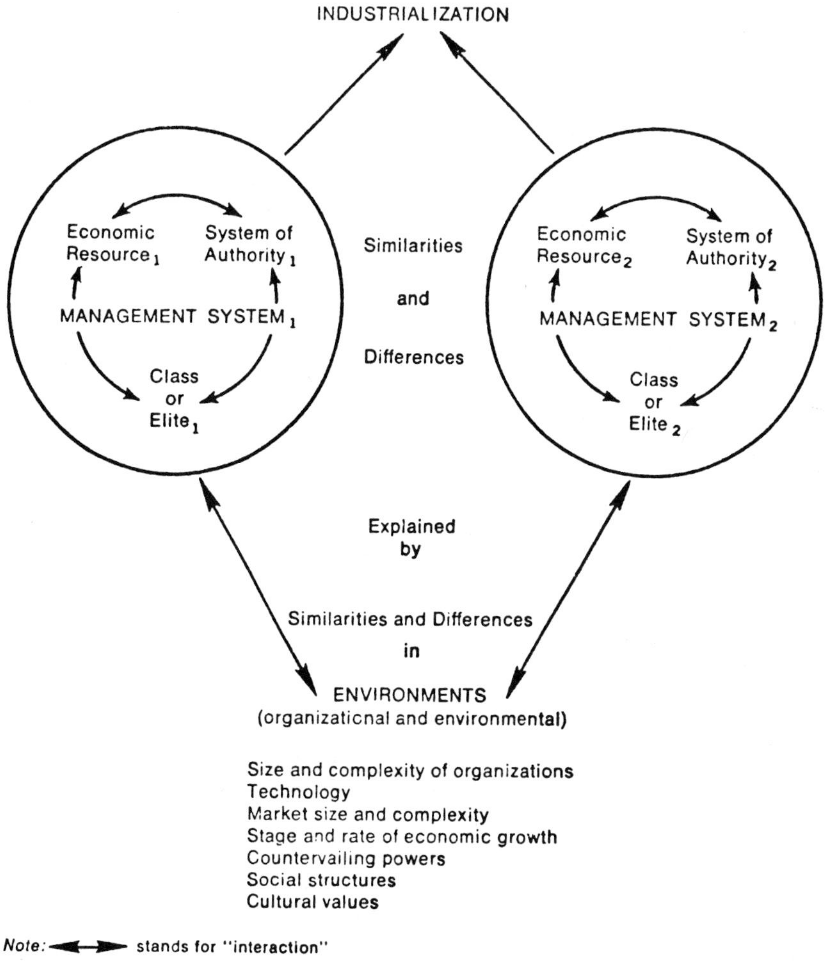

INDUSTRIALIZATION

Economic Resource$_1$ System of Authority$_1$

Similarities

MANAGEMENT SYSTEM$_1$

and

Class or Elite$_1$

Differences

Economic Resource$_2$ System of Authority$_2$

MANAGEMENT SYSTEM$_2$

Class or Elite$_2$

Explained by

Similarities and Differences in

ENVIRONMENTS
(organizational and environmental)

Size and complexity of organizations
Technology
Market size and complexity
Stage and rate of economic growth
Countervailing powers
Social structures
Cultural values

Note: ◄──► stands for "interaction"

Source: J. Boddewyn, *Comparative Management and Marketing,* 1969, p. 36.

modified for other purposes. Yet it successfully indicates that comparative studies need not be harnessed exclusively to generating general theories of management; they can be linked to the analysis of concrete contemporary problems such as economic growth.

Besides, Harbison and Myers' analysis focuses on managers— top managers—rather than on organizations or environments... Finally, Harbison and Myers' research methodology is neither particularly uniform nor easily duplicable. While the characterizations of "Management in Country X" as a resource, a system, and a class have been generally accepted as correct, one cannot say that they are substantiated with hard data. Besides, the country rankings are not very precise, and there is no rigorous hypothesis testing.

The Indiana-UCLA team of Farmer and Richman reveals the same interest as Harbison and Myers in management's contribution to general economic progress. Such progress, as seen by Farmer and Richman, results from the economic efficiency of firms, itself a function of the effectiveness with which managers perform the process of planning, innovating, organizing, staffing, directing, and controlling in such areas as marketing, production, and finance... The following diagram (Exhibit 2) represents the various relationships and comparisons proposed by Farmer and Richman.

This framework for comparative management analysis invites several remarks. First, Farmer and Richman attempt to shift attention away from what they call the "black box" view of management... They stress instead the fact that external factors constrain managerial endeavor and that therefore analysis and improvement of management systems should focus on the crucial environmental variables rather than on what goes on inside the management "box". Farmer and Richman's interest in the environment somewhat overwhelms the comparative management analysis that they suggest and otherwise facilitate by carefully delineating the dimensions of the managerial process. Essentially, these authors visualize management as a variable dependent on the environment, and their construct is more like a prelude to comparative studies... Farmer and Richman's listing of "critical elements of the managerial process" lumps together purely managerial aspects with organizational and even environmental considerations... Besides, Farmer and Richman have offered neither typologies of management nor hypotheses testable by means of comparative studies.

On the other hand, applied to the managerial process and the environment, Farmer and Richman's comparative framework nicely supplements Harbison and Myers concentration on actors, structures, and functions...

Exhibit 2. Farmer and Richman's Comparative Constructa

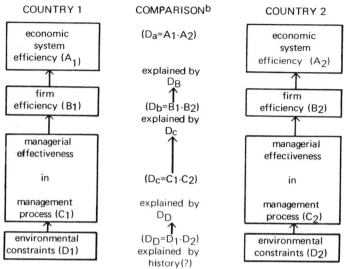

COUNTRY 1	COMPARISON[b]	COUNTRY 2
economic system efficiency (A_1)	($D_a = A_1 - A_2$)	economic system efficiency (A_2)
	explained by D_B	
firm efficiency (B_1)	($D_b = B_1 - B_2$) explained by D_C	firm efficiency (B_2)
managerial effectiveness in management process (C_1)	($D_C = C_1 - C_2$) explained by D_D	managerial effectiveness in management process (C_2)
environmental constraints (D_1)	($D_D = D_1 - D_2$) explained by history(?)	environmental constraints (D_2)

[a]This diagram presents a somewhat simplified version of the relationships analyzed by Farmer and Richman in COMPARATIVE MANAGEMENT AND ECONOMIC PROGRESS (pp. 32-45). In particular, the relationships between managerial activities and affectiveness and the environmental constraints are more complex than the above representation suggests. The arrows indicate the apparent direction of the influence.
[b]In this column, "D" stands for "the difference between countries 1 and 2, as far as a particular element is concerned."

Source: J. Boddewyn, COMPARATIVE MANAGEMENT AND MARKETING (Scott, Foresman and Co., 1969), p. 38.

Instead of focusing on the ecological analysis of aggregates such as "Indian management," as Farmer and Richman would have us do, Negandhi and Estafen propose to compare roughly similar *firms* in different countries on the basis of "effectiveness". They see the latter quality as the product of the means by which top managers carry out their planning, organizing, staffing, directing, and controlling activities—a "process" influenced by particular environmental factors and by the firm's "philosophy," that is, its members attitude toward, and relationship with, outsiders and insiders.

In this connection, Negandhi and Estafen suggest a comparative method to pursue empirical research on this subject. Focusing on the firm, their approach appears more manageable than Farmer and Richman's "Management in Country X"; however, Negandhi and Estafen seem to tend more toward comparisons of business firms than of managers, and their comparative research faces the very

149

difficult problems of holding various internal and evnironmental .factors constant.

Prasad's Commentary: The purpose of Harbison and Myers is to trace the logic of management development as it relates to the process of industrial growth. Their concern is more with the dynamics of development and the basic trends of managerial growth than with an analysis of particular practices at any point in time... Their approach is comparative to the extent that they do make international comparisons—of managers as well as the problems and prospects of generating them—of the management structure which manifests a particular system of authority as well as the forces which brought about such a system and those which tend to modify it, and finally, of the nature of the managerial elite and the inevitability of its becoming more professionally oriented as industrialization advances.

If we accept that management is made up of at least three components—the people (managers and others), the framework (authority structure and the organizational environment), and actions (the things which managers have to do in executing their roles, i.e., management process)—then the Harbison-Myers analysis deals with the first two of these. Somewhat in contrast to the pioneering approach of Harbison and Myers is the scheme of Farmer and Richman.

As they expressed it, the purpose of their model was to develop a new conceptual framework for comparative studies which will prove more useful in the analysis of critical comparative management problems. They employ four key concepts: comparative management problems (the question of relative managerial efficiency among cultures), internal management, external constraints, and, managerial efficiency (degree with which members of productive enterprises achieve their stated goals). The variables in this scheme are aggregate variables. The independent variables are the external constraints.

When one examines their model critically and objectively, one finds little that is comparative but much that is ecological. Since the model has yet to reach field work stage,[3] it is justifiable to say that it remains a skeleton of a scheme yet to be beefed up. One of the fundamental assumptions on which their scheme rests is the notion that "environment" determines "management effectiveness." All phenomena, including management, of course take place within given societal contexts, and there is a constant interaction between institutions and their environments. In its substance, the Farmer-Richman model appears more a scheme for comparing environmental systems than for comparing management.

There are two main contrasts between the Harbison-Myers and Farmer-Richman models: (1) The H-M model is *dynamic* in the sense that it is concerned not only with those forces which have brought about one or the other type of management in a country but also with those which are likely to modify it, while the Farmer-Richman model is static in the sense that it purports to inquire as to what environmental factors have produced a given level of managerial efficiency in a country; (2) The H-M model, from a social scientist's point of view, offers a typology of management, specific concepts, and a general logic whereas these are unfortunately not easily found in the Farmer-Richman model.

Exhibit 3 summarizes the salient features of the three models referred to in this paper. On the Negandhi-Estafen model, Boddewyn's comments are very appropriate; to which one can add that there is a lack of delineation of the relationship of the variables included in their model.

The Negandhi-Estafen model which has undergone a series of revisions essentially recognizes that a firm and its environmnet interact, that the effectiveness of the firm is a function of a selective set of environmental variables as well as a set of selective managerial variables, and the unit of analysis needs to be, initially, at the level of the firm or the organization rather than at the level of the country.

From the foregoing discussion, one can establish the following in terms of the significance of the comparative management models or frameworks:

Considerable thinking has gone into questions related to problems of the world as a whole.

Such thinking, as reflected in these models, each of which has strengths and weaknesses, manifests deliberate attempts to go beyond such questions as: How to Americanize management in foreign countries?

Two of the models (except Harbison and Myers') are built upon limited observation, limited description but with grandiose purposes.

From the field studies which have provided empirical data of one sort or another, there is not a great deal to beef-up the theoretical skeletons offered in these models.

Finally, while it is a very respectable goal to develop concepts which have universal meaningfulness and theoretical foundations, it behooves those interested in comparative management to ask whether more can be learned from the findings of comparative studies than from the comparative models. This is not to say that model-building should be abandoned.

The answer to the above question seems to be in the affirmative. That is there appear to be many useful and interesting things that one can learn from comparative studies whether or not they follow

Exhibit 3. Comparisons of Comparative Management Models

	Harbison-Myers	Farmer-Richman	Negandhi-Estafen
Locus of Comparison	International	International	International and Intranational
Level of Comparison	Macro	Macro	Micro
Managerial Dimension Compared	"Management Development"	"Managerial Efficiency"	"Management Process and Effectiveness"
Orientation	High-level Human Resource	Ecological	Value and Process
Key Variables			
Independent	Forces of Industrialization	Macro economic, legal-political, sociological, educational	Management Philosophy
Dependent	Management as resource, elite, and authority system	Managerial Efficiency measured in economic terms	Management Effectiveness
Purpose(s) of modeling	To trace logic of management development	To extend theory, identify problem-areas in an economy, aid planning by multinational firms	To test management theories, determine international transfer process/problems
Overtones	Social-historical	Ecological	Normative
Stress upon	Typologies	Environment	Adaptation
Field Work of Supportive Type*	Not since late 50's	None	Some

*It should be noted that Harbison-Myers model and studies were part of the Inter-University studies undertaken in the mid-1950's; however, since the publication of Management in the Industrial World (1959) search of literature provides no evidence of further field work supportive of their model. In the case of the Farmer-Richman model, while it is a fact that numerous doctoral theses both at UCLA and Indiana reflect the concern of the model, there is little evidence to support any of the major theses contained in the model while there are indications of relationships which can be postulated A PRIORI.

a model or construct. Let us examine a few of these studies and attempt to substantiate that answer.

Comparative Empirical Studies

Three comparative empirical studies (which are neither related to nor inspired from the comparative management "models" discussed in the previous section) are cited here merely to illustrate the point made earlier; namely, that useful knowledge can stem from studies without theoretical underpinnings. The three are those reported by Whitehill (1964), Lee (1968), and Prasad (1971). In addition, some findings of the intranational Comparative Survey in India are also cited. These were selected on the basis of the fact that they were independently undertaken, contain specific data, and suggest contrasts in value systems of American managers and workers with those from culturally distinct countries, Ethiopia and Japan.

Whitehill's report is based upon a survey of 2,000 production workers, equally divided between Japan and the United States, and employed by four roughly comparable firms. The research was based upon the evolving notion of a "theory of reciprocal role expectation." Data from Whitehill's report are given in Exhibit 4. On the basis of these, Whitehill inferred that (a) cultural factors indigenous to a given society tend to mold the attitudes of workers as to what they may reasonably expect from good management, (b) in exercising its position of leadership, management success in human relations will depend, at least in part, upon understanding in depth the nature and impact of the cultural environment, and (c) that organizational leaders must realize that forces affecting man's willingness to work are dynamic in nature and *can* be influenced by creative, alert administrators.

Lee's report, stemming from his doctoral research in three nations, is concerned with the specific problems associated with developing local or indigenous personnel for management positions in American-owned enterprises abroad. He identifies the following five differences between management selection and development in the developing countries and the U.S. as basic: Limited sources of managerial leadership potential, educational and technological deprivation, economic attitudes hostile to private enterprise objectives, divergent concepts of what an "ideal" manager should be, and resistance to traditional American development approaches, such as face-to-face criticism. The one factor which he has researched presumably by means of personal interview questionnaires is the one relative to the perception of "ideal manager." To

Exhibit 4: Employment Continuity, Identification with Employer, and Motivational Source of American and Japanese Workers

Factor	Percentage Responses by	
	American	Japanese
EMPLOYMENT CONTINUITY: if a worker, although willing, proves to be unqualified on his job, management has a responsibility:		
1. to continue his employment until he retires/dies;	23	55
2. to continue his employment for as long as 1 year so that he may look for another job;	19	23
3. to continue his employment for 3 months so that he may look for another job;	38	18
4. to terminate his employment, after 2-week notice.	20	4
IDENTIFICATION WITH EMPLOYER: I think of my company as:		
1. the central concern in my life and of greater importance than my personel life;	1	9
2. a part of my life at least equal in importance to my personal life;	23	57
3. a place for me to work with management, during working hours, to accomplish mutual goals;	54	26
4. strictly a place to work and entirely separate from my personal life.	23	6
MOTIVATIONAL SOURCE: I believe workers are willing to work hard on their jobs because:		
1. they want to live up to the expectations of their family, friends, and society;	10	41
2. they feel it is their responsibility to the company and co-workers to do whatever work is assigned them;	61	37
3. the harder they work, the more likely they are to be promoted over others to positions of greater responsibility;	9	11
4. the harder they work, the more money they expect to earn.	20	11

Source of Data: A.M. Whitehill, "Cultural Values and Employee Attitudes," 1964.
Note: Interesting details are available in A.M. Whitehill and S. Tajezawa, THE OTHER WORKER (Honolulu: East-West Press) 1968.

quote the researcher: "In 1966-67, I asked managers from America, Pakistan, and Ethiopia to rank 15 qualities or characteristics—selected from American business literature—of the so-called ideal manager." These fifteen factors, and how his respondents ranked them are shown in Exhibit 5, which compares the rankings of the foreign national manager groups (Ethiopian) surveyed with Amer-

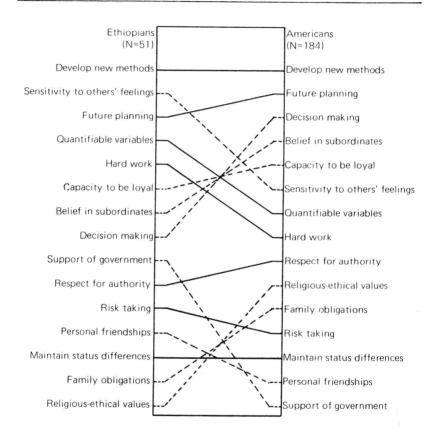

Exhibit V. Comparative ranking of Ethiopian and American managers

Ethiopians (N=51)	Americans (N=184)
Develop new methods	Develop new methods
Sensitivity to others' feelings	Future planning
Future planning	Decision making
Quantifiable variables	Belief in subordinates
Hard work	Capacity to be loyal
Capacity to be loyal	Sensitivity to others' feelings
Belief in subordinates	Quantifiable variables
Decision making	Hard work
Support of government	Respect for authority
Respect for authority	Religious-ethical values
Risk taking	Family obligations
Personal friendships	Risk taking
Maintain status differences	Maintain status differences
Family obligations	Personal friendships
Religious-ethical values	Support of government

Note: Dotted line denotes pair of ranking distribution found to be significantly different.

Source: J. Lee, "Developing Managers for Developing Countries," HARVARD BUSINESS REVIEW, Nov.-Dec. 1968, p. 61.

ican managers' rankings on each of the 15 ideal manager characteristics. Median ranks were used to show the order of ranking importance and connected to point up differences between the two groups. From the information contained in Exhibit 5, we can see that there were significant differences with respect to 8 of the 15 factors relative to the "ideal" manager image.

Prasad reports the findings of a questionnaire survey conducted in 1970-71, the intent of which was to elicit responses of corporate executives from two industrially advanced but culturally distinct nations, the U.S. and Japan. Specifically the question explored was simply: Is there a significant philosophical difference between the premises of American executives and those of Japanese executives so far as corporate decision making was concerned.

The questionnaire contained only two questions relative to: (a) the nature of executive decision making, and (b) "model" of executive decision-making. Questionnaires were sent to 100 chief executives of *Fortune*'s second largest industrialists, and to 100 chief executives of industrial organizations listed in the *Japan Company Directory*, 1970. These were randomly selected.

Sixty replies were received from the American executives and the number of replies from Japanese executives was fifty-two. Tabulated responses to the questions are shown in Exhibit 6. It is quite possible that in a number of instances, the questions were actually answered by assistants to these executives from both the United States and Japan. Nevertheless, the responses are deemed to reflect the thinking of executives.

The first question was phrased: Which one of the following *best* characterizes decision-making, in your opinion? The choices were, decision making is: (a) a vital part of the job of the chief executive, and (b) a vital part of the job of most managers in our company.

Examining data in Exhibit 6, it seems apparent that more than 60 percent of the American executives subscribe to the generally accepted view (in the United States) that decision-making is a vital part of most managers' jobs in business firms. By most managers it is generally understood that they may be at different organizational levels and affiliated with different functional areas of business. In contrast, among the Japanese executives a similarly large proportion of respondents opine that decision-making is a vital part of the job of the chief executive. If we were to examine the "ringi" system of decision-making characteristic of the Japanese business scene (Yoshino, 1968) this opinion would become tenable. A chi-square test indicated a significant difference, at the .001 level, between the American executives' view of the nature of decision-making and that of Japanese executives.

Exhibit 6.

	Response		American Executives		Japanese Executives
On the Nature of Decision Making	(a)	25	37.9 %	37	71.1%
	(b)	41	62.1	15	28.9
		66	100.0	52	100.0
	X^2=35.44				
On the "Model" of Decision Making	(a)	59	89.4 %	3	4.5 %
	(b)	7	10.6	49	95.5
		66	100.0	52	100.0
	X^2=85.45				

Source: S.B. Prasad, "Executive Decision-Making," Working Paper, 1971.

A more distinct difference shows up when we examine the responses to the second question. There is a marked contrast between the fundamental or the philosophical premise on which American executives and Japanese executives base their respective decision-making process. Whereas American executives tend to place primary emphasis upon problem-solving, Japanese tend to stress the problem-identification more than problem-solving as the philosophical foundation. A chi-square test indicated a significant difference at the .001 level between American executives' view of the "model" of decision-making and that of Japanese.

There are no doubt methodological limitations inherent in cross-cultural comparative studies of workers and/or managers. Whitehill's study as reported in the 1964 paper has served at least as a partial basis for his valuable descriptions, analogies, and inferences in the *The Other Worker*. Lee's findings, the basis of which are fully spelled out in his thesis, have served well to conceptualize specific management development programs offered in some of the African countries. Prasad's preliminary survey lends empirical support to the generally held notion that while American managers as well as Japanese managers are both equally pragmatic they seem to reach that point by following different paths.

Intranational Survey Findings

The broad framework within which the survey was conducted in 1967-1969 was the Negandhi-Estafen model. The phenomenon compared here is management process, specifically, the leadership patterns and policy-making processes. Survey method was primarily personal interviews with several members of the 34 organizations operating in India. Half of these were subsidiaries of U.S. multinational firms, and the other half were Indian-owned companies.

There are two kinds of comparisons undertaken in the survey; one was an overall comparison between the U.S. subsidiaries and the Indian firms, that is, on the basis of the nationality of equity ownership and management control. The other comparison was in terms of the degree of sophistication of the company's management. The companies surveyed were categorized as "most sophisticated" (MS), "somewhat progressive" (SP), and "not progressive" (NP), and the basis of the classification was a management philosophy score.

The management philosophy score was attitudinal, that is, management concern or lack of it, positive attitude or lack of it, toward seven *publics*: the employees, the consumers, the community at large, the Government, the suppliers, the distributors, and the stockholders. If a company had positive attitudes toward all seven of these its management philosophy score would be the maximum of 100; negative attitudes on all counts would earn the minimum of 0. On this numerical basis but subjectively the three ranks (MS, SP, NP) were classified according to the following range:

75 to 100 points: MS
40 to 74 points: SP
0 to 39 points: NP

The above scheme placed 17 of the American subsidiaries thus: MS (5), SP (11), and NP (1); and 17 of the Indian firms thus: MS (5), SP (7), and NP (5).

LEADERSHIP PATTERNS: Focusing upon "institutional leadership" (Selznick, 1953) a variety of questions were asked of the respondents in the survey. The style of the chief executive, based on information obtained from several members in each company, was classified according to one of the following: democratic, bureaucratic, or authoritarian. Data shown in Exhibit 7 indicate that all three of these forms were prevalent, although the democratic form appeared in proportionately more subsidiary firms than in Indian firms.

Exhibit 7: Leadership Patterns and Policy-Making Process in U.S. Subsidiary Firms and Indian Companies

	American Subsidiaries	Indian Companies
LEADERSHIP PATTERN		
Democratic	7 (4,3,0)	3 (3,0,0)
Bureaucratic*	6 (0,5,1)	5 (2,3,0)
Authoritarian	4 (1,3,0)	9 (0,4,5)
COMPANY-WIDE POLICY-MAKING BY:		
Chief Executive Only	6 (0,1,5)	13 (2,6,5)
Committee**	11 (5,6,0)	4 (3,1,0)

*The bureaucratic leader was one who attempted to influence his subordinates' behavior by stressing the maze of rules, regulations, and operating procedures; he was neither strictly democratic nor authoritarian but essentially procedure-oriented officer.
**Comprised of a small number of people including functional managers and one or two others including the chief executive.

Source of Data: Adapted from data of the comparative management study reported in A.R. Negandhi and S.B. Prasad, COMPARATIVE MANAGEMENT (1971).

POLICY-MAKING: Examining the overall comparisons (Exhibit 7) it can be seen that the chief executive in Indian firms formulated the company-wide policies by himself while a committee form was more predominant among U.S. subsidiary firms. However, the figures in the parentheses give a clue to another interpretation—irrespective of ownership-nationality, among the MS firms the committee form is dominant.

Viewing both of these variables we can also indicate close association between one and the other. Of course, a sticky question remains unanswered: Considering the MS firms alone, are the chief executives democratic in their style and do they promote group decision-making because they espouse sophisticated management philosophy? Or, do they espouse sophisticated management philosophy because they are democratic type? In other words cause-effect relationships seem blurred. Nonetheless, what is interesting is the revelation that U.S. subsidiary firms can be similar to indigenous firms and indigenous firms can be similar to U.S. firms in their sophistication, progressiveness, and management style.

Conclusion

The significance of the slowly emerging field of comparative management lies in recognizing that findings from comparative studies do enhance our knowledge of one or more dimensions of management in other countries. There are two complementary ways of conducting research studies: one, to build or develop a model and use it as a framework within which field research can be undertaken. On this count, the three well-known models offer some but not much promise. The second approach is to embark upon empirical studies, well defined, well designed, and on a small scale. The latter may very well provide us with the bricks with which to build elaborate structures at some point of time in the future.

---

1. Quoted from *Comparative Education Review*, Vol. 9, No. 3 (October 1965), p. 257.
2. Quoted from *American Sociological Review*, Vol. 28, August 1963, p. 532.
3. Interestingly, Harbison and Myers did not use the term model in their book; other have recognized the framework implicit in their field studies and identified their model. Negandhi and Estafen's was entitled as a model for determining the applicability of American management knowhow in differing cultures and/or environments; nevertheless, it is construed as a comparative management model. If one agrees with the notion that analyses of systems in terms of environment are *cultural* (environmental, ecological) rather than *comparative*, Farmer and Richman's model for research in comparative management would turn out to be an environmental rather than a comparative model. For purposes of this paper such meticulous differentiation as those above are ignored, and all three of these are viewed as comparative models.

REFERENCES

Bendix, Reinhard, "Concepts and Generalizations in Comparative Sociological Studies," *American Sociological Review*, Vol. 28, August 1963, pp. 532-539.

Boddewyn, J.J., *Comparative Management and Marketing* (Scott, Foresman and Company, 1969).

Farmer, Richard and B. Richman, "A Model for Research in Comparative Management," *California Management Review*, Vol. 4, No. 2, Winter 1964, pp. 55-68.

Harbison, Frederick and C. Myers, *Management in the Industrial World* (New York: McGraw-Hill Book Company, 1959).

Lee, James, "Developing Managers for Developing Countries," *Harvard Business Review*, November-December, 1968.

Negandhi, A.R., and B. Estafen, "A Model for Determining the Applicability of American Management Know-how in Differing Environments and/or Cultures," *Academy of Management Journal*, Vol. 8, No. 4, December 1965, pp. 319-323.

Prasad, S.B., "Comparative Managerialism as an Approach to International Economic Growth," *Quarterly Journal of AIESEC International*, Vol. 2, August 1966, pp. 22-30.

___, "Executive Decision-Making," Unpublished Paper, 1971.

Whitehill, Arthur M., "Cultural Values and Employee Attitudes: United States and Japan," *Journal of Applied Psychology*, Vol. 48, 1964, pp. 70-71.

Yoshino, Michael, *Japan's Managerial System* (M.I.T. Press, 1969).

Socioeconomic Indicators in Comparative Management*

Musbau Ajiferuke and J. Boddewyn
New York University

There have been very few extensive, quantitative and cross-cultural surveys of managerial attitudes. Apart from the still growing work of Bass and his associates at the University of Rochester (Bass, 1967), the best known cross-cultural survey is that of Haire *et al.* (1966). They used questionnaires to study attitudes, motivation and satisfactions among managers within 14 countries, and found great similarities in the first two. Of the differences noted in their analysis, 70 percent were accounted for by individual variations among the respondents, 28 percent were attributed to culture, and the remaining 2 percent were left unaccounted for. Furthermore, most of the countries were found to fall into identifiable clusters based on sociocultural groupings, except for Japan which stood by itself, and the developing countries of India, Argentina, and Chile which formed a cluster based on the level of industrialization. Haire *et al.* (1966: 9) concluded that of all the environmental factors having a bearing on managerial attitudes and motivations, cultural influence was substantial but not over-whelming.

Their study is widely regarded as a major contribution to the field of comparative management (Argyris, 1967). However, since their analysis, economic and noneconomic indicators have become more readily available (Russett, 1964) and have been used to analyze various phenomena in the social sciences (Bell, 1969;

*Reprinted from *Administrative Science Quarterly*, December, 1970 by special permission.

Simpson, 1964; Adelman and Morris, 1966). Because the data and interpretations of the Haire *et al.* (1966) study are frequently quoted, it seems desirable to test the validity of their explanation based on the rather crude variables of: (1) culture, loosely defined in terms of religion and language; and (2) level of industrialization, apparently defined in terms of percentage of nonfarm workers and of production of fabricated goods—an investigation welcomed by Haire *et al.* (1966: vi), but also indicated by questions raised about the value of cultural explanations in comparative management studies (Boddewyn, 1969; Ajiferuke and Boddewyn, 1970).

Hence, this analysis correlates selected sociocultural, political, and economic indicators with the attitudes and motivation measurements provided in the Haire *et al.* (1966) study, in order to find out which explanatory variables provide a good or better fit than theirs. Although the data collected by Haire and his collaborators are not completely reliable because of convenience samples, nor necessarily valid because some of their questions were rather badly framed, they were taken at face value for this analysis.

Measurement of Variables

The dependent variables are the four used by Haire *et al.* (1966) (1) attitudes and assumptions underlying management practices, (2) need importance, (3) need fulfillment, and (4) need satisfaction. The last three variables together measured managerial motivation and satisfaction in Haire *et al.* (1966) study, but they are considered separately here in order to highlight their individual relationships to the various independent, explanatory variables. Because there are several item measurements in each of the four variables, the summation of these items represents the score of each country on each dependent variable.

Eight independent or explanatory variables were selected for investigation. They were chosen because data on them were available for all of the 14 countries in the period around 1960 when Haire and his collaborators collected their data. Russett (1964) was used as the primary source of statistical data for the independent variables. However, the present study was somewhat handicapped by the fact that data were not available on many sociocultural factors associated with the social structure and cultural values of the 14 countries.

The following 8 variables were selected as representative of key sociocultural, political, and economic dimensions worth correlating with Haire *et. al.*'s (1966) findings:

1. Percentage of Roman Catholics in the population
2. Percentage of population in primary and secondary schools
3. Percentage of adult literacy
4. Percentage of population living in urban areas (20,000 and over)
5. Life expectancy
6. Percentage of population voting in national elections
7. Gross National Product per capita
8. Percentage of nonagricultural employment.

Obviously, these 8 independent variables could not be used at once in a multiple regression analysis involving only 14 observations. Besides, many of these variables were highly correlated with one another. Still, a relatively large number of independent variables was used because such a number made it possible to obtain good results by using a combination of three uncorrelated explanatory variables at a time. Here, variables having less than a .60 simple correlation were not regarded as highly correlated, and therefore could not be included in a combination. The choice of .60 rather than, say, .50 as the dividing line between a significant and a nonsignificant correlation was arbitrary, and was only made to allow for a greater number of combinations. However, if 50 percent had been chosen instead, the results of this study would not have been materially affected. Exhibit 1 gives the correlation matrix.

This procedure gave 13 combinations of three variables; and each of these combinations was correlated separately with the four dependent variables, resulting in a total of 52 regressions—with each regression involving one dependent and three independent variables.

Results

Only the best results obtained for each of the four dependent variables are discussed below; that is, of the 52 regressions, 48 were rejected as not giving as good results as four presented in exhibit 2.

Attitudes and Assumptions Underlying Management Practices

As exhibit 2 indicates, the multiple correlation coefficient in the regression measuring the degree of relationships between the dependent variable of attitudes and assumptions underlying management practices and the independent variables is .76. However, the reliability graph (Ezekiel and Fox, 1967; 296) gave a

Table 1: Correlation Matrix

	Attitudes and assumptions underlying management practices	Need importance	Need fulfillment	Need satisfaction	% of adult literacy	% of population in primary and secondary schools
Attitudes and assumptions underlying management practices	1.00					
Need importance	-.60	1.00				
Need fulfillment	.21	-.13	1.00			
Need satisfaction	-.61	.77	-.61	1.00		
% of adult literacy	.57	-.54	.43	-.62	1.00	
% of population in primary and secondary schools	.73	-.62	.44	-.73	.88	1.00
Life expectancy						
% of Roman Catholics in the population						
% of population living in urban areas (20,000 and over)						
% of population voting in national elections						
% of nonagricultural employment						
Gross National Product per capita						

	Life expectancy	% of Roman Catholics in the population	% of population living in urban areas (20,000 and over)	% of population voting in national elections	% of nonagricultural employment	Gross National Product per capita
Attitudes and assumptions underlying management practices	.59	-.25	.13	.16	.39	.55
Need importance	-.66	.42	-.10	-.56	-.58	-.58
Need fulfillment	.38	-.50	.43	.08	.41	.17
Need satisfaction	-.68	.68	-.39	-.54	-.73	-.58
% of adult literacy	.96	.06	.63	.35	.83	.51
% of population in primary and secondary schools	.85	-.18	.66	.36	.85	.69
Life expectancy	1.00	-.05	.55	.48	.84	.57
% of Roman Catholics in the population		1.00	-.12	-.25	-.20	-.28
% of population living in urban areas (20,000 and over)			1.00	.03	.71	.39
% of population voting in national elections				1.00	.65	.36
% of nonagricultural employment					1.00	.64
Gross National Product per capita						1.00

Table 2: Multiple Regressions

Variables	Regression coefficient	Computed t-value	Partial R²	Intercept	Multiple correlation	Adjusted R²
Attitudes and assumptions underlying management practices						
% of Roman Catholics in the population	−.002	−0.706	.05	11.600	.760	.451
% of population in primary and secondary schools	.032	3.450	.54			
% of population voting in national elections	−.004	−0.670	.04			
Need importance				33.988	.844	.626
% of Roman Catholics in the population	.015	2.498	.38			
Life expectancy	−.123	−4.296	.65			
% of population living in urban areas (20,000 and over)	.051	2.080	.30			
Need fulfillment				23.599	.745	.422
% of Roman Catholics in the population	−.015	−2.852	.45			
% of adult literacy	.032	2.590	.40			
Gross National Product per capita	−.001	−1.327	.15			
Need satisfaction				7.372	.967	.915
% of Roman Catholics in the population	.021	8.068	.87			
% of adult literacy	−.041	−7.058	.83			
% of population voting in national elections	−.008	−1.674	.22			

value of approximately .30 as the probable minimum correlation. This indicates that the true correlation between the variables is at least 30 percent in the universe from which the sample was drawn, with one chance in 20 of being wrong. With the computed t-value being significant for only one of the three independent variables, it is safe to assume that the true correlation coefficient is probably less than 76 percent. The adjusted coefficient of multiple determination R^2 is .45, which means that about 45 percent of the variation in these managerial attitudes and assumptions underlying management practices among the 14 countries is explained by the three independent variables retained. Of these, the percentage of population in primary and secondary schools is the strongest explanatory factor, accounting through the partial R^2 for 54 percent of this explanation of the differences in managerial attitudes and assumptions in the countries studied.

Need Importance

In the regression with the managers' need importance as the dependent variable, the multiple correlation coefficient is .84; but according to the reliability graph, the probable minimum correlation is over .50 with a 5 percent chance of being wrong. Because the computed t-values are significant for the regression coefficients of all three independent variables, the true correlation must be considerably higher than the minimum correlation of .50, however. Therefore, the computed correlation is probably on the conservative side. The adjusted R^2 of .63 indicates that 63 percent of the variation in the need importance of these managers is explained by the three explanatory factors, with life expectancy having the highest partial R^2 of .65 and providing the best explanation for the comparative differentials in the importance the managers attached to their various needs.

Need Fulfillment

In the regression with the managers' need fulfillment as the dependent variable, the computed multiple correlation coefficient is .75, while the reliability graph gives the probable minimum correlation as approximately .30, with one chance in 20 of being wrong. The regression shows significant t-values for the percentage of Roman Catholics in the population and for the percentage of adult literacy, while Gross National Product per capita has a t-value that is not significant. With two t-values out of three being significant, the true multiple correlation could be expected to be much greater than .30, but probably not as high at .75. The adjusted coefficient of multiple determination R^2 is .42. This means that 42 percent of the variation in need fulfillment of managers is explained by the three explanatory factors, with the percentage of Roman Catholics having the highest partial R^2, closely followed by the percentage of adult literacy. Hence, this measure of religion accounts for the largest proportion of explained variance in the managers' need fulfillment.

Need Satisfaction

In the regression where the managers' need satisfaction is the dependent variable, the multiple correlation is .97. The reliability graph gives the probable minimum correlation between the variables as approximately .90, with a 5 percent chance of being wrong. The computed t-values indicate that the percentage of Roman Catholics in the population and the percentage of adult literacy are significant, but that the percentage voting in national elections is not. The adjusted R^2 indicates that 92 percent of the variation in need satisfaction among managers is explained by the three independent variables, with the percentage of Roman Catholics in the population being the most explanatory factor, accounting for 87 percent of the explained variance in the dependent variable.

Interpretation of Results

Any conclusion drawn from these findings must necessarily be tentative because other important indicators are not yet available for testing, and because this study was restricted to 8 variables considered to be particularly important.

Attitudes and Assumptions Underlying Management Practices

The factor, percentage of population in primary and secondary schools, was found to be superior to any other in explaining the variations in managerial attitudes and assumptions. This result seems to confirm Haire et al.'s (1966) findings that the variance in managerial attitudes noted among the 14 countries, is explained by cultural differences if this educational measure is considered to be a cultural one. However, it should be remembered that for Haire and his collaborators, cultural differences meant primarily religion and language. Yet, the results show very clearly that religion, as measured by the percentage of Roman Catholics in the population, is a relatively weak explanatory variable accounting for merely 5 percent; while education as measured by percentage of the population in primary and secondary schools, provided 54 percent of the explained variance in the dependent variable. Therefore, it appears that certain educational characteristics of the 14 countries are a better cultural explanation than religion or language, for the attitudes and assumptions underlying management practices.

However, percentage of population in primary and secondary schools is not a pure cultural factor since it also reflects political options as well as economic and social conditions. Besides, this correlation with education, like others in this analysis, does not provide a perfect fit. Thus, one would expect that the greater the percentage of population in primary and secondary schools, the more democratic and participative management would be. Instead, when the attitude measurement of the countries, as provided by Haire et al. (1966), were related to the education variable, several discrepancies became apparent. For instance, West Germany has one of the highest education scores, even though the attitude measurements showed that German managers favored a traditional, autocratic type of management; whereas Spain, with a lower education score, tended towards democratic, participative attitudes regarding management practices. Either additional factors not considered in this study are influential here, or Haire et al.'s (1966) data are not reliable.

Managerial Motivation and Satisfaction

On the need importance of managers, the analysis showed the superiority of life expectancy as an explanatory variable, whereas the percentage of Roman Catholics in the population accounted for the greater proportion of the variance in need fulfillment and need satisfaction. Here, Haire *et al.* (1966: 76) claimed that "the factors underlying these differences seem to be not only the degree of economic development of the country, but also the culture of the country in relation to business—one might say the business climate." While their meaning of business climate is rather ambiguous, the findings of this study seem to parallel theirs in that they amount to a combination of economic and cultural explanations where life expectancy and percentage of Roman Catholics predominate. Language, however, was not considered in this analysis; and the economic indicator, life expectancy, used here was different from their use of percentage of non-farm workers and of production of fabricated goods.

Conclusions

This analysis generally supports the validity of the findings of Haire et al. (1966) in their emphasis on cultural and economic factors, even though the measurements used here occasionally differ from theirs. This study also indicates the usefulness of the various indicators now more readily available, and the desirability of their application in comparative-management research. However, the potential of this type of analysis is certainly not exhausted since many other independent variables and other techniques such as factor analysis and rank correlation can also be used. Finally, it is both difficult and dangerous to label factors as economic, political, social, or cultural since most of them have multiple dimensions. Therefore, it is best to refer specifically to the variable studied, for example, percentage of the population in primary and secondary schools, rather than spend too much time arguing whether or not it is an economic, political, social, or cultural one.

REFERENCES

Adelman, Irma and C.T. Morris, 1966, "A quantitative study of the social and political determinants of fertily." *Economic Development and Cultural Change*, 14: 129-158.

Ajiferuke, Musbau, and J. Boddewyn, 1970, "Culture and other explanatory variables in comparative management studies." *Academy of Management Journal*, 13: 153-163.

Argyris, Chris, 1967, "Managerial Thinking. By Mason Haire, E.E. Ghiselli, and L.W. Porter. Book Review, *Administrative Science Quarterly*, 12: 177-179.

Bass, B.M., 1967, "Use of exercises for management and organization psychology." *Training and Development Journal*, 21: 2-7.

Bell, Peter F., 1969, "A quantitative study of entrepreneurship and its determinants in Asia." *Canadian Journal of Economics*, 2: 288-298.

Boddewyn, J., 1969, *Comparative Management and Marketing*, Glenview, Ill.: Scott, Foresman.

Ezekiel, Mordecai, and K.A. Fox, 1967, *Methods of Correlation and Regression Analysis*, New York: John Wiley.

Haire, Mason, E.E. Ghiselli, and L.W. Porter, 1966, *Managerial Thinking*, New York: John Wiley.

Russett, B.M., 1964, *World Handbook of Political and Social Indicators*, New Haven: Yale University Press.

Simpson, Dick, 1964, "The congruence of the political, social and economic aspects of development." *International Development Review*, 6: 21-25.

Strategic and Long Range Planning in the International Firm

John S. Schwendiman
Dow Chemical Company

Introduction

In today's world of expanding international business activities and a constantly changing environment for the international firm, the challenge to the firm is to deal more effectively with the problems and opportunities which arise because of different national sovereignties, economic, social, and political conditions, value systems, institutional arrangements and business practices. Formalized international strategic and long-range planning can play a major role in an international management system in meeting these challenges and opportunities.

To help understand the nature and context of international planning, three general types of international firms can be defined:

(1) The *national firm with foreign operations.* In this firm the emphasis is on the domestic business, with foreign operations (exporting or perhaps some assembly abroad) of peripheral interest.

(2) The *multinational corporation*—which is essentially a conglomerate of individual country subsidiaries which are generally very autonomous. The parent firm views each country as an individual market, and when manufacturing is done abroad it is done only for the country in which the production facility is located.

(3) The *international corporation* takes a global perspective, tries to integrate operations across national borders, tries to equalize returns at the margin, and treats the domestic home market as but an integral part of its global operations.[1]

This is an admittedly arbitrary typology, and it would be difficult to place a particular firm in a given category. Indeed, different parts of the same firm may have different characteristics. But the typology is useful in assessing a top management's orientation to international business, and this in turn has a direct impact on the nature and task of the planning system.

K.A. Ringbakk has proposed the following definition of corporate planning:

Corporate planning is the process of developing objectives for the corporation and its subparts as well as developing and evaluating alternative courses of action to reach these objectives; doing this on the basis of a systematic evaluation of external threats and opportunities and internal audits of strengths and weaknesses.[2]

George A. Steiner suggests a more specific typology of corporate planning which will provide the basic definitions of types of planning used in this paper:

(1) *Strategic planning*—is conducted by the highest levels of management and is concerned with the development of fundamental goals and objectives and the major policies and allocations of corporate resources to meet the goals.

(2) *Intermediate- or long-range planning*—which takes the overall strategies and defines action programs and steps for the accomplishment of the strategic objectives over a relevant (four to five year, perhaps longer) time period.

(3) *Tactical planning*—the programming of action plans through one or two year or shorter time period profit plans or budgets.

(4) *Planning studies*—which are initiated at the request of top management to provide background for strategic and long-range planning.[3]

The major thrust of this paper concerns strategic and long-range planning, and the "ideal" model developed has as its referent the "international corporation."

The three sections which follow summarize briefly (1) a simple international planning process model and the key dimensions of international planning, (2) the methodology of the empirical research for the dissertation upon which this paper is based, and (3) the results of the research, a "state of the art" analysis of international planning practices in twenty-two major international firms in the automotive, chemical, and electrical equipment industries.

Figure 1 presents an idealized international planning process seen from a corporate perspective. The four major functions to be performed are (1) environmental assessment, (2) company assessment, (3) strategic planning, and (4) derivative long- and intermediate-range and tactical planning. A general flow is indicated, but it is merely to suggest that an assessment of "what is" should precede the planning of "what is to be," although the different stages, to some extent, may be handled simultaneously or in some other order. In each stage some of the key tasks to be performed are indicated.

Other stage definitions can be found in varying degrees of complexity,[4] but Figure 1 represents a generalization. While these are the basic steps that underlie the ideal formalized corporate planning system (and the elements may even be handled in a sense without a formal system) the actual operational steps followed by companies will differ because they must reflect and accommodate a variety of factors more or less unique to each company.[5] Nevertheless, these are the key factors which should be handled in a systematic way in order to assure the best results from planning efforts. The interrelations and feedback loops between the elements are not detailed here, although they are numerous. The objective of having a formal process is not to generate piles of reports of non-essential data to which no attention is paid. The reason for having a formalized process is to assure that no key factors are overlooked, so that top management especially can make decisions with the best possible understanding of their future effects. The importance weights attached to the different elements will vary from company to company.

In stage (C), that of strategic objective-setting, heavy emphasis is laid on the responsibility of top management to lead out in specifying various corporate policies and priorities. This is one key dimension which can present several problems, not the least of which is that corporate executives may often find themselves needing to deal with business strategies in environments very unfamiliar to them. The amount of back-up work and analysis will therefore have to be proportionately greater because of the danger of the "self-reference criterion"[6] —the tendency to make decisions to be implemented in a foreign environment on the basis of what one knows to be true of the domestic, familiar environment— coming into play. Top management is also responsible for determining the orientation which the firm will take toward international business. If top management opts for the "international

Figure 1: AN INTERNATIONAL CORPORATE PLANNING PROCESS

(A)
Environmental Assessment
1. Overall economic/political/social outlook (problems?) by country and region.
2. Analysis of present lines of business on a worldwide basis.
3. Technology trends and forecast.
4. Analysis of markets outside company lines—diversification possibilities.
5. Worldwide industry outlook: costs and prices.

(B)
Company (Divisional) Assessment
1. Strengths and weaknesses vis-a-vis industry and competition in each country and/or regional market.
2. Corporate resources—financial, human, etc.
3. Evaluation of progress on short-term plans.
4. Evaluation of progress on long-range action programs.

(C)
Strategic Objective-Setting
1. By top management—and based on a consideration of alternatives arising from a thorough integrated analysis from stages (A) and (B).
2. Product line strategies on a global basis.
3. Overall geographic strategy.
4. Diversification strategy.
5. Divestment strategy.
6. Priority setting.

(D)
Formulation of Long-Range Action Programs, Tactical Plans, and Budgets
1. Within the context of stages (A), (B), and (C).
2. At appropriate organizational levels and by geographic subunit, within narrowing constraints or objectives.
3. Worldwide capital budget, source and use of funds analysis, and cash management plans.

This flow of activities is considered on a yearly cycle basis.

corporation" form, the requirements for planning inputs will be different than if they opt for the "multinational" form where they are more or less managing a portfolio of foreign company investments. The demands on the executives themselves will be quite different also.

Other key factors in the international planning process are the overall organization for planning on a global basis, the role of the "planning staffs," and the degree of integration of domestic and international planning.

In his study of the rise of the international firms, Professor Jack Behrman sees a tendency toward greater centralization of planning and decision- making.[7] This would suggest the necessity for increased organizational means for coordinating "top-down" policy-making with the "bottom-up" kinds of inputs needed to carry out not only the integration of planning activities but the actual integration of operations in different counties.

One of the first questions concerning staff support of international planning is whether there should be a separate "international planning staff" or whether special people should be designated as "international planners." Ideally, the answer would be "no." The planning staff of a large international company should be so competent that members can deal with home market or international problems using the same benchmarks. Since such expertise is only developed over a long period of time, however, it may be desirable to have international specialists on the central corporate planning staff with counterparts in the other planning staffs throughout the company.

The question of integration of "domestic" and "international" planning can be put in perspective by considering its implications along the spectrum of orientation to international operations. For instance, in the national firm and in the multinational corporation, integration of planning and operations is less important than in the international corporation where one of the major objectives is to maximize the results from the firm taken as a whole rather than as a sum of its parts. An interlocking structure of planning groups, each headed by a key line manager (with the overall structure patterned after Rensis Likert's "linking pin" model of a management structure[8]) is one way of organizing an integrated planning structure.

Research Methodology

In a desire to expand upon K.A. Ringbakk's empirical study of organized corporate planning systems,[9] it was decided that a mail survey would be inappropriate. Consequently a sample of companies was chosen in which personal interviews with planning personnel and executives could be obtained. It was recognized that the sample would necessarily be small, and therefore statistical analysis of answers would not be possible.

Three industries were chosen to represent a spectrum of business practices. These were: automobiles, chemicals, and electrical equipment. Specifically excluded from the analysis were the international petroleum industry and international banking. This was done because of a need to limit the study and because each of these industries has a number of special characteristics.

Twelve U.S.-based international companies were chosen to represent the three industries. They were chosen to represent a spectrum from relatively small international involvement (7-10 percent of corporate sales) to substantial involvement (40-50 percent of sales). The companies were asked to participate *whether or not there was any formalized corporate planning system.* Hence, the combinations of characteristics provide a very wide spectrum. The U.S. companies which participated are: General Motors, Ford, Chrysler, duPont, Union Carbide, Monsanto, Dow, General Electric, Westinghouse, General Telephone and Electronics, Emerson and Electric, and Cutler-Hammer.

Ten European-based companies were chosen. These companies (with the exception of Daimler-Benz) are all classified by Jack Behrman in his study as being substantially international in corporate outlook.[10] The companies are headquartered in Switzerland, Germany, and the Netherlands, and represent the "Germanic" European firm. The companies included are: Volkswagenwerk, Daimler-Benz, Farbenfabriken Bayer, Farbwerke Hoechst, Ciba-Geigy, BASF, Philips, Siemens, AEG-Telefunken, and Brown-Boveri.

A research questionnaire was designed for open-end interviews with planners and/or executives in these companies. The twenty-seven questions are directly related to the key elements of the model presented in Section B, plus certain information on general organization structure and international orientation of the top management of the company.

In each company an appointment was arranged with that person or group of persons responsible for or most familiar with the international planning activities of the company. The interviews generally lasted two to three hours, but in some cases longer.

It was not possible to conduct an equally rigorous or complete interview at each company. Several of the companies do not have formal planning systems in the sense in which they are generally defined, and many questions were therefore unanswerable. In some cases it was possible to speak with only one person, while on other occasions many people participated. The subjects of the interviews ranged from staff people specifically involved in the detail of international planning to international group vice presidents and members of boards of directors.

By agreement with the companies, they will not be specifically identified in the summary of findings which follows.

State of the Art in International Strategic and Long-Range Planning

In most of the sample companies formalized international planning is still in its infancy. The European companies generally began their formalized planning efforts in the late 1960's, often in conjunction with an organizational structure change from the traditional functional structure to the U.S. division-type structure, while the U.S. companies began formal planning early in the decade.

The companies included range from the "national firm with foreign operations" to companies attempting to be "international corporations." Most of the companies would seem to fall somewhere between the "multinational corporation" and the "international corporation" on the spectrum. Most of the U.S. companies, at some stage early in their international involvement, had a form of international division. These generally have been modified or replaced by other structures. Product division international responsibility and regional management structures are common.

While it is true that every one of the companies is engaged in some kind of formal planning, only about one-half of the companies (evenly divided between the U.S. and Europe) have overall systems that even begin to approximate the thorough and integrated planning system "ideal" which was sketched in briefest form earlier. Two examples will highlight the range of approaches to planning.

(1) Company G (a U.S. company) has no corporate (master) plan. In this company there are several "separate and discrete" planning processes which are basically functionally oriented. There is a three-year profit-planning system which is administered through the controller's office. While there is a Vice President of Planning, he and his staff do not administer a "system." They are concerned primarily with new business development and special projects. The "long-range" plans of the company, such as product plans, capacity

plans, and capital budgets are *presented* to the top management committee. While there must necessarily be coordination in drawing up the different plans, still there is no overall formal framework or system. The international operations are handled fairly autonomously from the domestic operations. The head of international operations sets five year goals for the various subunits. European operations are run on an integrated basis while in Latin America planning and operations are on a country-by-country basis.

(2) Company W (a European company) has the most thorough and integrated planning system among the sample companies. The top executive committee plans overall strategy, but with "give and take" with the product division heads. The executive committee is particularly concerned with its role as allocator of resources and how this affects the long-run overall growth and profitability of the company. There is a six phase planning process. In *Phase I* the company's worldwide policies and objectives are defined by the executive committee and the "rules of the game" for the year's planning activities are set forth. *Phase II* occurs simultaneously and concerns the preparation of a comprehensive "planning data base" on environmental factors and company assessment vis-a-vis competitors. *Phase III* involves the preparation of five-year plans by divisions and country subsidiaries along the guidelines laid down by top management. Emphasis is on strategies and action programs to carry them out. *Phase IV* involves the integration of plans after some "give and take" and the presentation of an integrated corporate plan to top management. The top management considers the plans and proposed action programs and then communicates its decisions and priorities for the action programs back to the divisions and planning units. *Phase V* involves the preparation of one-year plans and budgets (using top management priorities on action programs), while *Phase VI* is a quite financially-oriented integration of the budgets. Figure 2 gives a typical breakdown of a divisional plan for a five year planning horizon. This document is the most environment-, strategy-, and action-oriented plan format encountered in the research.

In general, headquarters capability and proficiency in environmental analysis is not high. (The term "environmental analysis" is used here in a broad sense and includes economic, social, cultural, and political-legal factors as they impact on the business climate.) This situation, I suspect, arises because of a feeling that continuing environmental assessment at headquarters is really not necessary when there are people on the spot.

Before investment is initiated in a "new" country, the companies reported that either a consultant is hired or a task force of people is

Figure 2: CONTENTS OF A DIVISIONAL PLAN IN COMPANY W		
Chapter 1:	Introduction	(1-2 pages)
Chapter 2:	Assumptions	(1-2 pages)
Chapter 3:	Opportunities and problems, with objectives and strategies	(10-15 pages)
Chapter 4:	Time schedule for strategies	(1-2 pages)
Chapter 5:	Personnel and resource requirements	(3-5 pages)
Chapter 6:	Five-year budget	(3-5 pages)
Chapter 7:	Problems for higher management attention	(1 page)

sent to investigate the environment. Both of these approaches are "one-shot" methods. At one large U.S. company, for example, a legal-political analysis is made by the legal department when a new venture is proposed. But there is no follow-up or ongoing analysis as the approved project comes to life.

The space devoted to consideration of environmental factors in written plans is minimal. In several cases the treasurer's office is responsible for adding a paragraph or two about environment to proposals and plans. This seems to be "lip-service" environmental analysis. Most financial analysts approach country analysis from a foreign exchange and balance-of-payments point of analysis from a foreign eschange and balance-of-payments point of view. Such approaches may widely miss the key factors for a company's overall business strategy.

It is, of course, not inappropriate for systematic environmental analysis to be done locally, but in the sample companies this does not appear to be the practice. There was little indication that strategy planners either at headquarters or in the local country subsidiaries make a conscious systematic effort to relate strategy to environment (in a broad sense). More likely is that a few economic indices and projections form the basis for what planning does take place. The two major exceptions to this finding are the European company previously mentioned which makes environmental analysis a key part of its planning process at all levels, and Company K (a U.S. company) which keeps at headquarters a "priority check-list" of factors to watch in the different countries in which it operates.

Several companies noted, however, that environmental analysis is an area where much more attention will be given in the future. As one planner said, "The main problem is that information costs money and does not show an immediate return." Nevertheless, many of the companies are recognizing that money spent in obtaining good environmental data will more than pay for itself in the strategy adaptations that result. At Company H (a U.S. company) some of the corporate development staff are attempting to develop analytic matrices and checklists to help set priorities in gathering environmental information.

Most of the companies feel that their internal management information systems serve planning purposes fairly well. The overwhelming preponderance of data designated as "key data" are the items appearing on monthly, quarterly, and yearly financial statements (e.g., sales, costs, inventories, operating margin, cash position, etc.). Another general benchmark is the trend in market share. The cataloging of non-financial resources (personnel, research and development capabilities, etc.) does not appear to receive much formal attention.

The answers to the questions dealing with internal company assessment were a disappointment. It seems that an in-depth analysis of internal strengths and weaknesses vis-a-vis competitors in the market is generally lacking, both at the strategic planning level and at the division, regional, or even local foreign subsidiary level. There is little evidence in the written plans that much attention is paid to these factors.

In the research interviews there was little evidence that company top managements currently engage in formalized strategic planning processes, although several U.S. and European companies are trying to head in that direction with their planning systems. A significant problem slowing progress is typified in one of the European companies which introduced a formalized planning system within the last three years. The director of planning commented how difficult it is to get top management support of and inputs into the planning process. He explained, "All members of the top management group have thirty or forty years of experience in the company and have seen it grow from a small firm to an international company that is very successful. Their attitude often is: 'Why do we need planning? Look how well we have done without it!'" This planner commented that one of his objectives as a planner in this increasingly diversified and far flung international giant is to develop better evaluation tools and yardsticks for use in making decisions. It is becoming very difficult to rely on seat-of-the-pants decision-making as decisions become more and more complex.

The fact that the top management decision processes in the sample companies do not appear to be very formalized does not mean that great effort is not devoted to making corporate decisions. In one way or another allocations of scarce corporate resources are made. These decisions have long-range and strategic effects, but the term "strategic planning" does not really describe the process. It is probable that in several instances I was not able to gain a complete picture of the top management decision process. But what can be inferred from staff efforts and peripheral evidence is that most top managements of these large international companies do not take a very strong *formal* or leadership role in the development of corporate strategy.

Major problems in international planning receiving increasing attention include this lack of top management involvement in corporate-wide planning. Corollary to this is the problem of poor communication of top management goals within the organization. Language and communication barriers and different "cultural concepts" of planning in different countries also provide a problem which takes time to solve. The general problem of getting enough "good people" who can handle the planning function as well as being good operating businessmen was mentioned frequently. The lack of good environmental analysis is receiving important attention in many companies, while the general lack of integration of plans, not only between "domestic" and "international" but between international subunits as well is also seen as a critical need.

There are many problems, and many improvements will be made in the coming years. But formalized international strategic and long-range planning is here to stay. It is not a "cure-all" for all corporate ills. Rather, good planning should be seen as part of a broader modern management system and philosophy which will help the international firm achieve success in its world markets in the decades ahead.

FOOTNOTES

1. Charles P. Kindleberger, *American Business Abroad*, New Haven: Yale University Press, 1969, pp. 179-182.
2. K.A. Ringbakk, *Organized Corporate Planning Systems: An Empirical Study of Planning Practices and Experiences in American Big Business*, doctoral dissertation, University of Wisconsin, 1968, p. 31.
3. George A. Steiner and Warren M. Cannon, *Multinational Corporate Planning* New York: The Macmillan Company, 1966, p. 11-16.

4. See, for example, Ringbakk, op. cit., pp. 14-17, or George A. Steiner, ed., *Managerial Long-Range Planning*, New York: McGraw-Hill, 1963, or *Planning for Profits*, New York: Business International, 1967, or Frank F. Gilmore and Richard D. Brandenburg, "Anatomy of Corporate Planning," *Harvard Business Review*, November-December, 1962, pp. 61-69.

5.. Steiner and Cannon, op. cit., p. 25.

6. James A. Lee, "Cultural Analysis in Overseas Operations," *Harvard Business Review*, March-April, 1966, pp. 106-114.

7. Jack N. Behrman, *Some Patterns in the Rise of Multinational Enterprise*, Chapel Hill: University of North Carolina, 1969, pp. 86-87.

8. Rensis Likert, *The Human Organization*, New York: McGraw-Hill, 1967.

9. Ringbakk, op. cit.

10. Behrman, op. cit.

A Methodology for Computerization of International Market Research

C.G. Alexandrides
Georgia State University

A major problem of a U.S. firm in exporting is to identify global markets for its products.[1] The identification of export markets by means of statistical analysis requires sufficient international trade data. The lack of detailed international commodity data in the past has limited the application of statistical methods to market research for identification of global markets. However, the need for international market research is constantly increasing due to the internationalization of business. At present, several projects in this field are under implementation by governments, international agencies and universities.[2]

The objective of this article is to demonstrate a methodology for identifying world markets, and examining the U.S. export performance and the degree and trend of major foreign competition. For this purpose, a case study is used to illustrate the methodology.

The research methodology described in this article is made possible as a result of international commodity statistics recently made available by the United Nations and the Organization for Economic Cooperation and Development.[3]

Methodology

The research methodology is briefly described in the following six steps:

Step 1—Data Collection. The collection of pertinent economic, demographic and trade data is the first requirement of the methodology. Economic data, such as GNP, business cycle, industrial production index and relative prices are selected and/or constructed for major countries. Population data are available from 1950 with projections for 222 countries and territories. International trade data are obtained on a commodity basis (SITC 4 and 5 digits) from 1962 to present from the UN International Computing Center.

Step 2—Determination of Relevant Data. The independent variables used to explain variations in commodity imports are based on theoretical grounds. Consumer goods are related to GNP, population, and relative prices,[4] while capital goods to industrial production and business cycle.[5] The small number of observations does not allow for a great flexibility in using a larger number of independent variables, because disaggregated commodity import data for major countries are available only since 1962. Other independent variables may be used in explaining import variations of commodities depending upon theoretical grounds as well as empirical results of relationships between the nature of the commodity and the variable(s) used.

Step 3—Determination of Predictive Equation. An import equation is generated for a particular commodity by regressing the dependent variable (imports) on the independent variables. Extraneous factors of a more permanent type, such as tariffs and devaluations, are considered with the use of dummy variables, while factors of a temporary nature such as strikes are eliminated. Variables which do not explain significant variations in imports are eliminated from the analysis, since the objective is to generate predictive equations, and new regressions are run on the remaining variables.

Step 4—Import Projections. The predictive equation is used to forecast commodity imports into various countries for several years. At this stage, the objective of the model is not to make accurate year to year projections, but to give approximate total import demand for a number of years. Linear and curvilinear regression analysis is used in forecasting independent variables, when projections of these variables for certain countries cannot be obtained from UN and OECD sources.[6]

Step 5—Market Share Forecasting. Time series analyses are used to project commodity exports of the major exporting countries into the various countries for several years, and determine the average market share of main exporters for the projected period of time. Market share trends are obtained by comparing percentage changes in the share of each of the major exporting countries over a certain number of years.

Step 6—Determination of Global Markets. The selection of world markets for a commodity is based upon the projected total import demand in each market for a particular period of time, the anticipated U.S. performance in each market expressed by the total forecasted U.S. exports to each country over the same period, and the degree and trend of foreign competition.

Business and government organizations can build the methodology into a computerized international information system for analyzing over one thousand commodities in major world markets (See Figure 1).

A Case Study

The objective of the case study is to locate major world markets for electric switchgear by means of the described methodology. The variables used to explain variations in imports of switchgear are electrical production and business cycle. Business cycle was used as proxy variable for investment, as it is difficult to project investment activity in many countries.

The model used to forecast imports of switchgear in foreign countries is the following:

$M = a + b_1 \text{ EPI} + b_2 \text{ BC} + b_3 \text{ DUM}$

where

M = imports

EPI = electrical production index

BC = business cycle index

DUM = dummy variable for tariffs, devaluation, etc.

a = intercept of the regression line*

b_1 = regression coefficient of EPI

b_2 = regression coefficient of BC

b_3 = regression coefficient of DUM (difference in the intercept before and after structural change)

*a = 1. intercept of the regression line, if no DUM is used.
2. intercept of the regression line consistent with time period before structural change, if DUM is used.

The regression coefficients of the import functions for each country, based on UN and OECD data for 1962-1969,[7] are shown

187

in Table 1. Using OECD and UN projected rates of growth for GNP, the independent variables were projected for five years (1970-1974) as follows: (1) EPI = a + b IPI (Industrial Production Index);** and, (2) Business cycle index = $\frac{IPI}{\log \text{trend}}$ x 100. The projected variables were substituted into each import equation of each country to obtain five-year import demand projections.

A summary of the findings for twenty major world markets of switchgear is shown in Table 2. The table shows the major export markets, the projected total import demand and the U.S. exports for the five-year period in each market along with the rank of the countries based upon the projected import value, the U.S. share and its trend. The table also indicates the two major competitors with projected five-year exports, percentage share of the total import market and trend of their market shares.

The findings disclose that the largest world markets for switchgear during the 1970-1974 period should be France, Germany, Canada and The Netherlands. The largest markets of the U.S. for this commodity over the same period are expected to be the U.K., Mexico, Japan, and Germany. The U.S. will be holding a large share of the import market for switchgear in Japan, Mexico, South Africa, the U.K., and Brazil. The U.S. share of the projected import market should be increasing over the five-year period in Australia, Belgium and Luxembourg, Denmark. Italy, and Japan.

Summary

International market information that can be obtained through the methodology could be used by firms interested in developing export sales as selection criteria to choose the most promising markets. Furthermore, this information can be helpful to an exporting firm to improve its international marketing plan. Government agencies can also use this information as guidelines in the development of export expansion programs.

**IPI = c + d GNP

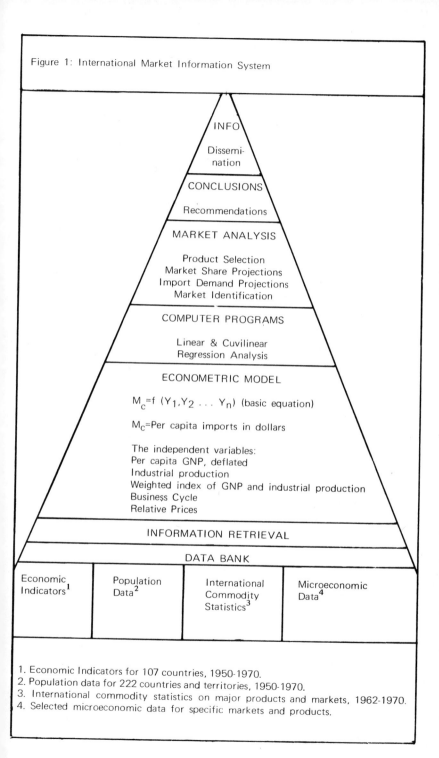

Figure 1: International Market Information System

INFO
Dissemination

CONCLUSIONS
Recommendations

MARKET ANALYSIS
Product Selection
Market Share Projections
Import Demand Projections
Market Identification

COMPUTER PROGRAMS
Linear & Cuvilinear
Regression Analysis

ECONOMETRIC MODEL

$M_c = f(Y_1, Y_2 \ldots Y_n)$ (basic equation)

M_c = Per capita imports in dollars

The independent variables:
Per capita GNP, deflated
Industrial production
Weighted index of GNP and industrial production
Business Cycle
Relative Prices

INFORMATION RETRIEVAL

DATA BANK

Economic Indicators[1]	Population Data[2]	International Commodity Statistics[3]	Microeconomic Data[4]

1. Economic Indicators for 107 countries, 1950-1970.
2. Population data for 222 countries and territories, 1950-1970.
3. International commodity statistics on major products and markets, 1962-1970.
4. Selected microeconomic data for specific markets and products.

Table 1. Coefficients of Switchgear Import Functions
$(M=a + b_1 EPI + b_2 BC + b_3 DUM)$

	Constant	Elec. Prod. Index Coefficient	Business Cycle Coefficient	Dummy Coefficient	r^2	t-value	F ratio	Level Significance
Australia	-5958.78	242.49 (37.87)[1]			.87	6.40		.01
Austria	-28745	401.98 (16.19)			.99	24.83		.01
Belg.-Luxbg.	-118274	525.34 (86.79)	962.42 (744.9)		.89	$6.05b_1$*** $1.29b_2$***	20.47	.01
Brazil	-27038.9	414.72 (110.59)		-7683.05[2]	.75	$3.74b_1$*** $1.64b_3$**	7.63	.05
Canada	-384934	1066.72 (127.75)	3179.19 (99.87)		.94	$8.67b_1$*** $1.64b_2$**	39.71	.01
Denmark	-24402	323.02 (33.89)			.94	9.53		.01
France	-81526.6	1052.28 (120.62)			.92	8.47		.01
Germany	-128915	1243.52 (106.16)	314.92 (249.42)		.98	$1.26b_1$* $11.71b_2$***	142.54	.01
Iran	-33464.3	128.34 (6.58)	223.25 (53.52)		.99	$19.48b_1$*** $4.17b_2$***		.01
Italy	-169364	923.71 (179.78)	1108.93 (832.16)		.85	$5.14b_1$*** $1.33b_2$*	14.74	.01

	Constant	Elec. Prod. Index Coefficient	Business Cycle Coefficient	Dummy Coefficient	r^2	t-value	F ratio	Level Significance
Japan	-21289.3	229.79 (37.84)			.93	11.84		.01
Mexico	-13552.9	241.14 (32.60)			.90	7.39		.01
Netherlands	-5229.61	375.56 (35.32)			.95	10.63		.01
Norway	-10456.1	209.06 (29.55)			.89	7.07		.01
South Africa	-35906	541.44 (47.11)			.96	11.49		.01
Spain	-6993.31	199.04 (27.70)			.89	6.93		.01
Sweden	-92600	605.01 (31.42)	563.5 (278.07)		.99	$19.25b_1$*** $2.03b_2$**	193.04	.01
Switz.	-33069.2	502.57 (162.26)			.61	3.12		.01
Taiwan	-26392.4	96.07 (17.64)	200.67 (115.19)		.92	$5.44b_1$*** $1.74b_2$**	28.21	.01
U.K.	-66235.8	856.92 (54.63)			.98	15.68		.01

1. Number in parenthesis is standard error of regression coefficient(s).
2. Devaluation of 1964.
 *Coefficient is significant at 0.15 level.
 **Coefficient is significant at 0.10 level.
 ***Coefficient is significant at 0.01 level.

Table 2

FIVE-YEAR TRADE OUTLOOK OF SWITCHGEAR IN MAJOR COUNTRIES
(1970-1974)

Country	Five-Year Import Demand Projections, 1970-1974 ($000's)	Rank	Five Year U.S. Export Projections $000's	Rank	U.S. Mkt. Share %	Trend	Major Competitors Country	Total 5-Yr. Export Proj ($000's)	Market Share %	Trend	Major Competitors Country	Total 5-Yr. Export Proj. ($000's)	Market Share %	Trend
Australia	187,743	13	34,196	10	18.2	Increasing	U.K.	33,810	18.0	Decreas.	Germany	29,694	15.8	Increasing
Austria	199,566	11	18,550	17	9.3	Static	Germany	111,975	56.1	Increas.	Switz.	20,708	10.4	Static
Belgium-Luxbg.	317,892	8	27,222	13	8.6	Increasing	Germany	161,781	50.9	Increas.	N'lds.	58,249	18.3	Increasing
Brazil	157,096	14	53,044	8	28.4	Static	Germany	33,603	18.0	Increas.	Italy	24,487	3.1	Static
Canada	657,307	3	55,870	7	8.0	Static	U.K.	17,090	2.5	Static	Germany	15,375	2.2	Static
Denmark	149,292	17	7,831	19	5.2	Increasing	Germany	62,032	41.6	Decreas.	N'lds	10,080	6.8	Static
France	1,353,638	1	81,363	6	6.0	Decreasing	Germany	264,889	19.5	Increas.	Italy	52,782	3.9	Increasing
Germany	876,863	2	109,640	4	12.5	Static	France	119,036	13.6	Increas.	Switz.	101,600	11.6	Static
Iran	157,991	16	12,343	18	7.8	Static	Germany	40,039	25.3	Increas.	France	19,288	2.2	Static
Italy	495,482	5	86,020	5	17.4	Increasing	Germany	259,440	52.4	Static	France	71,221	4.4	Increasing
Japan	159,663	15	113,695	3	71.2	Increasing	Germany	18,930	11.9	Increas.	Italy	10,505	6.6	Increasing
Mexico	195,407	12	116,236	2	59.5	Static	Japan	14,864	7.6	Static	France	12,310	6.3	Decreasing
Netherlands	530,347	4	38,374	9	7.2	Static	Germany	223,010	42.0	Static	Be-Lux.	120,003	22.6	Increasing
Norway	119,936	18	2,892	20	2.4	Static	Germany	46,466	39.7	Decreas.	Switz.	9,409	7.8	Decreasing
South Africa	249,217	20	28,884	14	34.9	Static	U.K.	74,111	29.7	Decreas.	Germany	32,670	13.1	Static
Spain	211,795	10	19,122	16	5.6	Static	Germany	54,060	32.2	Static	Italy	26,791	12.6	Static
Sweden	343,724	7	32,408	11	13.6	Decreasing	Germany	154,990	45.1	Decreas.	Switz.	21,606	6.3	Static
Switzerland	227,656	9	19,210	15	14.2	Decreasing	Germany	139,000	61.1	Decreas.	Germany	22,184	9.7	Static
Taiwan	95,501	19	19,210	12	20.1	Decreasing	Japan	87,095	91.2	Static	Germany	3,002	3.1	Static
United Kingdom	446,600	6	143,640	1	32.2	Decreasing	Germany	90,817	20.3	Decreas.	France	37,408	8.4	Static

FOOTNOTES

1. C. G. Alexandrides, "Major Obstacles to Export Expansion," *Atlanta Economic Review*, May 1971.
2. Examples of recent projects in this area include the computerization of international trade intelligence information by the British Board of Trade; the global marketing program of the U.S. Department of Commerce; and, LINK, the world trade forecasting model under the coordination of the Wharton School of the University of Pennsylvania. Also, international market research publications of the UNCTAD–GATT International Trade Center, OECD, and the international academic community.
3. The UN has standarized international commodity data on SITC only since 1962. See, UN, *Commodity Trade Statistics: Series D*, (Paris, annual). Also, OECD, *Foreign Trade Statistics: Series C*, (Paris, annual).
4. Charles P. Kindleberger, *International Economics*, (Homewood, Illinois, 1968), pp. 272-274.
5. F.A. Adams, et. al., *An Econometric Analysis of International Trade*, (Paris, OECD, 1969), p. 15.
6. UN Secretariat, "Total Population Estimates for World Regions and Countries Each Year 1950-1985," (New York, 1970), OECD, *The Outlook for Economic Growth*, (Paris, 1970).
7. Data were compiled from the following UN and OECD sources: UN, *Commodity Trade Statistics: Series D* (annual); UN, *Statistical Yearbood* (annual); UN, *Monthly Bulletin of Statistics*; OECD, *Main Economic Indicators: Historical Statistics*, 1957-1966, and *Main Economic Indicators* (monthly).

Environmental Determinants of Overseas Market Entry Strategies*

James D. Goodnow and James E. Hansz
Eastern Michigan University

Purpose

This research examines a hypothesis, modified from one originally stated by Isaiah Litvak and Peter Banting,[1] concerning the relationship of U.S. companies' entry strategies into overseas country markets and those countries' positions along an environmental "temperature gradient." Although Litvak and Banting's original hypothesis was put forth to explain why international agent middlemen evolve into merchant middlemen, the analytical framework is relevant to explain the evolution of other marketing channel phenomena.

Central Hypothesis

Specifically the present study seeks to examine the hypothesis that a firm will tend to pursue an entry strategy involving greater control over overseas production and marketing activities as the country's environment becomes "hotter" in the Litvak-Banting sense. ("Hot" countries are defined as those which are politically stable; high in market opportunity, economic development and performance, and cultural unity, and low in legal barriers, physiographic barriers and geocultural distance. Definitions of these environmental barriers are given in Appendix A.)

*Reprinted from the *Journal of International Business Studies*, Vol.3, No. 1, Spring 1972 by special permission.

Related Literature

Apart from the original Litvak and Banting article (which has been cited by Lazer[2] as well as Miracle and Albaum[3]), concepts for this project have been gathered from several sources. Environmental variables have been selected from those suggested in previous research done by Bartels,[4] Sherbini,[5] Farmer and Richman,[6] Stobaugh,[7] and Rostow.[8] The influence of stages of economic development on channel structure *within countries* has been studied by George Wadinambiaratchi,[9] Susan Douglass,[10] and Reed Moyer.[11] Although channel structure *between countries* is discussed in virtually every international marketing text, empirical analysis of the relationship between the economic, social and political climates of various overseas countries and the international channel strategies pursued by U.S. firms in the respective countries is not readily available.

Methodology

Several research methods were employed in this project. First, country environmental indicators were gathered from published sources (such as Sherbini's comparative analysis,[12] the U.S. Departments of Commerce and State,[13] The United Nations,[14] the International Monetary Fund,[15] and *Business International*[16]) and expert opinion (e.g., country desk officers of the U.S. Department of Commerce). Second, the countries were grouped through the use of proxy variables representing each of the seven multivariate categories suggested by Litvak and Banting. (See Appendix A for a list of variables.) To be more specific, a hierarchical clustering computer program was used to "objectively" classify countries into similar groups which lie along a "country temperature continuum." A brief technical description of this multivariate statistical technique is presented in Appendix B.

Third, questionnaires were sent to the directors of the international divisions of the 750 largest U.S. based corporations (company size based upon 1970 sales volumes listed in *Fortune*). The purpose was to identify, for each country in which the firm's major product line is sold, the type of entry strategy used by the firm. These entry strategies include indirect methods, such as sales through outside parties like export-import houses, combination export managers, and piggybacking arrangements; more direct methods, such as having wholly or jointly-owned overseas assembly or production facilities or maintaining permanent overseas sales and distribution facilities; or a combination of the above strategies.

Fourth, the U.S. corporate channel strategies were observed for three clusters of countries ("hot," "moderate," and "cold") to test the central hypothesis.

Results

Cluster Analysis of Countries

The cluster analysis program compared the 100 selected countries on the basis of 59 characteristics. Each variable was standardized and given equal weight in the hierarchical grouping process explained in Appendix B. At each stage in the grouping process the two most similar countries (or groups of countries) were clustered together. First there were 100 groups, then 99, 98, 97 and so forth until all countries had been combined into a single group. For each stage in the grouping process an information loss function was calculated. A portion of this function indicating the changes of within-group variance is illustrated in Table I. The fourth column indicates the percent change in the information loss as each new cluster was formed. The sharp jumps in the information loss function starting with the reduction of four groups to three groups suggested that either three or four groups would be "optimal" (at least in a heuristic sense).

For the sake of simplicity in our presentation we have chosen the three major clusters of countries. Using the Banting and Litvak nomenclature, we have designated them as "hot," "moderate," and "cold" countries. A listing of the countries included in each cluster is presented in Table II. An asterisk has been placed next to the 20 countries which merged with the 30 "coldest" countries when the number of groups was reduced from four to three.

The first cluster, which we call "hot" countries, is made up of the EEC nations, Austria, Denmark, Iceland, Norway, Sweden, Switzerland, United Kingdom, plus Canada, Australia, New Zealand and Japan. These countries are characterized by very stable governments, relatively few restrictions on foreign investment, temperate climates and cultures similar to the United States.

The second cluster of 34 nations which might be called the moderate countries, contains most of the Caribbean and Latin American countries as well as Finland, Hong Kong, Ireland, Israel, Lebanon, Malaysia, Portugal, Singapore, Spain, South Korea, Taiwan, Turkey, the Union of South Africa and Yugoslavia.

The third set of 50 nations, which might be called the "cold"

Table I
INFORMATION LOSS
FUNCTION FROM CLUSTER ANALYSIS OF 100 COUNTRIES

Number of Groups	Total Error	Change	Percent Change
100	4.33		
		4.33	100
99	7.37		
		3.04	70
98	8.17		
		.80	11
97	9.49		
		1.32	16
96	10.84		
		1.35	14
—	—	—	—
—	—	—	—
—	—	—	—
11	117.01		
		5.57	5
10	122.58		
		8.31	7
9	130.89		
		7.06	5
8	137.95		
		1.85	1
7	139.80		
		15.05	11
6	154.85		
		9.20	6
5	164.06		
		13.89	8
4	177.94		
		66.47	37
3	244.42		
		133.42	55
2	377.84		
		780.05	206
1	1157.89		

Table II. Countries Belonging to the Three Major Clusters

"HOT" COUNTRIES

Australia	Japan
Austria	New Zealand
Belgium-Luxembourg	Netherlands
Canada	Norway
Denmark	Sweden
France	Switzerland
Iceland	United Kingdom
Italy	West Germany

"MODERATE" COUNTRIES

Barbados	Lebanon
Brazil	Mexico
Chile	Netherlands Antillies
Colombia	Nicaragua
Costa Rica	Panama
Cyprus	Portugal
Dominican Republic	Singapore
Ecuador	South Africa
El Salvador	South Korea
Finland	Spain
Guatemala	Taiwan
Guyana	Trinidad
Honduras	Turkey
Hong Kong	Uruguay
Ireland	Venezuela
Israel	Yugoslavia
Jamaica	Malaysia

"COLD" COUNTRIES

Afghanistan	Laos
*Algeria	Liberia
Angola	*Libya
*Argentina	Malagasy Republic
*Bolivia	Malawi
*Burma	*Morocco
*Cambodia	Mozambique
Cameroon	Nepal
*Ceylon	Nigeria
Congo (Kinshasa)	*Pakistan
*Egypt	Paraguay
Ethiopia	*Peru
Gabon	*Philippines
Ghana	Saudi Arabia
*Greece	Senegal
Haiti	Sierra Leone
*India	*South Vietnam
Indonesia	*Sudan
Iran	*Syria
*Iraq	Tanzania
Ivory Coast	Togo
Jordon	*Tunisia
Kenya	Uganda
*Kuwait	Upper Volta
	Zambia

*Members of the "warmer" group of "cold" countries—which tend to be more developed economically but less stable politically. Preliminary analysis indicates that companies prefer more direct marketing routes in these countries than in other "cold" countries.

countries, consists of all the African countries (save South Africa), most of the Middle East, the Indian subcontinent, most of Southeast Asia, plus Argentina, Bolivia, Haiti, Paraguay, Peru, and Greece.

In general, as one moves from the first to the third cluster, the government becomes more unstable, the markets become poorer, the economy becomes less stable, cultural homogeneity declines, legal and geographic barriers go up and cultures become different from the U.S.

What makes the second group unique from the third? Most of the countries in the second group have had a longer period of freedom from foreign domination. Thus, they have had an opportunity to strengthen their economies, to become better educated, and to improve their health and material well-being. Their cultures tend to become more homogeneous—especially with respect to language. They also tend to be geographically closer to the U.S. Many of the countries also require local assembly of goods or local sourcing for purchases of components.

(For a more comprehensive view of the similarities versus the differences among the three clusters, see Table III. This table shows the average value of each of the 59 proxy variables for each cluster, and the average value for all 100 countries.)

Analysis of Company Market Entry Strategies

We received answers from 250 of the 750 firms in our universe. Usable questionnaires came from 222 firms. Sixteen firms had policies of not responding to any questionnaires; three needed more clarification of our questionnaire; five had no overseas activity (including Anaconda and Kennecott which were withdrawing from Chile); and four were received too late for tabulation. The usable questionnaires were quite evenly distributed according to company size and industry.

A frequency distribution of company market entry strategies was calculated for each country. Firms using a combination of strategies in a given country were put into one of three categories:

A. Combination of a majority owned plant with one or more other strategies.

B. Combination of direct export through company owned overseas facilities, licensing and/or joint venture with one or more other strategies.

C. Combination of direct export through overseas agents or distributors with indirect export.

We also created a special category for those firms which wrote in "exports from third countries."

Marketing subsidiaries were included as a form of direct export through company-owned overseas facilities.

We then prepared a frequency distribution of company market entry strategies for the average country in each of our three clusters.

Before comparing company responses with country clusters, the following observations from our data shed light on market entry behavior which may be unique to larger firms:

1) Large companies do not make extensive use of indirect exporting (i.e., exports through outside parties in the U.S.). Indirect exporting was used at a minimum by one percent of the 222 companies when going to Canada and at a maximum by about 10 percent when going to the countries of Indochina.

2) Minority and/or 50:50 joint ventures as well as licensing are not as popular as majority-owned subsidiaries except in countries like Japan and India where majority ownership is forbidden to foreigners in many industries. Licensing agreements are preferred to joint ventures 2:1 in the "hot" and "moderate" countries and 5:1 in the "cold" countries.

As shown on Table IV, the percent of firms having plants in the typical country in each cluster declines as one moves from Cluster I ("Hot" Countries) to Cluster III ("Cold" Countries). This is consistent with the Banting-Litvak hypothesis.

As firms move from Cluster I to Cluster III, firms substitute direct export for local manufacturing, which is also consistent with Banting's and Litvak's ideas.

Further analysis of Table IV reveals that as firms move from "Hot" to "Cold" countries, firms move away from the use of licensees and joint venture partners while they make significantly greater use of strategies involving decreased control over sales such as overseas agents and distributors as well as U.S. based intermediaries. We did not receive enough "write-in" replies about the use of company-owned sources in third countries to attach any statistical significance to multinational sourcing in each of the three clusters.

Significance of Research Results

Despite some shortcomings in our research which we shall mention momentarily, our findings generally support the Banting-Litvak hypothesis that the degree of control exercised by firms over

Table III. Cluster Profiles of the 59 Variables for the "Hot," "Moderate," and "Cold," Categories.

VARIABLE Cluster Size	"HOT" 16	"MODERATE" 34	"COLD" 50	TOTAL SAMPLE 100
A. POLITICAL STABILITY				
X_1 Political stability of central government[A]	Estremely stable	Stability depends on key persons.	Government in control despite internal factions.	Government in control despite internal factors.
X_2 Years since independence[B]	379	55	35	49
X_3 Years under current constitution[B]	357	51	12	80
X_4 Type of government[A]	Parliamentary	Parliamentary	Benevolent dictator or revisionist	Coalition-parliament
X_5 Military vs. civilian control[A]	Civilian 100%	Civilian 100%	Civilian 72% Military 28%	Civilian 86% Military 14%
X_6 Dictatorships?[A]	None	None	46% dictatorships	24% dictatorships
X_7 Direction of dominant political party[A]	Conservative	Conservative	Liberal	Liberal
X_8 Percent of countries having minor riots, insurrections[A]	25%	44%	46%	42%
X_9 Percent of countries having major wars, revolutions[A]	0%	6%	26%	15%

Table (cont.)

X$_{10}$ Median number of anti-business pressure factions[A]	0	1	1	1
X$_{11}$ Average annual % increase in population[C]	1.1%	2.5%	2.7%	2.4%
B. MARKET OPPORTUNITY MEASURES				
X$_{12}$ Total population[C] (in millions)	24,984	10,572	21,641	18,413
X$_{13}$ Percent adult male literacy[C]	85.1%	49.6%	22.7%	41.9%
X$_{14}$ Televisions/1000[D]	232	57	11	62
X$_{15}$ Radios/1000[D]	310	176	91	155
X$_{16}$ Telephones/100[D]	285	58	13	72
X$_{17}$ Automobiles/100[D]	203	42	16	55
X$_{18}$ Trucks/100[D]	38	13	7	14
X$_{19}$ Newspapers/100[D]	352	123	18	107
X$_{20}$ GNP annual growth rate[C]	5.3%	6.3%	7.3%	6.7%
X$_{21}$ GNP/capita[C]	$2,467	$782	$414	$868

C. ECONOMIC DEVELOPMENT AND PERFORMANCE MEASURES

X_{22} GNP (in billion U.S. dollars)C	$56,331	$6,368	$3,860	$13,108
X_{23} Gross private domestic investment as % if GNPC	21.5%	17.2%	14.3%	16.4%
X_{24} Average annual % increase in consumer price indexC	5.0%	18.0%	27.5%	20.5%
X_{25} Energy consumption per capita as a % of U.S.A.D	40.8%	10.3%	5.1%	12.5%
X_{26} Steel consumption per capita (annual)D	.4 metric tons	.07 metric tons	.03 metric tons	.11 metric tons
X_{27} Cement production per capita (annual)D	.5 metric tons	.2 metric tons	.06 metric tons	.18 metric tons
X_{28} Exports and imports as a % of GNPC	42%	46%	34%	38%
X_{29} Raw materials as % of exportsC	38.6%	81.6%	90.5%	79.2%
X_{30} Male life expectancy at birthC	68.5 yrs.	57.4 yrs.	44.6 yrs.	52.8 yrs.
X_{31} Infant mortality/1000C	21.4 deaths	55.8 deaths	71.2 deaths	58 deaths
X_{32} Inhabitants/physicianC	787	2,256	17,757	9,771

X_{33} Currency reserves (in billion U.S. $)E	2.7	0.4	0.2	0.7
X_{34} Trend in 5-year balance of paymentsE	1 year surplus	1 year surplus	2 years deficit	1 quarter deficit
X_{35} Currency convertibilityA	Freely convertible	Less than 10% open/black mkt. differential	Less than 10% open/black mkt. differential	Less than 10% open/black mkt. differential
X_{36} Development of local capital marketsA	Open stock exchange	Limited capital market	Limited capital market	Limited capital market
D. CULTURAL UNITY MEASURES				
X_{37} Percent of countries with ethnic homogeneityF	50%	47%	28%	38%
X_{38} Percent of countries with religious homogeneityF	93%	71%	54%	66%
X_{39} Percent of countries with racial homogeneityF	100%	41%	82%	71%
X_{40} Percent of countries with linguistic homogeneityF	81%	71%	28%	51%
X_{41} Percent urban population	61%	42%	19%	34%

E. LEGAL BARRIER MEASURES

X_{42} Percent of countries belonging to strong common market[H]	75%	24%	18%	29%
X_{43} Capital repatriation policy	Liberal restrictions	Liberal restrictions	Restriction based on time	Liberal restrictions
X_{44} Policy towards foreign ownership[A]	100% allowed and welcomed	100% allowed not welcomed	Some local ownership required	100% allowed, not welcomed
X_{45} Legal discrimination against foreigners[A]	Equal treatment with locals	Minor restrictions	Some controls on foreigners	Minor restrictions
X_{46} Tariff protection for local industry[A]	Little or no protection	Some infant industry protection	Considerable infant industry protection	Some infant industry protection
X_{47} Percent of countries expropriating foreign property (1966-71)[A]	0%	15%	30%	20%
X_{48} Percent of countries where local content and/or assembly required[A]	6%	38%	10%	19%
X_{49} Percent of countries with strong price control or anti-trust programs[A]	56%	50%	58%	55%

F. PHYSIOGRAPHIC BARRIER MEASURES

X_{50} Road density (road kilometers/sq. kilometer)[G]	81	25	5	24

X_{51} Rail density (rail kilometer/sq. kilometer)G	7	3	0.6	2
X_{52} ClimateG	Temperate	Tropical	Tropical	Sub-Tropical
X_{53} Population/square kilometerC	130	301	37	142
X_{54} Land area (million sq. kilometers)C	1.3	.6	8	.8
G. GEOCULTURAL DISTANCE MEASURES				
X_{55} Air distance from Chicago to national capital (in miles)I	~	5,397	8,268	6,981
X_{56} Percent of countries with ocean portI	81%	100%	70%	82%
X_{57} Percent of countries whose primary language is GermanicJ	75%	29%	0%	13%
X_{58} Percent of countries whose primary language is RomanticJ	19%	59%	10%	28%
X_{59} Percent of countries where Judeo-Protestant culture is predominantJ	63%	9%	0%	13%

Sources: A. Country specialists at the U.S. Department of Commerce (opinion survey results)
B. National Education Association, OTHER LANDS, OTHER PEOPLES plus recent newspapers.
C. United Nations STATISTICAL YEARBOOK, DEMOGRAPHIC YEARBOOK and NATIONAL ACCOUNTS STATISTICS.
D. Business International INDICATORS OF MARKET SIZE FOR 130 COUNTRIES.
E. International Monetary Fund, INTERNATIONAL FINANCIAL STATISTICS.
F. Sherbini et. al, COMPARATIVE ANALYSIS IN INTERNATIONAL MARKETING.
G. OXFORD ECONOMIC ATLAS OF THE WORLD.
H. Cateora and Hess, INTERNATIONAL MARKETING (revised edition).
I. Examination of a world globe.
J. Christian Science Monitor, WORLD MAP SERIES.

sales in other countries is related to the external environment and that the degree of control declines as the environment becomes less favorable. To further support the hypothesis, we found that close to two-thirds (60.9%) of the firms in our sample sold their goods in the average "hot" country; somewhat under half (43.3%) sold in the average "moderate" country; and slightly over one-third (34.4%) sold in the average "cold" country. Thus, the external environment not only influences channel selection, it also influences whether a firm chooses to enter a market at all.

It is important to bear in mind that our method of analysis focuses on macro as opposed to micro behavior. We have looked at

Table IV. Percent of U.S. Firms Surveyed Using Selected Market Entry Strategies

Market Entry Strategy	Average* "Hot" Country	Average* "Moderate" Country	Average* "Cold" Country
Majority-Owned Plant	14.5%	6.1%	1.5%
Combination (Majority-owned plant plus other strategies)	11.0	2.9	0.7
Export Via Company-Owned Overseas Channels	19.2	29.9	32.4
Joint Venture	3.0	2.2	0.7
Licensing Agreement	7.6	4.2	3.5
Combination (Export via company-owned channels, joint venture, and/or license and/or less direct exporting)	16.4	12.8	10.4
Indirect Export	2.9	5.3	6.4
Combination (Overseas agents, distributors, indirect exports)	0.9	0.7	0.4
Export Via Overseas Agents or Distributors	24.2	35.6	43.4
Company-Owned Sources in Third Countries	1.9	0.9	2.2

*These percents represent the proportion of U.S. firms employing a particular market entry strategy to a typical country in each respective cluster.

Preliminary analysis of our data indicates that the larger companies tend to take more control over market entry strategies in all markets than do smaller firms. Their additional resources make it possible for them to take more risks.

market entry strategies of a large group of firms in *groups* of country markets. Then we looked at firms' strategies for individual countries in each of the clusters, there were some rather important exceptions. For example, Mexico, Brazil, Colombia, Venezuela, Spain, and South Africa outrank some of the countries in cluster I with respect to the numbers of firms with at least one majority-owned plant. Japan ranked lower (due obviously to its extensive foreign investment restrictions). Argentina, the Phillippines, Peru, and India (all in the "cold" cluster) also have significant numbers of majority-owned plants.

This suggests that the weighting system used in our cluster analysis is not necessarily that used by businessmen when making decisions about specific countries. For example, geocultural distance factors like common or familiar language and/or distance from the U.S. may have been weighted more heavily by business decision makers than economic and political factors.

Moreover, the way businessmen weigh the various variables probably changes from situation to situation. For example, local legislation requiring local assembly or local sourcing will constrain the firm to a limited number of international channel options.

We have also overlooked such factors as the degree of competition from local manufacturers of substitute products, the extent of the firm's financial resources, and the nature of the product.

This suggests that our findings—although they tend in general to substantiate the Banting-Litvak hypothesis—do not fully explain the rationale behind international business decisions with respect to market entry strategies.

Some Directions For Future Research

Our research efforts uncovered several problem areas which may be improved in future research. Apart from the traditional problems with secondary data from the United Nations and other statistical sources (e.g., slow data collection and reporting by governments, and differences in measuring systems), the problem of missing data for some variables forced us to estimate values of these variables for certain countries or to eliminate countries from our sample. As country-by-country statistical information gathering reporting improves, clustering techniques will yield more meaningful insights.

The instrument we used to gather data from companies failed to include the concept of overseas manufacture for export to third countries. A more complex questionnaire could show which countries are being used as manufacturing bases for which third countries. Such information would be valuable to point out the growing importance of multinational sourcing.

We are not certain as to the relative importance of the selected variables in determining country membership in each of the clusters nor are we aware of each country's rank within each cluster. To answer these questions, we plan to perform a stepwise multiple discriminant analysis in the near future.

We are also planning to experiment by varying weights assigned to each variable to find out whether cluster membership changes so as to better explain the rationale behind the behavior of the business firms we have observed. Moreover, we plan to observe differences in country-by-country market entry strategies according to size of the firm (in 1970 worldwide sales volume) and according to major branch of industry (2 digit Standard Industrial Classification) for the firm's major product category.

Later researchers may wish to conduct personal interviews to go beyond our statistical skeleton to find out how firm decision-makers perceive local competition and how they weigh variables (those we have observed plus others) in making market entry strategy decisions. It would probably be valuable to conduct an experiment similar to ours in other industrialized countries as well as sometime in the future in this country in order to test the degree to which one can generalize the Banting-Litvak framework from a dynamic perspective.

The social sciences, including the study of international business, have yet to develop invariant laws. The Banting-Litvak hypothesis is an example of a hypothesis which has been developed, but not empirically tested until now. This study has employed a multivariate statistical technique, hierarchical cluster analysis, to empirically examine the hypothesis. The authors feel that such an inductive approach is not only useful in testing current theories in international business, but could also be applied to generate additional theories in the field.

APPENDIX A
LITVAK-BANTING ENVIRONMENTAL CHARACTERISTICS AND SELECTED PROXY VARIABLES

1) *Political Stability*—"A system of government which permits representation of major segments of its society, enjoys the confidence of its people, generates conditions for continuity of business enterprise, and is sympathetic to private enterprise."

Indicators:

X_1—Index of future political stability expected by U.S. Government country experts (20=stable; 0=unstable).

X_2—Number of years since independence.

X_3—Number of years under current form of government or current constitution.

X_4—Type of Government: (Parliamentary=1; Coalition Parliamentary = 2 Benevolent Dictatorship=3; Dictatorship=4).

X_5—Military vs. civilian government? (1=military; 0=civilian).

X_6—Dictatorship vs. parliamentary government? (1=dictatorship; 0=parliamentary)

X_7—Direction of dominant political party (moderate to extremist, 1-6).

X_8—Minor riots or insurrections in the past five years? (yes=1; no=0).

X_9—Major wars or revolutions in the past five years? (yes=1; no=0).

X_{10}—Number of pressure groups which could bring change of government (0-7).

X_{11}—Average annual rate of increase in population over last five years.

2) *Market Opportunity*—"A sufficient number of customers with incompletely satisfied needs and the necessary resources with which to satisfy those needs for the product or service in question."

Indicators:

X_{12}—Total population.

X_{13}—Percent adult male literacy.

X_{14}—Televisions/1000.

X_{15}—Radios/1000.

X_{16}—Telephones/1000.

X_{17}—Automobiles/1000.

X_{18}—Trucks/1000.

X_{19}—Newspapers/1000.

X_{20}—GNP annual growth rate.

X_{21}—GNP/capita.

3) *Economic Development and Performance*—"The level of a country's economic growth, efficiency, equity and stability, which shape the environment for private enterprise."

Indicators:

X_{22}—Level of GNP (in U.S. dollars).

X_{23}—Gross private domestic investment as a % of GNP.

X_{24}—Percent annual inflation (average annual change in consumer price index for past five years).

211

X_{25}–Energy consumption per capita (as a percent of U.S.).

X_{26}–Steel consumption per capita.

X_{27}–Cement production per capita.

X_{28}–Exports plus imports as a percent of GNP.

X_{29}–Raw materials as a percent of total exports.

X_{30}–Male life expectancy at birth.

X_{31}–Infant mortality rate/1000.

X_{32}–Inhabitants per physician.

X_{33}–Level of currency reserves in U.S. dollars.

X_{34}–Trend in balance of payments (number of surpluses vs. deficits for past five years).

X_{35}–Index of convertibility of currency (20=freely convertible; 4=over 100% open/black market differential).

X_{36}–Index of development of local capital markets (10=well developed; 0=no capital market and capital flight exists).

4) *Cultural Unity*–"The values, goals, social relationships and interactions within a country's people in terms of shared heritage, unassailed by competing groups."

Indicators:

X_{37}–Index of number of ethnic groups comprising one percent of population (1=1-6 groups; 2=7-9 groups; 3=10 or more groups).

X_{38}–One religion at least 75% predominant? (1=yes; 0=no).

X_{39}–One major racial stock at least 90% predominant? (1=yes; 0=no).

X_{40}–One common language spoken by at least 85% of the adult population? (1=yes; 0=no).

X_{41}–Percent urban population.

5) *Legal Barriers*–"A proliferation of public measures in the form of laws and regulations which either deliberately or unintentionally restrict or discourage existing business activities and the future environment for private enterprise."

Indicators:

X_{42}–Regional trading group to which country belongs (1=member of EEC, EFTA, CACM or Andean Common Market; 0=not a member of above groups).

X_{43}–Index of liberality of laws affecting repatriation of earnings (12=no restrictions; 0=no repatriation).

X_{44}–Index of policy towards foreign ownership (12=100% allowed and welcomed; 0=no foreign ownership allowed).

X_{45}–Index of legal discrimination against foreign investors (12=foreigners treated equally as locals; 0-no foreign investment allowed).

X_{46}–Index of tariff protection (8=extensive protection; 2=little or no protection).

X_{47}–Confiscations and expropriations of foreign owned property in past five years? (1=yes; 0=no).

X_{48}–Laws requiring local assembly and/or local sourcing of components? (1=yes; 0=no).

X_{49}–Strong price control or antitrust program? (1=yes; 0=no).

6) *Physiographic Barriers*—"The obstacles to the development of efficient business operations created by the physical landscape or land forms of the country."
Indicators:
X_{50}—Road kilometers per 100 square kilometers.
X_{51}—Railroad kilometers per 100 square kilometers.
X_{52}—Temperate vs. non-temperate climate (1=temperate; 2=sub-tropical; 3=tropical).
X_{53}—Population per square kilometer.
X_{54}—Total land area.

7) *Geocultural Distance*—"Barriers created by geographical separation, cultural disparities between countries and problems of communication resulting from differences in social perspectives, attitudes and language."
Indicators:
X_{55}—Distance (by air) from Chicago (representing center of U.S. business) and capital city of country.
X_{56}—Landlocked or coastal boundaries? (1=coastal; 0=landlocked).
X_{57}—Germanic language? (1=Germanic; 0 otherwise).
X_{58}—Romance language? (1=Romance; 0 otherwise).
X_{59}—Judeo-Protestant culture predominant? (1=Judeo-Protestant; 0=Otherwise)

APPENDIX B

HIERARCHICAL GROUPING:
A NUMERICAL TAXONOMY TECHNIQUE

The central hypothesis asserts that countries lie along a "temperature continuum" and that a firm's market entry strategy for a particular country will be influenced by the country's position on the continuum. The objective of the hierarchical grouping program is to cluster similar countries together with the hope that these clusters would differ in "temperature" from "hot" to "cold."
The grouping problem of numerical taxonomy is essentially the following. Given a set of n objects (persons, species, countries, etc.), each measured on *several* variables, one may ask to what extent there exist natural groupings among the objects. Theoretically, an optimum grouping of the objects can be defined for each number of groups from 2 to n-1 which maximizes the average inter-group distance and minimizes the average intra-group distance. However, the computational burden for calculating the optimum grouping from a problem with only 20 objects is prohibitive even with the aid of a computer. Ward, however, proposed a compromise.[17]

1) To reduce the number of groups from n to n-1 in a manner that would minimize the loss and to repeat the process until the number of groups was systematically reduced from n to 1, if desired, and

2) To evaluate loss in terms of whatever functional relation best expressed an investigator's criterion for grouping.

Thus, Ward's heuristic rule of defining the previous groupings at each stage of the process as the basis for determining the next reduction makes possible a solution which is an approximation of the theoretically optimal solution.

The choice of a proximity measure as the criterion for grouping from the many available is not an easy one.[18] A popular measure is some form of Euclidean distance. Utilizing the squared Euclidean distance measure as the proximity criteria with the Ward algorithm allows one to compare each country in the sample according to its "profile" across m variables with every other country's "profile". Hence, we can group the countries into their naturally proximate cluster (in n space) according to some loss function.

Thus, given x_{ik}, where k is the subscript representing the m variables measured for each of the countries (i=1,...,n), the Euclidean squared distance between country i and country j measured across m variables can be expressed as

$$\Delta^2 = \sum_{i=1}^{m} (x_{ik} - x_{jk})^2$$

The resulting n by n matrix, Δ_{ij}^2 , is then used to determine which two countries (defined as groups) are most alike vis-a-vis their profiles on the m variables. These two countries (groups) are then combined and the matrix.

Δ_{ij}^2 , is then adjusted. The now (n-1) by (n-1) matrix can be re-analyzed to determine which two groups of countries should be combined. The process can be continued in stepwise fashion so that within-cluster variation is minimally increased at each stage until all countries are in a single group.

The sequence through grouping stages of the error-sum-of-squares (within cluster variation) is used to determine the number of clusters that is optimal in a variance (information-loss) sense. Examination of the error-sum-of-squares series (as a function of the number of clusters) reveals the number of clusters at which the slope of the series becomes intolerable in an information-loss sense.[19]

FOOTNOTES

1. Isaiah A. Litvak and Peter M. Banting, "A Conceptual Framework for International Business Arrangements," *Marketing and the New Science of Planning*, ed. Robert L. King (Chicago: American Marketing Association, 1968 Fall Conference Proceedings), pp. 460-467.
2. William A. Lazer, *Marketing Management: A Systems Viewpoint* (New York: John Wiley and Company, 1971), pp. 611-614.
3. Gordon E. Miracle and Gerald S. Albaum, *International Marketing Management* (Homewood, Illinois: Richard D. Irwin, 1971), pp. 397-400, 403-404.
4. Robert A. Bartels, *Marketing Theory and Metatheory* (Homewood, Illinois: Richard D. Irwin, 1970), Chapter 18, pp. 154-295.
5. A.A. Sherbini, "Classifying and Comparing Countries," in *Comparative Analysis for International Management*, Marketing Science Institute (Boston: Allyn and Bacon, Inc., 1967), Pt. II, pp. 55-145.
6. Richard N. Farmer and Barry M. Richman, *Comparative Management and Economic Progress* (Homewood, Illinois: Richard D. Irwin, 1965).
7. Robert Stobaugh, "How to Analyze Foreign Investment Climates," *Harvard Business Review* (September-October, 1969), pp. 100-108.
8. W.W. Rostow, *The Stages of Economic Growth* (Cambridge, England: Cambridge University Press, 1960).
9. George Wadinambiaratchi, "Channels of Distribution in Developing Countries," *The Business Quarterly*, 30 (Winter 1965), pp. 74-82.
10. Susan P. Souglass, "Patterns and Parallels of Marketing Structures in Several Countries," *M.S.U. Business Topics*, (Spring 1971), pp. 38-48.
11. Reed Moyer, "The Structure of Markets in Developing Economies," *M.S.U. Business Topics*, 12 (Autumn, 1964), pp. 43-60.
12. Sherbini, op. cit.
13. For example, *Economic Trends* for each country published annually by the U.S. Department of Commerce and *Background Notes* for each country published yearly by the U.S. Department of State.
14. For example, The U.N. *Monthly Bulletin of Statistics* and the U.N. *Statistical Yearbook*.
15. Specifically, The IMF *Financial Statistics*.
16. Specifically, the *Indicators of Market Size for 130 Countries* (Published in late 1970 and early 1971).
17. Joe H. Ward, Jr., "Hierarchical Grouping to Optimize an Objective," *Journal of American Statistical Association*, 59, (March 1963), pp. 236-244.
18. Paul E. Green and V.R. Ras, "Note on Proximity Measures and Cluster Analysis," *Journal of Marketing Research*, 6 (August 1969), pp. 359-364.
19. Donald J. Veldman, *FORTRAN Programming for the Behavioral Sciences* (New York: Holt, Rinehart, and Winston, 1967), Chapter 12.

Marketing Factors in Manufactured Exports from Developing Countries

Jose R. de la Torre, Jr.
Georgia State University

It has been amply demonstrated that if the aspirations of the less developed countries of the world are to be fulfilled, relatively high priority must be given to the development of manufactured exports. The disadvantages of dependency upon primary products for export earnings, the limitations of reliance on import substitution as the main vehicle for industrialization, and, more generally, the constraints which insufficient foreign exchange earnings impose on promoting viable economic growth are most frequently cited as evidence of this need.

The factors which affect the feasibility of viable export industries in developing countries are numerous and varied. They range from the economic to the behavioral and will differ from country to country. However, some of these factors are common to many developing countries and the problems they pose justify efforts to search for common solutions.

This article examines the experience of three countries in exporting manufactured goods. Central to the paper is the proposition that the marketing characteristics of a product are a major determinant of its export potential for developing countries, particularly as these characteristics affect how, by whom, to what extent, and under what conditions successful export efforts are undertaken. What follows is an analysis of the relationships which appear to exist between a product's marketing characteristics—the independent variable—and various indices of export performance.

*Reprinted from "Marketing Factors in Manufactured Exports from Developing Countries," in Louis T. Wells, Jr., (ed.), *The Product Life Cycle and International Trade*, Boston, Mass.: Graduate School of Business Administration, Harvard University, 1972 by special permission.

Classical and neoclassical economic theory supports the argument that developing nations enjoy a comparative advantage in goods whose manufacture makes extensive utilization of labor. Presumably, labor is an abundant and a relatively cheap resource in the less developed countries. If no factor reversals occur and production functions remain constant throughout the world, the larger the input of the cheaper resource (labor) in the manufacturing process of a given good, the greater the potential for a country that exhibits such factor proportions to specialize in that good's production and export.[1]

The relative factor-abundance theorem can also be brought to bear on the technological inputs to the manufacuring process. Less developed countries are generally poorly endowed with a research and development capability. Consequently, the theory would indicate that, barring any factor movement, those industries with low technological requirements will be better suited for export purposes.

More recently a new body of theory has emerged in the literature which attempts to explain trade patterns in manufactured goods on the basis of stages in a product's life—the product life cycle theory. The product life cycle (PLC) model states that as new products or processes are introduced, the consuming country is likely to be the producing country because of the close relationship between innovation and demand, the producer's concern with flexibility in changing his inputs and outputs, the low price elastisity of demand for the output of individual firms, and the desirability for swift and effective communications between producer and customers, suppliers, and even competitors at this stage. The model further indicates that as the product matures it becomes increasingly standardized; the number of producers increases since entry into the market is facilitated by the increasing availability of technology; mass production utilizing standard processes becomes the rule, lowering production costs; demand increases while becoming more price-elastic; prices tend to decrease as competition stiffens and a buyer's market develops; and profit margins are substantially reduced. In addition, product differentiation may gradually appear as producers strive to maintain their shares of the market. At this stage, if economies of scale are being fully utilized, the principal difference between production costs at any two locations is likely to be a result of differences in factor costs.

During the product's introductory stage, demand in other countries has been created and satisfied through exports from the first producing country. But a point is reached when transport and tariff costs offer an incentive to begin production in one or more of these other markets. When the possibility of lower labor costs is also considered, the aggregate cost incentive may more than offset the negative effects of producing at lower volumes. The original producer may then consider entering one or more of these second countries by investing in production facilities, especially if he is to maintain his share of the market in the face of the threat of local competition. If the cost savings are sufficient, the trade flows may even reverse themselves, with the original producing country now being an importer from the lower cost location.

A seemingly logical extension of the PLC model would suggest that mature products possess a series of characteristics which make them more suitable for export from developing countries—notably a lower requirement for technological inputs and/or higher degree of technological stability, an increase in the lower skilled labor content, and a higher degree of price consciousness on the part of the consumer at this later stage. However, one aspect of the product remains of critical importance to developing countries: the changes in marketing requirements which occur as products advance through different stages in their life.

As a product reaches maturity producers are faced with increasing competition. Let us assume, for the time being, that consumers are also likely to become more aware of their ability to substitute one manufacturer's product for that of another and will tend to search for the most economic one. Of course, if all producers accepted such uniformly rational behavior on the part of the consumer as given, a situation would exist where prices are determined by lowest cost. The producer's strategy would then be limited to an attempt to find a least-cost location for production. A likely production location for these mature products would be developing countries with low technological capabilities but large supplies of low-cost unskilled and semiskilled labor.

Certain textile products offer good examples of developments of this kind. Standardized textile products, such as yarn, thread, and raw cotton cloth, are produced cheaply in low-wage countries. Advanced nations have had to turn to high tariffs and import quotas in order to save certain elements of their national textile industries from competitive gains made by less developed country producers.

But manufacturers of mature products are well aware of the diverse behavioral patterns of most consumers, whether they be individual or industrial buyers. They realize that by appealing to a particular need in the buyer's emotional or intellectual make-up—through advertising, personalized promotion, slight design changes, service assurances, and a host of other methods—they are able to exert some influence over the consumer's buying decision. This is particularly true for those products exhibiting performance characteristics which are not readily perceived and are difficult to evaluate. The manufacturer thus attempts to create a loyal following among his prospective customers in order to extract a premium sufficient to cover his added promotional expenditures, attain a certain advantage over his competition, and gain an added profit. The case of common aspirins provides an example of a product where a few manufacturers have achieved a commanding lead over the cheaper unbranded item. This lead was obtained through extensive advertising, the establishment of brand images, the maintenance of better production quality control, and small, but consumer-significant, product improvements, such as buffering additives.

The basic PLC model does not deal explicitly with the effect that a product differentiation strategy could have on export potential. The analysis above indicates that the possibilities of such a strategy would imply that similarly mature products would exhibit substantial differences from a marketing viewpoint. How these differences affect export performance and potential from developing countries is the central question to be resolved.

Marketing Factors and Export Behavior

The research showed that a product's marketing characteristics affect not only its potential for export development, but the nature of the original export decision, the market to which it was originally exported, the various markets which have been reached at a later point in time, the channels through which it is exported and the degrees of control which are exercised over them, and, critically, the types of companies which are responsible for the export activity. In order to illustrate these relationships between marketing characteristics and export behavior, it is necessary to define what is meant by differences in marketing characteristics and to identify suitable measures of these differences.

Product Differentiation and Marketing Entry Barrier[2]

Firms engaged in manufacturing mature products may utilize different competitive strategies in the market place. The dominance of any one marketing strategy, or of particular elements within that strategy, will have an effect on the relative difficulty faced by prospective competitors. A newcomer wishing to enter the market, whether that newcomer be another domestic producer or an exporter from another country, must be prepared to overcome a "marketing entry barrier."

In order for a new firm (an exporter in a developing country, for example) to enter a market for a particular product where the existing firms are competing at a given level of product differentiation, the newcomer may have to accept a lower price than is commanded by the established firms. Or, on the other hand, it may have to incur extremely high marketing costs per unit of sales volume. Finally, the firm may have to contend with both forms of disadvantages. Moreover, the duration of the added disadvantages, and not only their absolute value, is also critically important.

For analytical purposes, all relatively labor-intensive, mature products which may be considered *a priori* as having export potential for developing countries may be divided into two broad categories: (1) those which are sold or traded in conditions basically determined by price considerations, e.g., gray cloth, and (2) those where product differentiation plays a significant role in the market place, e.g., standard mechanical typewriters.

The boundary areas encompassing both groups are described by Bain as follows. Products for which well-established and widely based markets generally exist constitute the undifferentiated category. Barriers to entry were classified by Bain as "negligible" when a new entrant suffered a product differentiation advantage which was between 0 and 5% of price and which lasted no longer than two years.[3] Many products in this category are considered industrial goods. Examples given by Bain are copper, rayon, cement, flour, most textiles, fountain pens, steel products, women's shoes, and men's lower priced shoes.

Differentiated products are further subdivided into two groups: (a) products with "moderate" entry barriers, where the extent of the disadvantages is estimated by Bain at 5% to 10% of price for two to five years; and (b) products with "great" entry barriers, upwards of 10% for more than five years in most cases.[4]

If should be noted that the disadvantage faced by the potential exporter when entering the market for any such products does not consist simply of a price differential that would be easily overcome. Instead, the percentage figure attached to each entry barrier level is merely intended to reflect, in quantitative terms, the total effect of factors such as brand loyalty, captive distribution channels, and advertising expenditures.

Bain's examples of products with moderate entry barriers include canned fruits and vegetables, men's higher priced shoes, metal containers, rubber tires, petroleum derivatives, and soap; those with great entry barriers include typewriters, cigarettes, liquor and automobiles.[5]

Bain's classification of products into these three categories constitutes the independent variable employed in the study. This measure was correlated with various export parameters to determine whether a product's export behavior is related to its marketing characteristics.

The Effect of Marketing Characteristics on Exports

Products with a relatively higher marketing entry barrier require a more difficult or more costly marketing effort on the part of those attempting to initiate the export process than do products with a lower barrier. The exporting firm and its executives need to possess better knowledge of the market, of the competitive situation, and of the requirements for successful entry. Heavy demands are placed on their ability to plan, implement, and control marketing functions. Close contacts with market sources, capable of providing rapid feedback and information on market conditions, are essential.

Export Performance. The skills, knowledge, and contacts necessary to overcome the marketing barriers to entry are not abundant resources in developing countries. As a result, developing countries will experience relatively better performance in exporting those manufactured goods characterized by low marketing requirements.[6]

Export performance is, of course, a vague term. It has volume, growth, and profitability connotations. Ideally, data on profit margins, contributions, and the like would serve for comparing performance from a profitability viewpoint. But these data would be difficult if not impossible to obtain. Instead, it is necessary to rely on measures of export intensity and growth to determine the relative competitive ability of industries in sectors with differing marketing characteristics.

Any attempt to ascribe export performance to a single factor is bound to be unsuccessful. Obviously, many variables enter into determining why certain products perform better in export markets than others. What is intended here is to show that marketing characteristics are one of the important determinants of export behavior.

A useful measure of a country's *propensity to export* manufactured goods is the percentage of its total industrial production destined for export markets. Furthermore, a relative measure of any given sector's export performance can be obtained from *its* propensity factor normalized by the propensity factor for the total national manufacturing activity. Thus, an *export propensity index*[7] is obtained for comparative purposes.

A sample of 32 industrial sectors and subsectors in Colombia was analyzed for these purposes. The following formula was applied for computing the various export propensity indices.

$$e_i = \frac{X_i / P_i}{\sum\limits_{i=1}^{n} X_i / \sum\limits_{i=1}^{n} P_i}$$

where: e = export propensity index
X = export volume in dollars
P = total production volume in dollars
i = a grouping signifying either an industrial sector (32 in our sample), or a group of sectors classified under a particular heading (e.g., according to marketing entry barrier)
n = total number of manufacturing sectors in the country

Using as the normalizing factor (the denominator in the formula above) the export propensity of all Colombian industrial sectors, the resulting index for the 32 sectors in the sample was 2.10. This reflects the fact that while the sample sectors accounted for 60% of all manufactured exports from Colombia, they represented only 28.5% of total industrial production.[8]

After each of the 32 sectors was allocated to the appropriate group among Bain's three marketing entry barrier categories, the aggregate export propensity index for each group was computed. For group I sectors, whose products were principally classified as having "negligible" marketing entry barriers, the index was 2.75. The aggregate indices for group II and III sectors ("moderate" and "great" entry barriers) were 1.12 and 1.45 respectively. If these two groups are combined, their index was 1.22. Table I summarizes these results.

All three indices were greater than unity since the 32 sample sectors included a large number of industries actively exporting, as evidenced by the aggregate sample index of 2.10. But it is evident that those firms manufacturing products classified in group I were more involved in export markets than the others. The comparison between groups II and III yields contradictory results. However, given the small size of the group III sample, and the fact that only those group III sectors which were exporting were included in the sample, the results may be biased in their favor. Also, foreign firms constituted a large proportion of this group, and their incidence, as discussed below, has a marked effect on exports.

Table 1. Export Propensity of 32 Manufacturing Sectors in Colombia

	Produc- tion(a) (A)	Exports(b) (B)	Percent- age (B/A)	Export pro- pensity index
All manufacturing sectors	$2,404.70	$58.14	2.42 %	1.00
All sample sectors	686.22	34.81	5.07	2.10
Group I sectors	392.03	26.12	6.65	2.75
Group II sectors	203.34	5.48	2.71	1.12
Group III sectors	90.85	3.21	3.52	1.45

(a) Data relate to 1964, in millions of dollars.
(b) Data relate to 1968, in millions of dollars.

Sources: Departamento Administrativo Nacional de Estadisticas (DANE), ANUARIO GENERAL DE ESTADISTICAS—1964, Bogota, 1967.
    Banco de la Republica, Fondo de Promocion de Exportaciones, INFORMES NO. 7 Y 8,—1968, Bogota, February, 1969.

Data were also obtained from a small sample of individual firms in which extensive in-depth interviews were conducted. The sample included 69 companies—38 in Colombia, 16 in Nicaragua, and 15 in Mexico—randomly selected, in the first two cases, from national exporters' directories. The sample firms were classified according to Bain's typology as applied to their respective product lines. The firms were also classified as "domestic" when management control was in the hands of nationals of the country, usually implying that ownership was also primarily national. Alternatively, they were classified as "foreign" when management control was vested in a foreign partner, regardless of the percentage of foreign ownership.

The data obtained from this sample also provide some supporting evidence as to the effect marketing characteristics have on export performance. Two measures of performance, export growth and export sales as a percentage of total sales ("export intensity"), are shown in Table 2 (A&B) for the domestic firms in the sample, classified according to their marketing entry barrier classification. The evidence indicates a slight tendency for firms in the lower marketing entry barrier group to perform better than the others.

Export Initiative. Marketing characteristics also influence the nature of the original export decision. The higher the marketing entry barrier, the greater the need for or dependence on external agents or forces to initiate the firm along the export path, since products with higher marketing requirements demand a higher level of marketing skill on the part of the exporter. If the local manufacturer or potential exporter is unable or unwilling for any of a variety of reasons to supply such skills, the initiative will have to come from outside the firm.

The data provided by the sample indicate that the initiative for the first export attempt was located within the firm more frequently among group I companies (30%) than among group II (25%) or group III (none) firms. Thus, the higher the marketing entry barrier, the more domestic firms rely on elements external to their organization to initiate export activities.

Export Destination. In addition to their effect on the nature of the original export decision, marketing characteristics are a determinant of the market to which the first export effort is directed. Market knowledge is an important element in determining the ability of a firm to introduce its products in a new environment successfully. And this factor becomes more critical the higher the marketing entry barrier of the product.

Let us assume that market knowledge can be represented by market proximity. It seems likely that people in any given country would tend to have a better knowledge about the markets, the people, and the opportunities available in neighboring countries than they would have about more distant nations. Familiarity would tend to diminish some of the fears and uncertainties generally associated with foreign markets. Therefore, a positive correlation should exist between market proximity, as measured in Table 3, and the firm's first export market.[9] The sample data show that initial export activity was more frequently aimed at bordering markets (65%) than at either intermediate (13%) or distant (28%) markets.[10] Of course, other factors such as lower transport costs and preferential duties through common market arrangements may account for part of this behavior. But insofar as the three sample countries are concerned, these cost and tariff advantages also exist with respect to certain market areas other than those classified as bordering.

Table 2-D presents the same data for domestic firms classified according to the marketing entry barrier. The evidence from the table is clear. Domestic firms show a tendency to limit themselves to neighboring markets in their first export attempts in direct proportion to the height of the marketing entry barrier.

A similar tendency exists when the extent of the firm's present commitment to various export markets is considered. The data in Table 2-E lend further support to the proposition than when complex product marketing requirements are superimposed on a

Table 2. Marketing Factors and Export Behavior of Domestic Firms

Measures of Export Behavior	% of Firms in Each Marketing Behavior Category that Fell into the Particular Export Behavior Class(a)			
	I. Negligible	II. Moderate	III. Great	All firms
A. Export intensity(b)				
0%-10%	74 %	77 %	100 % (2)	76%
10%-25%	7	15	–	10
25%-50%	11	8	–	10
More than 50%	7	–	–	5
	100 %	100 %	100 %	100%
No. of firms responding	27	13	2	42
B. Export growth rate(c)				
Negative	14 %	44 %	50 % (1)	28%
0%-20%	36	11	–	24
More than 20%	50	44	50 % (1)	48
	100 %	100 %	100 %	100%
No. of firms responding	14	9	2	25
C. Source of initiative for export decision				
Within the company	30 %	25 %	– %	28%
External	70	75	100 % (1)	72
— foreign buyer	42%	38%	100%	40%
— government	17	8	–	15
— licensor	4	17	–	8
— other	7	12	–	9
	100 %	100 %	100 %	100%
No. of firms responding	24	12	1	37
D. Proximity factor in first export market(d)				
Bordering	54 %	75 %	100 % (2)	61%
Intermediate	15	17	–	15
Distant	42	17	–	31
	100 %	100 %	100 %	100%
No. of firms responding	26	12	2	40

E. Export markets(d)

Regional(e)	57 %	57 %	100 % (2)	59%
Rest of L.A.	61	43	50 (1)	55
United States	39	50	–	41
Other developed	18	7	–	14
Other	4	–	–	2
	100 %	100 %	100 %	100%
No. of firms responding	28	14	2	44

(differentiating between domestic and export markets)

F. Level of control over marketing channels(f)

	Dom. mkt.	Exp. mkt.	Dom. mkt.	Exp. mkt.	Dom. mkt.	Exp. mkt.	Dom. mkt.	Exp. mkt.
High	35 %	8 %	27 %	8 %	100 % (2)	– %	30 %	8%
Intermediate	22	28	27	25	–	50 (1)	22	28
Low	43	64	47	67	–	50 (1)	48	64
	100 %	100 %	100 %	100 %	100 %	100 %	100 %	100%
No. of firms responding	23	25	15	12	2	2	40	39

G. Change in level of control over channels(f) (toward a:)

	Dom. mkt.	Exp. mkt.	Dom. mkt.	Exp. mkt.	Dom. mkt.	Exp. mkt.
Higher level	30 %	15 %	– %	24%
No change	22	46		23
Lower level	48	38	100 % (2)	47
	100 %	100 %	100 %	100%
No. of firms responding	23	13	2	38

(a) The absolute numbers are provided in parentheses for the group III firms, since there were only a small number.
(b) Export sales a percentage of total sales.
(c) Average yearly compounded rate of growth for 1965-1968 period.
(d) Percentages may add to more than 100 because of multiple answers.
(e) Represents exports to those countries formally associated with the exporting country through regional integration agreements.
(f) See text for explanation of control levels.

SOURCE: Interviews.

situation involving a sophisticated market, the manufacturer in the developing country faces increasing difficulties in export marketing. The percentage of domestic firms in group I involved in nonregional markets is slightly higher than the percentage of group II domestic firms similarly involved. If "other Latin American countries" are excluded, the performance of domestic firms falls drastically from group I to group III.

Distribution Channels. In order to export products that are characterized by the use of high differentiation strategies, producing firms have to rely to a great extent on their marketing skills and on their knowledge about market conditions in importing countries. The more sophisticated a product's marketing requirements, the greater the need that exists for the firm to have access to an organization closely related to the market to which exports are intended. As a result, exporting firms will have either to enter the market themselves or to hand over their export business to other firms that are capable of performing the necessary marketing functions.

Domestic firms in developing countries are generally unable or unwilling to take upon themselves the increased marketing requirements of differentiated products when dealing with export markets. These same firms, which for a variety of reasons exercise different degrees of control over their domestic marketing activities, will, when moving into export markets, surrender a significant portion of this control to foreign-based firms. Regardless of the level of control exerted over domestic channels of distribution, exporting firm exercise a lower level of control over distribution and other marketing functions as they move into export markets; and this decrease in control is more dramatic the higher the marketing entry barrier that characterizes the product.

From the standpoint of the domestic market, many factors influence the decision of whether to attempt to control distribution channels. Certainly, the firm's committment to a differentiation strategy is one such factor. All other things being equal, many firms engaged in differentiating their products may attempt, as an element of that strategy, to control their domestic channels of distribution. But other factors will also influence the domestic behavior of firms. The lack of sophistication among domestic marketing institutions may force a manufacturer to take a more active role in the distribution of its products. Also, differences in industrial structure and consumer habits exist between advanced and developing countries. As a result, some products principally considered intermediate in advanced countries may be purchased to a larger extent by end users in a developing country, e.g., textiles.

228

Table 3. Classification of Market Areas According to Market Knowledge and Proximity

Market Knowledge	Market Proximity	Market Areas		
		Colombia	Nicaragua	Mexico
Higher	Bordering	Panama Ecuador Venezuela	Honduras Costa Rica El Salvador	U.S. Guatemala
Medium	Intermediate	Caribbean Central America	Guatemala Panama Caribbean	Rest of C.A.
Lower	Distant	All others	All others	All others

The choice of distribution channels may also be affected by differences in demographic structure and income distribution. Nonetheless, control of distribution channels constitutes an integral part of the firm's marketing strategy and, most importantly, it represents a critical variable in the export process.

The principal tendency observable among the domestic operations of the sample firms was the dominant use of controlled channels. The data show that company stores, exclusive distributors, and direct sales to consumers were the most commonly used channels in all groups.[11] In addition, there were few differences among the three marketing entry barrier groups. Control over export channels of distribution, however, shows more variance according to product characteristics and type of user.[12]

The interviews showed that domestic companies forfeit control of their marketing functions to some extent when they move into export markets. But the yielding of control was especially associated with those product lines that are more market-oriented. The decrease in control of export channels by the exporting firms, observed to be most prevalent for the highly differentiated products, was associated with a greater role of organizations outside of the producing country. These organizations usually consisted of independent foreign buyers and foreign affiliates of domestic firms.

This behavior is consistent with our previous findings. Domestic enterprises could easily cope with the problems of exporting relatively undifferentiated products, where price was the major purchase consideration. But their ability to compete successfully in foreign markets with highly differentiated manufactured goods was considerably lower. Evidence of the differences is presented in

Tables 2-F and 2-G. The tables show the absolute levels and the frequency of differences in the level of control exerted by domestic firms over marketing channels when comparing domestic with export markets.

The Role of Foreign Enterprise[13]

The evidence presented thus far corroborates the claim that marketing characteristics are an important factor in the development of exports of manufactures from developing countries. The existence of this relationship between marketing characteristics and export behavior tends to support the hypothesis that market knowledge and marketing skills are necessary conditions for exploiting certain export markets. The lower performance of domestic firms in exporting highly differentiated products, as opposed to exporting products with negligible marketing entry barriers, has been atributed to the fact that the requisite marketing skills and knowledge seem to be relatively scarce resources in developing countries. However, it is the individual firm, and not the country, which is ultimately responsible for the performance of its products in export markets, and the degree of marketing skill available varies from firm to firm.

Foreign firms have greater access to market information, distribution channels, and marketing skills for export markets than do domestic firms. They generally form part of a multinational group or network of affiliates which has greater experience and broader exposure to worldwide competitive markets than do domestic enterprises. Since foreign firms are able to apply these skills to exports from developing countries, they export relatively more than domestic firms. Moreover, the higher the marketing entry barrier and the more distant or sophisticated the market of destination, the more pronounced is the advantage of the foreign firms.

Comprehensive data recently released by the U.S. Department of Commerce and reported in a study performed for The Council for Latin American[14] provide evidence of the impact foreign firms have had in developing manufactured exports from the region. Manufacturing affiliates of U.S. multinational firms accounted for almost two-thirds of the increase in exports of manufactured goods from Latin America in the decade between 1957 and 1966. Their exports increased 704.8%, from $83 million to $668 million, during this period, while domestic firms increased exports by only 51.0%.

A better idea of the role played by foreign firms in the export process can be obtained from Table 4. In 1966 total value added by all U.S. affiliates in Latin America accounted for only 6.76% of the region's gross domestic product, while their share of total exports was 35.0%. A similar relationship exists for manufactured goods alone. U.S. affiliates accounted for 9.5% of Latin America's gross manufacturing value added, while their share of manufactured exports was 41.4%.

Further analysis of the data in Table 4 provides interesting insights into the activites of foreign subsidiaries in the region. A measurement of the relative importance of foreign firms in the export sector is provided in the comparison of the percentage participation of foreign firms in export markets with their participation in the economy as a whole.[15] This index (RXI) can be obtained at various levels of aggregation ranging from an overall index for all economic activities to that for any given industrial sector. The RXI index for all economic activities throughout Latin America (5.19) is somewhat larger than the index for the manufacturing sector (4.35). The key to this discrepancy must lie in the nature of foreign investment in Latin America.

Most foreign investment in nonmanufacturing activities is in either extractive industries or agricultural production.[16] These investments are often made with the intention of serving export markets, whether they be home or third country markets. This fact is demonstrated by the data in Table 4. Exports by non-manufacturing U.S. subsidiaries represent 63.5% of their total sales. On the other hand, exports by manufacturing subsidiaries represent only 10.2% of their total sales. This difference reflects the fact that, in contrast with firms active in extractive industries and agricultural production, most foreign firms engaged in manufacturing activities in the countries under consideration entered originally for import-substitution.

Foreign manufacturing affiliates show a higher propensity to export than domestic firms, as evidenced by the RXI index. Since most foreign manufacturing subsidiaries in these countries were originally established primarily to substitute local production for imports, a situation that also applies to most domestic manufacturing firms, there is little reason to suspect that major differences exist between domestic and foreign firms regarding their principal committment to domestic markets. The advantage of foreign firms in exporting manufactured goods seems to be the result of a greater ability in international markets, and not the result of differences in the original motivation for the investment.

But the higher the marketing entry barrier characterizing the product, the higher is the foreign firm's advantage in export

Table 4. U.S. Affiliates Participation in Latin America's Economic Activity, 1966 (millions of dollars)

	All Economic Activities	Manufacturing (a)	Nonmanufacturing
Gross domestic production	$94,203	$22,346	
Gross industrial value added			
Sales by U.S. affiliates: total	$12,567	$6,548	$6,019
Less: Current expenditures for material, supplies and services	6,202	4,424	1,778
Value added: wages and salaries, taxes, depreciation, and income	$6,365	$2,124	$4,241
Percentage participation (A)	6.76 %	9.50 %	—
Total exports	$12,830	$1,613	$11,217
Total exports by U.S. affiliates	4,497	688	3,829
Percentage participation (B)	35.05 %	41.41 %	34.14 %
Relative export importance index (B/A)	5.19	4.35	—

(a) Includes only ISIC (International Standard Industrial Classification) classifications 2 and 3.

Sources: United Nations, STATISTICAL YEARBOOK, 1968, and IMF, INTERNATIONAL FINANCIAL STATISTICS. U.S. Department of Commerce preliminary data. Taken from Herbert K. May, THE EFFECTS OF UNITED STATES AND OTHER FOREIGN INVESTMENT IN LATIN AMERICA, a report for The Council for Latin America, New York, January 1970.

markets. Data obtained from 32 industrial sectors and subsectors in Colombia (Table 5) provide strong corroboration of this view. While foreign firms are responsible for 49.8% of the exports of those industrial sectors included in group I, they account for 80.6% and 90.2%, respectively, of all exports among groups II and III.

However, such a comparison is not sufficient since it does not take into account the relative participation of foreign firms in the total production of each group of sectors. Column C in Table 5 gives a measure of the relative export importance index for all three groups. Group II sectors show a substantially higher index than group I. While foreign firms among group II sectors accounted for a slightly larger percentage of national production than group I foreign firms (31.2% vs. 30.0%) their contribution in the export sector was substantially higher (80.6% vs. 49.8%). The RXI index for foreign firms in group III sectors, however, is lower than for the other two groups. This result appears to contradict the hypothesis that foreign firms perform increasingly better in the export field the higher the marketing entry barrier.

Various explanations can be offered for this apparent contradiction. Perhaps most fundamental is the fact that the percentage of foreign participation in any sector of economic activity is higher at the higher marketing entry barrier levels. When the original premises of the analytical model are considered, this should not come as a surprise. The conditions which require that superior market knowledge and marketing skills be brought to bear on the problems of exporting goods which are highly differentiated are also present in producing and marketing within the domestic market. As a result, those industrial sectors which are characterized by high marketing inputs will, in all likelihood, have a tendency toward domination by firms which possess considerable marketing experience.[17] Given this high foreign incidence among group III sectors (the denominator in the formula above), the RXI index will necessarily result in a low value.

But the model also indicates other reasons, not totally unrelated, for such dominance. Both the product life cycle mode and the requirements of a product differentiation strategy imply that a certain degree of industrial concentration or oligopolistic behavior characterizes industries with high marketing barrier to entry. While no attempt is made here to determine causality or prove any such proposition, others have shown that some correlation exists between oligopolistic conditions and high product differentiation.[18] Accordingly, oligopolistic industries will have a tendency to extend their activities to world markets on the same basis that they compete in their domestic markets.[19]

Table 5. Foreign Subsidiaries' Participation in Export Activity: Colombia—32 Industrial Sectors, 1968

Industrial Sectors Classified by Their Products' Marketing Entry Barrier	Production		Exports			Relative Export Importance Index (C=B/A)
	Total Volume (millions)	% Partici- pation by Foreign Firms (A)	Total Volume (thousands)	Volume by Foreign Firms (thousands)	% Partici- pation by Foreign Firms (B)	
I Negligible	$392.0	30.0%	$26,126	$13,004	49.8%	1.66
II. Moderate	203.3	31.2	5,481	4,422	80.6	2.58
III Great	90.8	7i.3	3,207	2.893	90.2	1.27
Total	$686.2	35.8%	$34,813	$20,319	58.4%	1.63

(a)Production data relate to 1964, the most recent year for which detailed component data were available.
(b)Export data relate to 1968.

Sources: Banco de la Republica, Fondo de Promocion do Exportaciones, INFORMES NO. 7 Y 8,—1968, Bogota, Febrero 1969.
.ıes by Oficina de Planeacion Nacional, Office of the Presidency of the Republic.
Departamento Administrativo Nacional de Estadisticas, ANUARIO GENERAL DE ESTADISTICAS—1964, Bogota, 1967.

The in-depth interviews provided further evidence of the differences in export behavior between domestic (Table 2) and foreign (Table 6) firms. The observed differences were consistent with the findings reported above and lend further support to the argument that foreign firms will have relatively higher indices of export performance with respect to domestic firms the higher the marketing entry barrier.

Conclusions

The central theme of this paper has been that marketing factors play a critical role in establishing the conditions that determine suitability of a manufactured product for export from developing countries. Products characterized by a high degree of product differentiation require the application of more skills and knowledge in the export effort than is the case for those with low or no product differentiation. Since these marketing skills and knowledge are relatively scarce resources in developing countries, these countries perform less well in exporting highly differentiated products than in exporting products with negligible marketing entry barriers.

Individual firms are ultimately responsible for the performance of their products in export markets, and varying degrees of marketing skills are likely to prevail from firm to firm. As a result, export performance is bound to differ among different types of firms. Foreign firms, because of their membership in a multinational group or network of affiliates, have greater access to the required market information, distribution channels, and marketing skills for export markets than do domestic firms. Therefore, foreign subsidiaries export relatively more than domestic enterprises. And this higher level of export performance is more pronounced the higher the marketing entry barrier of the product and the more distant or sophisticated the market of destination.

Marketing factors clearly are not the only determinants of export performance. Neoclassical and product life cycle models provide other variables, such as product maturity and labor content, that significantly affect export performance. Data from the interviews also revealed the multivariate and complex nature of the problem.[20] What this research shows is that marketing factors need to be considered as important variables when policies are being evaluated to promote exports of manufactures from developing countries. Specifically, the findings of this research have direct relevance to two broad policy areas: strategy formulation in the multinational firm and economic planning in developing countries.

Table 6. Marketing Factors and Export Behavior of Foreign Subsidiaries

Measures of Export Behavior	% of Firms in Each Marketing Behavior Category that Fell into the Particular Export Behavior Class(a)			
	I. Negligible	II. Moderate	III. Great	All Firms
A. Export intensity(b)				
0%-19%	25%	40%	50% (1)	35%
10%-25%	38	20	-	25
25%-50%	12	-	-	5
More than 50%	25	40	50 (1)	35
	100%	100%	100%	100%
No. of firms responding	8	10	2	20
B. Export growth(c)				
Negative	20%	29%	- %	23%
0%-20%	20	14	100 (1)	23
More than 20%	60	57	-	54
	100%	100%	100%	100%
No. of firms responding	5	7	1	13
C. Source of initiative for export decision				
Within subsidiary	50%	35%	- %	36
Parent company	33	35	33 (1)	34
External	17	30	67 (2)	30
--foreign buyer	12%	20%	- %	14%
--government	6	10	67 (2)	16
	100%	100%	100%	100%
No. of firms responding	9	10	3	22
D. Proximity factors in first export market				
Bordering	89%	60%	- %	64%
Intermediate	-	10	-	5
Distant	11	30	100 (3)	32
	100%	100%	100%	100%
		10	3	22

E. LEGAL BARRIER MEASURES

X_{42}	Percent of countries belonging to strong common market[H]	75%	24%	18%	29%
X_{43}	Capital repatriation policy	Liberal restrictions	Liberal restrictions	Restriction based on time	Liberal restrictions
X_{44}	Policy towards foreign ownership[A]	100% allowed and welcomed	100% allowed not welcomed	Some local ownership required	100% allowed, not welcomed
X_{45}	Legal discrimination against foreigners[A]	Equal treatment with locals	Minor restrictions	Some controls on foreigners	Minor restrictions
X_{46}	Tariff protection for local industry[A]	Little or no protection	Some infant industry protection	Considerable infant industry protection	Some infant industry protection
X_{47}	Percent of countries expropriating foreign property (1966-71)[A]	0%	15%	30%	20%
X_{48}	Percent of countries where local content and/or assembly required[A]	6%	38%	10%	19%
X_{49}	Percent of countries with strong price control or anti-trust programs[A]	56%	50%	58%	55%

F. PHYSIOGRAPHIC BARRIER MEASURES

X_{50}	Road density (road kilometer/sq. kilometer)[G]	81	25	5	24

Recently U.S. firms, faced with increasing competition at home from producers in other countries, have begun to search for lower cost locations for their manufacturing activities.[21] These so-called "off-shore" manufacturing facilities have been established in developing countries and could be the first real indication of the full closing of the product life cycle theory. Taiwan, Hong Kong, South Korea, and other Asian locations have thus far experienced most of this activity, but Latin American countries increasingly are being considered as possible "off-shore" locations.[22]

This research indicates that multinational firms are in a very favorable position to exploit some of the opportunities that are being created for exports from developing countries. Where marketing considerations play an important role, multinational firms have an advantage over domestic enterprises. They have the necessary marketing experience, market knowledge, and established marketing channels in their home markets, as well as in other countries in which they operate, to market manufactures made by any of their subsidiaries on a world-wide basis. Where political, economic, and trade limitations are not prohibitive, these firms can follow a production location policy that reflects the maturity and marketing characteristics of their products. In the most advanced nations they would produce, for internal consumption and for export, high technology new products. As products mature and production costs become critical for .survival, locations in developing countries would become ideally suited for world-wide production. For those products where differentiation is important a major role remains for the multinational enterprise.

The poorer performance of domestic firms in the export sector is not suggested as a sign of business incompetence on the part of the local entrepreneur. His behavior is entirely rational given the environmental and information constraints under which he is operating. A government, intent on promoting manufactured exports, may be able to assist local firms in overcoming these constraints by extending the argument for infant industry protection to the export sector. By providing subsidies to export activity (commensurate with import-substitution-industrialization benefits) and by designing programs to increase the amount of information available about export opportunities, the returns and risks of export business may be brought in line with those prevailing in the domestic sector.

If developing countries are to succeed in promoting exports of manufactures, they must be conscious of the role that foreign investment can play in the process. The evidence suggests that multinational firms can provide an important contribution to developing countries, not to mention their own profits, through their capacity for export development. Because of its access to export markets, a foreign subsidiary may continue to justify whatever cost it represents to the host country long after the benefits from the initial contributions of capital and technology have passed.

FOOTNOTES

1. The theory is commonly known for the name of two of its early proponents: E.F. Heckscher, "The Effects of Foreign Trade on the Distribution of Income," American Economic Association, *Readings in the Theory of International Trade*, Blakiston Co., Philadelphia, 1949; and B. Ohlin, *Interregional and International Trade*, Harvard Economic Studies, Vol. XXXIX, Cambridge, Massachusetts, 1933.
2. Many of the issues raised in this section are derived from a study of twenty manufacturing industries in the U.S. reported by Joe S. Bain in *Barriers to New Competition*, Harvard University Press, Cambridge, 1956.
3. Ibid., p. 127.
4. Ibid., pp. 128-129.
5. Many firms in this last category which export to the U.S. market have capitalized on the foreign origin of their products in order to differentiate them from domestic competition. This is the case with typewriters (Olivetti), liquor (Scotch whiskey), and automobiles (Volkswagen).
6. Of course, the manufacturer could rely entirely on an importer to perform all the necessary marketing functions. In that case, the hypothesis could be modified to include exports of high marketing barrier products provided that foreign assistance takes place in the process. This alternative is explored in more detail in the next section.
7. The rationale for an index, while unnecessary in this example, derives from the possibility of comparing export propensity factors for similar sectors in various countries.
8. If agricultural industries are excluded from total industrial production the 32 sample sectors account for 39.5% of the balance.
9. Similar propositions linking the export markets to proximity have been repeatedly tested in the literature. See, for example, Hans Linnemann, *An Econometric Study of International Trade Flows*, Amsterdam, North Holland, 1966; and William H. Gruber and Raymond Vernon, "The R&D Factor in a World Trade Matrix," in Vernon (ed.) *The Technology Factor in International Trade*, National Bureau of Economic Research, New York: Columbia University Press, 1970.
10. Percentages add to more than 100 because of multiple answers in four cases.
11. The differentiation made between high-control and low-control channels was based on whether the manufacturer has any direct control over the final sale to the consumer. Obviously, company stores were highly

controlled channels where the manufacturer could directly influence the nature of the seller-buyer relationship. Private branding or the use of a manufacturer's agent would rank at the low-control end of the spectrum.

12. The criteria for determining control levels among export channels were similar to those utilized for domestic channels. Operating retail outlets or sales organizations in export markets were considered as the highest control level, the use of an export firm as the lowest level, and an active local distributor as the middle range.

13. A broader coverage of the issues raised in this section of the strategic considerations affecting the export decision in the multinational firm can be found in Jose R. de la Torre, "Exports of Manufactured goods from Developing Countries: Marketing factors and the Role of Foreign Enterprise," unpublished DBA thesis, Harvard Business School, 1970.

14. Herbert K. May, *The Effects of United States and Other Foreign Investment in Latin America*, a report for The Council for Latin America, New York, January 1970.

15. An index (RXI) was obtained according to the formula,

$$RXI = \frac{\%\text{ foreign participation in the export sector}}{\%\text{ foreign participation in total economic activity}}$$

16. For 1966, Department of Commerce data presented in the May report reveal that 61.4% of the outstanding investment at year end in Latin America by nonmanufacturing affiliates belongs to petroleum, mining, and smelting affiliates. These same firms accounted for 77.8% of estimated total sales of nonmanufacturing affiliates.

17. A good example is provided by the detergent industry. In most countries this industry is in the hands of the three international giants, Colgate-Palmolive, Procter & Gamble, and Unilever. This situation prevails in spite of the fact that the technology for detergent production is readily available and capital requirements are low ($200,000 will suffice for an optimal size plant). A Harvard Business School case series on the detergent industry in Central America (BP-817, 820, 822, and 825) illustrates the difficulties encountered by one domestic producer when faced with competition from the much more experienced international firms.

18. Verification of the existence of correlation between product differentiation and industry concentration is presented in William S. Comanor and Thomas S. Wilson, "Advertising Market Structure and Performance," *The Review of Economics and Statistics,* Vol. XLIX, November 1967.

In addition, most of Blain's examples of industries with high product differentiation appear also to be oligopolistic in nature, e.g., automobile, farm machinery, office equipment, cigarettes, etc. However, not all oligopolistic industries practice product differentiation, e.g., steel, copper, paper, synthetic fibers, etc.

19. Preliminary results obtained by Frederick T. Knickerbocker in connection with his dissertation research, "Oligopolistic Reaction and Multinational Enterprise," unpublished manuscript, Harvard Business School, April 1970, tend to support this view.

20. For example, capacity utilization, defined as the percentage of the firm's full-time productive capacity in use at the time, showed a strong negative

correlation with export performance. These data suggested that a firm would not turn to export markets as long as its home market (usually more lucrative due to import-substitution benefits and protection) could absorb the firm's output.

In addition, Hal B. Lary, *Imports of Manufactures from Less Developed Countries*, National Bureau of Economic Research, Columbia University Press, 1968, shows the validity of the labor content argument.

21. The new trend in this direction, while quite meager at this point, is becoming noticeable. See Nathaniel H. Leff, "Investment in the LDCs: The Next Wave," *Columbia Journal of World Business*, November-December 1969.

22. Over 75% of all foreign subsidiaries in the sample were engaged in exports to their parent company market.

Multinational Marketing Control*

Warren J. Keegan
Columbia University

The multinational enterprise with its operating subsidiaries spread over the globe presents formidable problems to managers responsible for marketing control. Each national market is different from every other market. Distance and differences in language, custom, and practices creates communications problems. The size of operations and number of country subsidiaries often results in the creation of an intermediate headquarters, the so-called regional or area headquarters, which adds an organizational level to the control system. This article reviews the multinational marketing control practices of large U.S. multinational companies, compares these practices with domestic marketing control, and identifies the major factors which influence the design of a multinational control system.

Control and Planning

Every plan is conceived in the context of uncertainty about most of the major internal and external forces which influence marketing success. For example, market growth, customer response to a new product, competitive moves, government regulations, and costs are just a few of the uncertain factors about which assumptions must be made in order to formulate a plan. Therefore, when a company

*Reprinted from the *Journal of Informational Business Studies* Vol. 3, No. 2, Fall 1972 by special permission.

plans, it must also make provisions to monitor the results of plan implementation programs, and make adjustments to plans where necessary. Planning necessitates control.

Control occurs in the context of an organization trying to achieve established goals or objectives.

In the managerial literature, control is defined as the process of assuring "that the results of operations conform as closely as possible to established goals." (Newman, Summer, and Warren, 1967), or as "the process by which managers assure that resources are obtained and used effectively and efficiently in the accomplishment of the organization's objectives (Anthony, 1965). The marketing literature parallels these definitions. A recent marketing textbook, for example, defines control as "the process of taking steps to bring the actual and desired ·results closer together." (Kotler, 1967).

Each of these definitions posits a process of activities and steps that are directed toward insuring that planned organizational programs do in fact achieve desired objectives. Control activities are directed towards programs initiated by the planning process. In the ongoing enterprise, however, the data measures and evaluations generated by the control process are also a major input into the planning process. Thus the two activities, planning and control, are intertwined and interdependent. The planning process can be divided into two related phases: (1) strategic planning is selection of opportunities defined in terms of products and markets, and the commitment of resources, both manpower and financial, to achieve these objectives; (2) operational planning is the process in which strategic product market objectives and resource commitments to these objectives are translated into specific projects and programs. The relationship between strategic planning, operational planning and control is illustrated in Figure 1.

In domestic operations, marketing control has become increasingly important and challenging. Because the enterprise is getting larger, the distance between top managers and marketing operations is growing. Top managers must take steps to insure that they receive information which measures their success. The growing size of enterprise makes this an increasingly challenging task. Secondly, the environment is changing rapidly making it essential that control systems generate data that will be timely enough to allow management to take steps to correct problems.

In multinational operations, marketing control presents additional challenges. The rate of environmental change in a multinational company is a dimension of each of the national markets in which the company operates, and the multiplicity of environments, each changing at a different rate and each exhibiting unique characteristics adds to the complexity of this dimension. In addition, the multiplicity of multinational environments challenges the multinational marketing control system with much greater environmental heterogeneity and therefore greater complexity in its control. Finally, multinational marketing brings special communications problems associated with the great distances between markets and headquarters, and differences among managers in languages, customs and practices.

Budgeting

The basic formal marketing control technique used by each of the companies I studied was budgeting. This confirms findings of other multinational operations (Mauriel, 1969: McIness, 1971). This practice is an extension to international marketing of a basic technique used by companies in domestic marketing. It involves expressing planned sales and profit objectives and marketing programs in unit and money terms in a budget. The budget spells out the objectives and the expenditures which will be made to achieve objectives. Control consists of measuring actual sales and expenditures. If there is no variance or a favorable variance between actual and budget, no action is usually taken. If variance is unfavorable, this is a red flag that attracts the attention of line and staff executives at regional and international headquarters and they will investigate and attempt to determine the cause of the unfavorable variance and what might be done to improve performance.

The principal measures of marketing performance in the companies studied are sales, share of market, and expenditure on various marketing programs, such as advertising and selling. In larger markets data is reported for subsidiaries and, where significant sales are involved, on a product-by-product basis. Share of market data is often produced by the same independent market audit method used in the U.S. In smaller markets, share of market data is often not available because the market is not large enough to justify the development of an independent commercial marketing audit service. Local managers are asked to estimate their share of market position. In these markets, it is possible for a country manager to hide a deteriorating market position or share of market behind absolute gains in sales and earnings. I did not detect a general analytic solution to this potential problem. In evaluating performance actual performance is compared to budgeted performance as described in the previous section. Thus, the key question is how is the budget established? According to one researcher, most

Figure 1: Relationship of Strategic Planning and Control

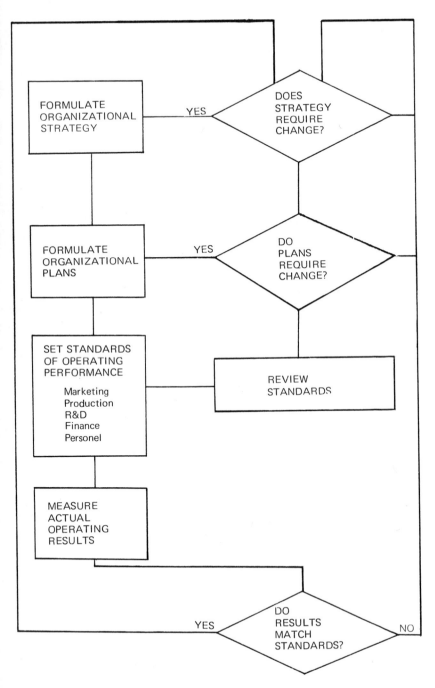

companies in both domestic and international operations place heavy reliance upon two standards—last year's actual performance and some kind of industry average of historical norm (Mauriel, 1969).

In the companies studied, corporate management developed their own estimate concerning the kind of growth that would be desirable and attainable. In one company, this estimate was based upon exhaustive studies of national and industrial growth patterns carried out by the corporate economics department. In two of the companies, this estimate was more of a best guess by top management based largely upon historical growth patterns.

In one of the companies studied, there is enough business volume in a number of products to justify staff product specialists at corporate headquarters who follow the performance of products worldwide, i.e., both domestic and foreign. They have staff responsibility for their product from its introduction to its withdrawal from the company's product line. Normally, a new product is first introduced in the largest and most sophisticated markets. It is subsequently introduced in smaller and less-developed markets. As a result, the company's products are typically at different stages of the product life cycle in different markets. A major responsibility of staff specialists is to insure that lessons learned in more advanced markets are applied to the management of their products in smaller less developed markets. Wherever possible, they try to avoid making the same mistake twice, and they try to capitalize on what they have learned to apply it wherever applicable. They also insure that useful ideas from markets at similar stages of development are fully applied. In a second respondent company with a much smaller international headquarters, a marketing vice president at international division headquarters focuses upon key products in key markets. Key products are those which are important to the company's sales, profit objectives, and competitive position. They are frequently new products which require close attention in their introductory stage in a market. If any budget variances develop with a key product, the marketing vice president intervenes directly to learn about the nature of the problem and to assist local management in dealing with the problem.

In theory, if conditions in the subsidiary's business environment change during a planning period, the budget should be changed to reflect changes in underlying assumptions. In practice, budgets of the companies studied are not changed during an operating period. Companies recognize that refusing to change a budget can result in unfavorable variances that are not controllable by the subsidiary management but the view of most companies is that it is better to allow these unfavorable variances to occur than it is to allow budget revision during an implementation period. When a company does not permit budget revision, it is emphasizing the importance of careful planning and of achieving plan objectives. If uncontrollable and unforeseeable changes do occur, these can be noted as mitigating reasons or even as a full explanation for failure to achieve budget.

In preparing a budget or plan, the following factors are of major importance:

a) Market Potential—How large is the potential market for the product being planned? In every domestic market, management must address this question in formulating a product plan. An international company which introduces a product in more than one national market must answer this question for each market. In most cases, new products are introduced on a serial rather than simultaneous basis, and can be defined as new international products as opposed to new products per se. A new international product is analogous to a product which has been introduced in a test market. The major opportunity of a test market is the chance to project the experience in the test market to a national market while its major pitfall is that the characteristics of the test market will be unlike those of the national market, thus invalidating the projections made. The same opportunities and pitfalls apply in an amplified way to new international products.

b) Competition—A marketing plan or budget must be prepared in light of the competitive level in the market. The more entrenched the competition, the more difficult it is to achieve market share and the more likely is a competitive reaction to any move which promises significant success in the target market. This is particularly important as a variable in international market planning since many companies are moving from strong positions of competitive strength in their base markets to foreign markets where they have a minor position and must compete against entrenched companies. Domestic market standards and expectations of marketing performance are based on experience in markets where the company has a major position. This is simply not relevant to a market where the company is in a minor position trying to break into the market.

c) Impact of Substitute Products—One of the sources of competition for a product in a market of course is the frequent existence of substitute products. As a product is moved into markets at different stages of development, improbable substitute products often emerge. For example, in Colombia, a major source of competition for manufactured boxes and other packaging products are woven bags and wood boxes made in the handicraft sector of the economy. Marketing officials of multinational companies in the packaging industry report that the garage operator producing a handmade product is very difficult competition—given costs of materials and labor—in Colombia.

d) Process—The manner in which estimates of performance are communicated to subsidiary management seems to be of more importance than the way in which they are derived. In one of the companies studied, an "indicative" planning method is used. Headquarters estimates of regional potential are disaggregated and communicated to subsidiary management as "guidance." The subsidiaries are in no way bound by guidance, and are expected to produce their own plan. This method produces excellent results because it combines a global perspective and estimate with specific country marketing plans that are developed from the objective to the program by the country management teams themselves. Headquarters in providing "guidance" does not need to understand a market in depth. For example, it is not necessary that the headquarters of a manufacturer of electrical products know how to sell electric motors to a Frenchman. What headquareters can do is gather data on the expected expansion in generating capacity in France and use experience tables drawn from world studies that indicate what each megawatt of additional generating capacity will mean in terms of the growth in demand in France for electrical motors. This estimate of total market potential together with information on the competitiveness of the French subsidiary can be the basis for a "guidance" in terms of expected sales and earnings in France. The guidance may not be accepted by the French subsidiary. If the indicative planning method is used properly, the subsidiary would educate the headquarters if its guidance was unrealistic. If headquarters does a good job, it will select an attainable but ambitious target. If the subsidiary does not see how it can achieve the headquarters goal, discussion and headquarters involvement in the planning process will either lead to a plan which will achieve the guidance objective or it will result in a revision of the guidance by headquarters.

In another company studied, headquarters communicated sales and earnings expectations rather than guidance to subsidiaries. In the case of one product, these expectations were high, and were based upon successful experience in the U.S. market. Subsidiaries accepted the expectations and budget programs to achieve them even though they did not have plans developed to achieve the budgeted goals. The problem in this company was the fear subsidiaries had of challenging headquarters expectations. They felt it was better to fail to achieve headquarters expectations than to challenge them. The result in this case was an almost worldwide failure to achieve product plan objectives. If subsidiaries had taken headquarters initial goals for the product in question as guidance rather than as expectations, the result would have been a dialogue at the plan formulation stage between headquarters and subsidiaries which would have led either to the development of realistic plans to achieve headquarters guidance or alternatively, the downward revision of the product's sales and earnings goals.

Variables Influencing Control

The major variables influencing the design of a control system in the companies studied are as follows:

1) Domestic practices and the value of standardization—One of the major assets of any organization are its operational and success-ful managerial practices. If a company has successfully developed and used a control system in its home or domestic operation, this system is clearly a candidate for export because (1) it works, (2) there are people who understand it and (3) these people can in most instances be persuaded to transfer their "know-how" to a foreign subsidiary. Each of the companies studied used a standard reporting format for both domestic and foreign operations. The amount of detail and frequency of reports was a function of the size of the foreign subsidiary. One of the respondents had designated seven key and another fourteen major markets in its 100-country multi-national country group. The amount and frequency of reporting was greatest for key markets, less for major markets, and still less for ordinary markets.

The advantage of a standard system (adapted for market size differences) is that it allows comparisons to be made on a global basis, and it facilitates the easy transfer of people and ideas since all managers in the organization are working with the same system.

2) Communications system—A major development affecting control in international marketing operations is the communica-tions infrastructure. A century ago, international marketers had at their disposal various means of surface travel—horse, carriage, and train, as well as various means of over-the-water travel, sailboats and, by that time, steamships. Electronic communications were limited to the telegraph. The businessman who wanted to control international operations had two choices. He could either travel himself by land, sea, or a combination of both, or he could transmit written messages either by post or telegraph. Given the speed, cost,

and comfort of the communications methods available a century ago, it is understandable that businesses operated on a highly decentralized basis. Operating policies consisted of sending out handpicked men with instructions as to their general areas of operations. These men were versed in the ways of the company and therefore it was assumed that company policies and procedures would be implemented by them. They had total responsibility for carrying out the company's operations in their area. At the end of the designated operating period, which was typically a year, the results of operations would be reported. In those days, subsidiaries were controlled according to Saint Augustine's rule for Christian conduct, "'Love God and do what you like!' The implication of this is... that if you love God, then you will only ever want to do things which are acceptable to Him." (Jay, 1967). Men who were sent out to manage company affairs were expected to be so versed in the company approach to business that they would automatically approach things in the approved manner.

Today, the communications infrastructure is vastly enlarged. In addition to surface and sea travel, the airplane is now the major form of long-distance travel in the world. Face-to-face and written communications possibilities are vastly extended by highspeed jet aircraft. Indeed, the jet aircraft is a major revolution in communications infrastructure because it makes it possible for businessmen involved in international operations to maintain regular face-to-face contact with operating units all over the world. Given the importance of face-to-face communications in the information-acquisition process (Keegan, 1967), it seems reasonable to conclude that the jet aircraft has been a major tool in making it possible to manage a global enterprise. Indeed, the very limited success of small businesses in international operations can be attributed in large measure to the reluctance or inability of the small-businessman to invest money and time in travel to get on-the-spot familiarity with customers, agents, and distributors in foreign markets. The larger enterprise spends enormous sums to maintain contact with managers in foreign markets who are in direct contact with employees, customers, agents, and distributors in their market.

In addition to the face-to-face communications possibilities, electronic communication is also vastly expanded. The teletype and telephone make it possible for rapid, direct, highspeed voice and data communication to take place on a global basis. Increasingly, the communications systems of large corporations (and large companies account for an estimated 80% of U.S. foreign direct investment) are being developed so that communication of voice and data are available on a worldwide basis. In many large companies internal communications systems allow direct dialing of any company telephone in several companies are extensive enough to enable them to manage inventories on a worldwide basis.

3) Distance—All other things being equal, the greater the distance between headquarters and an operating unit, the more automonous the operating unit will be from headquarters. This follows from physical and psychological differences. The physical distance imposes a time-and-cost barrier on communications. To travel to a distant point takes more time and therefore is more costly. To communicate by telephone, Telex, or other telecommunications method is also more costly and time-consuming as distances increase. Therefore, there is less communication, particularly face-to-face communication, and therefore a greater delegation of responsibility as distances increase in international operations. Nevertheless, one of the major changes in the environment of international business is the development of communications technology which has reduced the time-and-cost barriers of distance by increasing the speed and raising the quality of Telex, voice, T.V., and air-travel methods of communications.

4) The product—A major factor affecting the type of marketing control system developed for international operations is the product being controlled. A product which is technically sophisticated can be more extensively controlled because the way in which the product is used is highly similar around the world. This similarity creates opportunities to apply standards of measurement and evaluation on an international basis. Computers, for example, are products which are applied today in the same manner in technologies wherever they are located in the world. The process-control computer for the petro-chemical industry is the same type of application in Rotterdam as it is in Baton Rouge, Louisiana. The technology for the application of microcircuitry is a universal technology which is applied in the same way in Japan as it is in the United States.

Environmental sensitivity is the relevant product dimension influencing the extent to which "international" control can be exercised. If a product is similar or identical in the way it is applied and used around the world, that is, if it is environmentally insensitive, then international standards and measures of performance can be tested. A computer and many industrial products fit this category. If a product is sensitive to environmental differences, then it is more difficult to apply international standards. Drugs and packaged food are two examples of environmentally sensitive products which normally require adaptation to meet the preferences of different cultures and systems of medical practice.

5) Environmental differences—All other things being equal, the greater the environmental difference, the greater will be the delegation of responsibility and the more limited the control of the operating unit. For example, most United States companies with operations in Canada apply their most extensive control of international operations to Canadian operations. Indeed, many U.S. companies with extensive international operations, some of which are semi-autonomous with regard to U.S. headquarters, operate in Canada as if Canada were a part of the U.S. market. A major reason for this is because the Canadian market is perceived as highly similar to the U.S. market. Therefore the standards of measurement and evaluation applicable to the U.S. market are seen as being applicable and relevant to Canadian operations.

The development which has most accelerated the extension of control of international operations in regions which are highly different from the home-country area is the regional headquarters. This headquarters copes with environmental difference by focusing upon a group of countries which is formed to maximize within-group similarities and between-group differences.

6) Environmental stability—The greater the degree of instability in a country, the less the relevance of external or planned standards and measures of performance. When a country moves into a period of sweeping political change, previous plans and policy are simply delegating total on-the-spot discretion to local management to do whatever they thought best when a country went into a period of revolutionary change or turmoil. Their experience had been that local management usually achieved much more than headquarters expected.

7) Subsidiary performance—A major variable influencing the kind of control exercised over international operations is the performance of subsidiary units. A subsidiary which is achieving budget is normally left alone. When a subsidiary fails to achieve budget, the variance between budgeted and actual performance is a red flag which triggers intervention by headquarters. In addition, managers of successful profit centers have more leverage in holding off headquarters involvement in their operations. Subsidiaries reporting unfavorable variances find that headquarters is anxious to determine the cause of the problem, to correct the problem, and to maintain closer surveillance of operations to insure that further difficulties do not emerge and develop undetected. Therefore, all other things being equal, a well-managed, successful subsidiary operation will be more loosely controlled than an operation in difficulty. At the same time, the sophisticated multinational company headquarters wants to know how everybody, including

successful units, is doing. It needs data on performance to help establish standards and comparisons to use in evaluating the performance of subsidiaries.

8) Size of international operations—A researcher who studied nine U.S. based international companies found a strong relationship beween the firms share of total sales derived from international operations and the frequency of higher level participation in local decision making. (Algmer, 1970). The larger the international operation in terms of sales and earnings, the greater is its ability to support its own headquarters staff specialists. The greater the specialization of a headquarters staff, the more extensive and penetrating is its control, or measurement and evaluation of performance. A large multinational company will have three or four levels of staff expertise focusing upon the same functional aspect of its operations in large-country markets: country, region, and international and/or corporate. This fully developed staff organization is shown in Figure 2. A smaller company simply cannot afford to create a highly specialized multi-level staff and will have, as a consequence, less control over its operations. A large multinational company assigns control responsibility to both line and staff executives. Normally, marketing control falls into the province of product group specialists and general managers. In one of the companies studied, however, the headquarters staff is so large that a special marketing control department has been created. This department collects and analyzes key marketing data on 20 major markets and more abbreviated data on 80 smaller markets. In smaller country markets, small staff organizations require a considerable simplification and abbreviation of the control process since the expertise and time required to generate and evaluate data are simply not available. One of the challenges to the large multinational company is the development of methods and procedures for the control of small subsidiaries which do not place an excessive data collection and reporting burden on the small subsidiary.

Each of the companies studied has established regional headquarters groups which are responsible for the operations of all country subsidiaries in their region. They feel that their regional marketing staff are able to carefully and closely track the performance of operating units in their region because of their familiarity with the basic characteristics of their region. In structuring regions, each company tries to maximize the within-group similarities and between-group differences. The major variables determining regional boundaries are distance, or physical proximity, language, and stage of market development.

Lack of knowledge of basic market conditions is one of the major obstacles to the development of an effective control relationship between headquarters and subsidiary in international marketing. When headquarters commits itself to measure and evaluate subsidiary performance, this decision commits headquarters to participation in subsidiary planning. Measurement and evaluation of current performance is intimately involved in the cycle of planning for operations and programs in future time periods. In order to become effectively involved in this planning control cycle, headquarters must understand the basic characteristics and conditions of the subsidiary market. If there is inadequate understanding, headquraters may adversely or inadequately influence the design of the country marketing plan for future periods and may misunderstand the significance of operating results in current periods. The result of headquarters misunderstanding can involve major failures (when headquarters succeeds in imposing an inappropriate plan on subsidiaries, or in influencing subsidiaries to accept inappropriate objectives). Perhaps even more dangerously, headquarters misunderstanding can result in a failure of subsidiaries to achieve their full potential in a market. If headquarters does not understand the basic characteristics of a market, it will not be able to pinpoint subsidiary underperformance. This problem in international operations is a counterpart of the problem of managing product divisions in different technologies in a divisionalized company. In order to manage a product division, corporate management must understand the basic technology of the products being managed. If they do not understand the technology, divisional management has a virtually free rein in developing its plan and explaining its performance. For example the disasterous unchecked expenditure of over $250 million by the Convair Division of General Dynamics was attributed to the lack of knowledge of the airframe industry by corporate management.

Each of the companies studied are expanding their headquarters understanding of *headquarters* foreign markets in one important way: They are actively involved in the subsidiary planning process. This involvement insures that headquarters executives learn about each subsidiary's and each region's market conditions. One of the companies studied is assigning approximately equal numbers of domestic and foreign executives to its international headquarters in a deliberate effort to obtain an effective mix of U.S. product and system know-how and international environmental knowledge in the headquarters group.

ORGANIZATION CHART SHOWING THE RELATIONSHIP OF STAFF AND LINE
PROFIT CENTERS IN A LARGE MULTINATIONAL COMPANY

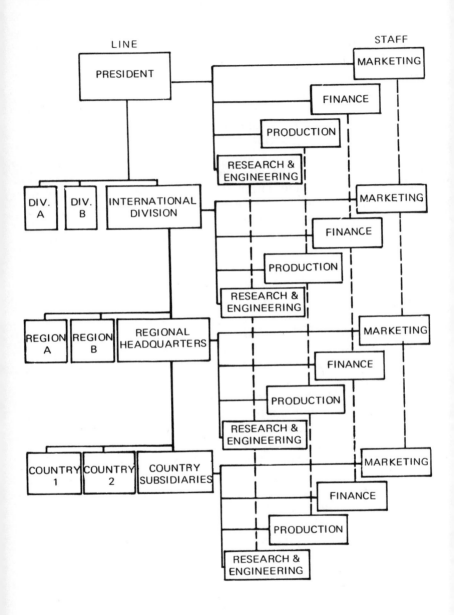

Consistency

Strangely enough, one of the major problems in control systems in international marketing is an attempt by headquarters management to apply a consistent standardized approach to control worldwide. Although it was Emerson who remarked, "Foolish consistency is the hobgoblin of little minds," this view is not widely held. There is a general feeling on the part of managers that a well-run company should evidence the consistent application of tools and practices. This is understandable. If there is a best way to control international operations, should it not be applied on a universal scale?

There is no single best control system. There is a best way to control international operations only if these operations are homogeneous. Most companies which have extended themselves to more than one continent find their operations to be highly differentiated in terms of the kinds of markets which they have, the length of experience of subsidiaries, and a host of other factors. The skilled and sophisticated international enterprise recognizes this, and develops control relationships with regions and subsidiaries based on the major variables influencing controls discussed earlier in this chapter. If a subsidiary is large and has a highly developed headquarters staff of its own, if the management of this subsidiary is highly competent, if the market in which this subsidiary operates is highly differentiated from other markets and requires a differentiated response in order to achieve company sales and profit objectives, a differentiated control system is needed. If a company's technology, its size and position in markets, its commuications relationships, its markets, and the competence of local management are uniform around the world, then a uniform control system is appropriate. Since these conditions are rarely if ever achieved, it follows that all control systems should be differentiated to respond to relevant differences. The secret of success is in developing systems which are responsible but which are not unique for each market.

Conclusion

The basic tool for controlling multinational marketing operations is the budget. The use of budgeting is an extension of a domestic practice suggesting once again that marketing tools and concepts are universal. Since the budget is derived from the marketing plan, it is clear that effective multinational marketing control begins with effective involvement in the national marketing planning process in each country market. To be effectively involved in the national marketing planning process the multinational marketer must understand the relevant dimensions of each national market environment. This understanding at headquarters is expanded by the assignment of managers with international experience to headquarters jobs in marketing, and by working with subsidiaries in the development of local marketing plans. As understanding expands, the multinational marketer is better able to play a role in establishing realistic and challenging goals and helping subsidiaries overcome obstacles to their objectives. The major advantage of the multinational marketer in this task is his ability to draw upon worldwide operating experience.

REFERENCES

1. Ackoff, Russell L., *A Concept of Corporate Planning,* Wiley Interscience, New York, 1970.
2. Alsegg Robert J., *Control Relationships Between American Corporations and Their European Subsidiaries,* AMA Research Study 107, American Management Association, 1971.
3. Ahroni, Yair, *The Foreign Investment Decision Process,* Division of Research, Graduate School of Business Administration, Harvard University, Boston, 1966.
4. Anthony, Robert N., *Planning and Control Systems: A Framework for Analysis,* Division of Research, Graduate School of Business Administration, Harvard University, Boston, 1965.
5. Aquilar, Francis J., Robert J. Howell and Richard F. Vancil, "Formal Planning Systems - 1970," (a collection of research reports presented at the Third Annual Workshop for Planning Executives), Harvard Business School, Boston, Mass.
6. Aylmer, R.J., "Who Makes Marketing Decisions in the Multinational Firm?" *Journal of Marketing*, Vol. 34, October, 1970, pp. 25-30.
7. Beer, Stafford, *Cybernetics and Management* (Science Editors, John Wiley & Sons, Inc., New York, 1964).
8. Behrman, Jack N., *Some Patterns in the Rise of the Multinational Enterprise*, Research Paper 18, Graduate School of Business Administration, University of North Carolina at Chapel Hill, March, 1969.
9. Bonini, Charles P., Robert J. Jaedicke, and Harvey M. Wagner, *Management Controls: New Directions in Basic Research*, McGraw-Hill, 1964.
10. Bonini, Charles P., "Simulation of Organizational Behavior" in *Management Controls*, Bonini, Jaedicke, and Wagner.
11. Brooke, Michael Z., H. Lee Remmerss, *The Strategy of the Multinational Enterprise*, American Elsevier Publishing Co., Inc., New York, 1970.

12. Bower, Joseph L., *Managing the Resource Allocation Process: A Study of Corporate Planning and Investment*, Division of Research, Graduate School of Business Administration, Harvard University, Boston, 1970.

13. Butler, W. Jack, and Dearden, John, "Managing a Worldwide Business," *Harvard Business Review*, May-June, 1965, pp. 93-1022.

14. Cain, William W., "International Planning: Mission Impossible?" *Columbia Journal of World Business*, July-August, 1970.

15. The Conference Board, "Measuring the Profitability of Foreign Operations," *Managing International Business*, No. 7, New York, 1970.

16. Deming, Robert H., *Characteristics of an Effective Management Control System in an Industrial Organization*, Division of Research, Graduate School of Business Administration, Harvard University, Boston, 1968.

17. Greiner, L.E., Leitch, D. Paul, Barnes, Louis D., "Putting Judgment Back Into Decision," *Harvard Business Review*, March-April, 1970, pp. 59-67.

18. Hawkins, David F., "Controlling Foreign Operations," *Financial Executive*, February, 1965, pp. 25-32, p. 56.

19. Horngren, Charles T., *Accounting for Management Control: An Introduction*, Prentice-Hall, 1965.

20. Jay, Anthony, *Management and Machiavelli*, Holt, Rinehart and Winston, New York, 1967.

21. Keegan, Warren J., "Multinational Marketing Management," Marketing Science Institute *Working Paper*, January 1970.

22. Keegan, Warren J., "Scanning the International Business Environment: A Study of the Information Acquisition Process," unpublished doctoral dissertation, Harvard Business School, June, 1967.

23. Keegan, Warren J., "Multinational Marketing Planning: Headquarters Role," *Columbia Journal of World Business*, Jan.-Feb. 1971.

24. Kotler, Philip, *Marketing Management: Analysis Planning and Control*, Prentice-Hall, Englewood Cliffs, N.J., 1967.

25. McIness, Jim, "Financial Control Systems for Multinational Operations: An Empirical Investigation," *Journal of International Business Studies*, Fall, 1971, pp. 11-28.

26. Mauriel, John J., "Evaluation and Control of Overseas Operations," *Management Accountant*, May 1969, pp. 35-39.

27. Miller, Ernest C., *Objectives and Standards of Performance in Marketing Management*, AMA Research Study 85, American Management Association, 1967.

28. Newman, W.H., Summer, Charles E., Warren, Kirby E., *The Process of Management*, Second Edition, Prentice-Hall, Inc., Englewood Cliffs, N.J., 1967.

29. Perlmutter, Howard V., "The Tortuous Evolution of the Multinational Corporation," *Columbia Journal of World Business*, January-February, 1969.

30. Rocour, Jean-Luc, "Management of European Subsidiaries in the U.S.," *Management International*, No. 1, 1966.

31. Ruttenberg, David, "Tailoring Controls to Types of Multinational Companies," unpublished paper, Carnegie-Mellon University, December 1968.

Perspectives International on World Companies

Judd Polk
U.S. Council of the
International Chamber of Commerce

We have heard a lot about the international corporation in recent years. Much has been written and some of the most thoughtful people in the universities and in the business world have addressed themselves to the implications of the international company. It is not surprising, though, that all of this work is bound to lag behind the impact of the rapid growth of international companies on the world economic scene. In fact the international company itself is a reflection rather than a source of a new phenomenon, namely the internationalization of production.

As we inform ourselves about this supposedly new phenomenon, we pursue its implications without reference to—in fact often inconsistently with—the really new phenomenon of which it is a part, namely the internationalization of production. The international company is old, as we have every reason to recall when standing on this ground once managed by such ancestors of our modern international company as the Hudson Bay Company. What is new and important is the degree of cohesion in international production. The scope of these operations inevitably implies an emergent world economy.

The question of the economic area whose resources are being allocated is crucial to the question of how best to allocate them. The emergence of national markets in contrast to their regional components is an event so recent that even the youngest of us here have witnessed it at least in part. For example, in the United States we are currently in a phase of national development in which national resources are being nationally allocated in such a way that the financial capabilities, the technology, the managerial skills and the energies of all regions of the country are contributing to the distinctive pace of development in the West and Southwest. Any significant use of resources in a country, whether under public or private sponsorship, be it dam or computer services, embraces and answers the question, what is the most effective national, not regional or local, use of the given funds or real resources? Yet as recently as a generation ago the nation was not the reference area for typical examinations of alternative prospective yields.

It is already the implicit suggestion, now worth putting explicitly, that our commitment to international operations in response to our communications, industrial, technological and, I think one must add, community capability requires us to assess international, not just national, competing opportunities if we are to reach a tenable resource commitment. This all came about as a matter of communications, and maybe of all forms of communication finance was the first to reflect the fact that the human family is one world and communicates with the speed of light. Once you are communicating, you are a community. International business expresses and consolidates a sense of international community. And the existence (in 1969) of some $375 billion in international investments, with an output profile of some $450 billion, illustrates the real force to date of the invitation, perhaps economic compulsion, to commit resources to production in an international rather than a national frame of reference.

Internationalization of World Output Through Investment

U.S. direct investment regularly accounts for most (three-fourths) of our long-term private investment, and half of our total investment in all forms, government and private, abroad. It grows with surprising regularity at about 10% a year overall, and it commands yields that run regularly at 10% or more worldwide. It gives rise to a sales volume that is on the average apparently about double this book value. In location, about a third of all this investment is in Canada, a third in Europe, and a third everywhere else. By industrial classification, about a third is in manufacturing, a third oil, and a third all other. A substantial amount—about 30%—is in the less developed countries, but a substantial portion of this is concentrated in oil and other extractive activities.

The counterflow of foreign investment here is regularly improving in a very encouraging way, but continues to run regularly less than U.S. investment abroad. Hence, the growing net investment (or creditor) position of the United States. This has more than quadrupled in the 19 years shown, indicating a derived growth rate of 8% or so a year; in dollar terms, it has grown by over $50 billion since 1950, with an inferred positive impact on current earnings of more than $5 billion a year—that is, our continuing investment abroad has added $5 billion to our overall earning ability. This is a figure of some importance in view of the continuing controversy over whether foreign investment is affordable in competition with other balance-of-payments priorities.

In maturities and risk, foreign investment here follows a pattern almost exactly the reverse of the U.S. position. About half (somewhat more actually) is in short-term low-yield low-risk. Of the other half, the bulk of it is in portfolio, and the growth of this investment has until recently been largely in terms of market-value appreciation. Direct investment—half of it British and Canadian—runs about 15% of the total and has grown about 7% a year.

U.S. figures permit the calculation of a separate European investment balance sheet— ours there, theirs here. Unlike the overall picture in which United States' net creditor position has grown, that is in which U.S. investment has regularly exceeded the flow of foreign investment here, Europe's total investment here has been in excess of ours there. As in the pattern indicated above, it is heavily dominated by (a) liquid holdings and (b) highly marketable portfolio.

A Sound Investment Structure: The Maturities Spectrum

The marked bias of foreign, and most importantly, European, investment toward liquidity is vividly apparent in this summary of investment figures covering foreign investment in the United States and U.S. investment abroad:

Asset Structure (billions of dollars)

	Liquid		Portfolio		Direct	
	Total	%	Total	%	Total	%
U.S. Investment Abroad	21.7	19	25.2	21	70.8	60
Foreign Investment in U.S.	49.8	55	29.2	32	11.8	13

As seen in the summary figures, U.S. private short term commitments now constitute 48% of total foreign investment here. For the United States' investment abroad, short-term assets are only 13% of the total.

The foreign, predominantly European, profile of maturities is dominated by their underlying acute liquidity preference. As absorbed in the U.S. monetary structure, the funds become committed to a credit spectrum normal to an up-to-date industrial structure. U.S. banks and other institutions (notably the financial market) intermediate this cash, that is commit it to production—in short, invest it. All this is as it should be. Without such intermediation, the funds would not participate in any earning process and would not warrant any payment of interest. For example, were they segregated and sterilized, they would amount to an interruption of the basic cycle of spending and production. This is close to the difficulty in Germany now, with neither inter-mediation nor sterilization suitably handled.

In the United States the growing short-term liabilities have a functional role in the context of rapidly growing international assets. These liabilities, which appear as mere deficit when viewed under the specialized focus of certain balance-of-payments accounting procedures, are seen as part of a normal banking function as soon as the accounting context is broadened to cover not just the balance of payments but the international structure of investment. Had the process been more simply one of Europeans depositing their own liquid funds in American banks with the banks subsequently investing in U.S. long-term assets, it would perhaps have been irresistible to Europeans to accept the intermediation process as the correct interpretation of events. But the fact that U.S. investors acquired foreign long-term assets in a simultaneous though usually not identical series of operations appears to have displayed (perversely) the weakness of the American banking position to foreign viewers. Actually, the American banking position has been greatly strengthened by the build-up of strong foreign *earning* assets. As seen in the tables, U.S. assets now total about $146 billion. To estimate the yield at 10% or $14.6 billion is, I think, conservative. Compared to 1950, United States has acquired net—that is, after subtracting foreign investment here—some $41 billion in foreign assets. The corresponding *increase* in U.S. investment earnings may be inferred to be over $4 billion a year. Against this fortification of foreign asset and earning position, U.S. short-term liabilities have grown *net*—that is, after subtracting U.S. short-term assets—by $22 billion, or about five times the increase in annual earning power of U.S. investments abroad. Five years would not seem to be a very long bridge of intermediation. Moreover, comparison to the domestic banking situation, although because of the less stable international situation it cannot be made one to one, would indicate that the 50% short-term asset to liability ratio is extremely high—a decided under-extension of supportable credit.

Implications for the World Economy

We do not have precise figures on the extent to which actual international investment trends have led to the establishment of an internationalized producing and market system in the world. But our indicators are quite good enough to demonstrate emphatically that American entrepreneurs are involved in production activities abroad that result in well over $200 billion a year in sales. In the same spirit of internationalizing our perspectives, we can note here that something like $100 billion—acutally a tenth of the production in geographic United States—is to be associated with foreigners' investment activities there. Both of these estimates of international activity are based on U.S. figures. Not covered are the investing and producing activities of other countries in foreign areas other than the United States. For these the available information is very sketchy. Nonetheless an order of magnitude can be inferred on the basis of general considerations such as achieved levels of GNP, trade and aggregate scraps of information on investment. I think $150 billion would be a minimal guess for this category of other (foreign) international production. Taken altogether we get an order of magnitude of $450 billion. This figure does not take into account the product of communist countries' producing operations abroad, a figure which though presumably very limited at present may well grow.

Governmental policy for international activities has fallen far behind the world that these activities have done so much to create.

By far the most important economic fact of this generation is the rapid rise of international production.

As a basic foundational fact, what we are wanting here is a figure for a gross world product (GWP). This lack is not fatal; we can make aggregate national product figures serve the purpose. But the lack illustrates the interesting point that when we need to be considering the consequences of operating an emergent world economy on the basis of national policy perspectives, we are driven to draw a picture of these activities from figures rooted in national rather than world perspective.

A world production figure can be approximated as follows in 1970:

Billions of dollars

U.S. GNP	$1,000
Rest of industrial "West"	1,000
Russia, Eastern Europe & China	650
Less developed countries	350
Total:	$3,000

Sources: These order-of-magnitude estimates have been elicited from information on national GNP or per capita production, as provided for different areas by U.S. Department of Commerce, The International Bank, the United Nations' YEARBOOK OF NATIONAL ACCOUNTS, O.E.C.D. National Accounts, and Joint Economic Committee's SOVIET ECONOMIC PERFORMANCE.

The figure of $450 billion, representing international production, when read against the aggregate GWP level of about $3,000 billion reveals that this internationalized component of aggregate world production amounts to a sixth of all activity. I think it may be accepted that at this level of relative importance, internationalized activities suggest not just a special area of overlap among national economies but rather the solid underpinning of an emergent world economy.

Beyond sheer size, the international sector of world production is a very dynamic one, growing steadily at an annual rate of close to 10%—a pace almost double the basic economic growth rates we are familiar with in the various national economies. The implication of these rates of growth is that world production continues to be internationalized at a fairly brisk pace. Projections of the rate suggest that within a generation a majority of production will have been internationalized. Moreover if the dynamism of the international sector can be maintained it will as it grows exert a more and more powerful influence on general growth rates, putting within reach fairly hopeful answers to both the capital and consumption requirements of the world's rapidly growing population.

In fact, the entire current output of the world appears to represent as a productive impulse only about half the strength that would be needed to bring world living standards generally to a subsistence standard statistically defined in the United States as "near poverty." If we use a round figure of $1,200 per capita as reflecting a near poverty level of living in larger units (seven numbers) we have a sort of crude standard of the quantity of modern productive impulse a man needs to hold his own in his hostile natural environment.

This $1,200 impulse we need to correct upwards by some 25 percent as a "GNP correction" to allow for maintenance of equipment and social infra-structure. We need also to make a correction to allow for some progress against pollution and for the realistic costing of resource-wastage. I am at a loss to quantify this properly and I gather that ecological analysis does not yield any ready quantification. Nevertheless I have gotten the impression that national accounts figures would be at least 50 percent higher if pollution and resource-wastage were covered at present. We can note that a relatively poor world—the world of say our near-poverty concept—is not as pollution-prone as the advanced industrial countries; accordingly allowance for pollution that would seem too slight in the case of the industrial countries may be somewhat more adequate as a world standard. As a first approximation, then, we reach a figure per capita of $1,200 basic near-poverty product, plus $300 social backstopping and equipment maintenance, plus $750 for pollution and resource-wastage, for a total of $2,250. Using a world population factor of three and one-half billion, we get a near-poverty income requirement of just under $8 trillion.

The present GWP estimate of $3 trillion reflects productive capacity evidently about one-third adequate. The $8 trillion figure would not be reached for another 20 years, even if the internationalizing of production is permitted to continue unimpeded. Population growth—a plus 67 percent at the United Nations' medium rate of 2.6 percent a year—would then have added $5 trillion to this requirement. Given these assumed growth rates for population and production, we do not get an equivalence until about the year 2010 at a level of $22+ trillion.

A further general upward correction to the $8 trillion requirement ought to be made in order to offset the maldistribution bias of highly interdependent societies. One possible measure of such bias is the margin of poverty on non-poor societies. At what level of total output the peripheral poverty would disappear raises intricate structural questions involving the relationship between production and distribution. If the history of amelioration we have

Value of U.S. Investments Abroad and Foreign Investment in U.S., 1950-1969 (Billions of Dollars)

	1950	1960	1964	1965	1966	1967	1968	1969 prelim
U.S. ASSETS (investments abroad), Total	31.5	68.0	99.1	106.7	111.8	122.7	135.9	146.0
Direct investment (book value-mainly subsidiaries of U.S. companies)	11.8	31.9	44.4	49.5	54.7	59.5	65.0	70.8
Other long-term private (market value-mainly "portfolio";incl. inv. where U.S. equity is less than 10%)	5.7	12.6	20.5	21.9	21.0	22.2	24.5	25.2
Total long-term private (with yeilds typically about 10%)	17.5	44.4	64.9	71.4	75.7	81.7	89.5	96.0
Short-term private	1.5	5.0	10.9	10.2	10.6	11.9	13.0	14.1
Total private	19.0	49.4	75.8	81.5	86.3	93.6	102.5	110.2
Government short-term (incl. monetary)	1.7	4.4	4.5	4.8	4.5	5.4	7.4	7.6
Other government (f.e. Eximbank, IBRD)	10.8	14.1	18.8	20.3	21.0	23.6	25.9	28.2
Total government	12.5	18.5	23.3	25.1	25.5	29.0	33.4	35.8
U.S. LIABILITIES (foreign in U.S.), Total	17.7	41.2	56.9	58.8	60.4	69.7	81.2	90.8
Direct investment	3.4	6.9	8.4	8.8	9.0	9.9	10.8	11.8
Other long-term	4.65	11.5	16.6	17.6	18.0	22.1	29.5	29.2
Total long-term	8.0	18.4	25.0	26.4	27.0	32.0	40.4	41.0
Private short-term	6.5	12.0	17.5	18.2	20.8	23.0	27.0	37.9
Government short-term	3.1	10.8	14.4	14.2	12.6	14.8	13.9	11.9
Total short-term	9.7	22.8	31.9	32.4	33.4	37.8	41.0	49.8
U.S Creditor position (Assets-Liabilities)	13.8	26.8	42.2	47.9	51.4	53.0	54.6	55.2

Sources: U.S. Department of Commerce, SURVEY OF CURRENT BUSINESS, various issues.
U.S. Council of the International Chamber of Commerce.

Value of U.S. Investments in EUROPE and EUROPEAN Investments in the U.S.
(Billions of Dollars)

	1950	1961	1967	1968	1969
U.S. ASSETS (investments in Europe), TOTAL:	12.4	21.3	35.6	39.7	41.4
Direct investment (book value-mainly subsidiaries of U.S. companies)	1.7	7.7	17.9	19.4	21.6
Other long-term private (market value-mainly "portfolio," incl. inv. where U.S. equity is less than 10%)	1.4	3.7	4.7	5.3	5.2
Total long-term private (with yield typically above 10%)	3.1	11.4	22.6	24.7	26.7
Short-term private	.5	1.3	2.8	3.4	3.6
Total private	3.6	12.7	25.4	28.2	30.3
Government short-term (incl. monetary)	.2	.8	2.6	3.7	3.0
Other government (f.e. Eximbank, IBRD)	8.6	7.8	7.6	7.8	8.0
Total government	8.8	8.6	10.1	11.5	11.1
U.S. LIABILITIES (European investment in U.S.) Total	9.1	27.4	41.0	48.2	55.5
Direct investment	2.2	5.1	7.0	7.8	8.5
Other long-term	3.1	10.1	13.2	18.6	18.9
Total long-term	5.3	15.3	20.2	26.3	27.4
Private short-term	2.8	5.6	10.9	14.3	21.7
Government short-term	1.0	6.6	9.9	7.6	6.3
Total short-term	3.8	12.2	20.8	21.9	28.0
U.S. CREDITOR POSITION (Assets - Liabilities) Total	3.3	-6.2	-5.5	-8.3	-14.1
On long-term	6.4	3.9	10.0	6.2	7.3
On short-term	-3.1	-10.1	-15.4	-14.8	-21.4

Sources: U.S. Department of Commerce, SURVEY OF CURRENT BUSINESS, various issues and Balance of Payments Supplement (1963)

seen in the highly advanced countries is used as a guide, reductions in the incidence of poverty require very large increments in GNP.

But our experience with 20th century production has very real elements of encouragement. The rate of growth we have seen effective in the rebuilding of Europe in the 1950's, in the Japanese "miracle," in the earlier Italian and German success stories, and very persuasively in the international producing activities we have been looking at here—this pace of growth suggests that we can produce adequately for world welfare.

This is all subject to a big if—we all have reservations to make whenever the game of growth rates is being played. If only the right

Gross World Product (GWP)

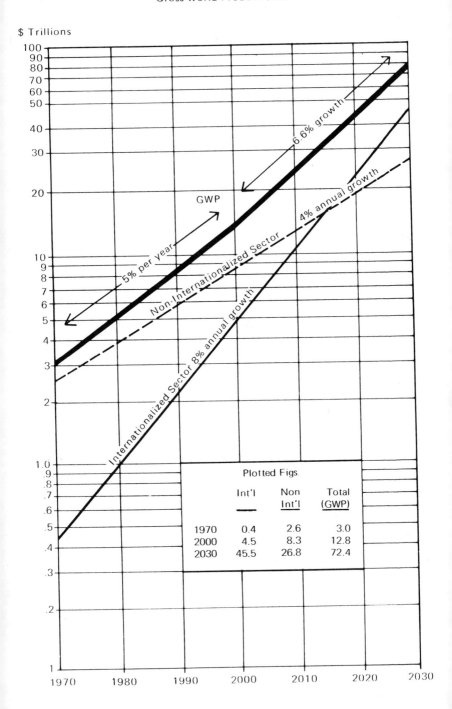

$ Trillions

Plotted Figs.			
	Int'l	Non Int'l	Total (GWP)
1970	0.4	2.6	3.0
2000	4.5	8.3	12.8
2030	45.5	26.8	72.4

6.6% growth

4% annual growth

GWP

5% per year

Non-Internationalized Sector

Internationalized Sector 8% annual growth

things are produced, if only reasonably equitable distribution is achieved—and above all if international politics do not force an economic fragmentation of the world. These and doubtless many other ifs are all relevant.

I think the industrialized countries have reached the point in their international orientation where an impeccably international policy is in their best national interest.

At the present high level of world interdependence almost any country is brought up against the fact that to discriminate against foreigners is to discriminate against itself. The effective operation of a national economy depends on the world setting of which it is only a part.

The Multinational Corporation in the Future

Ernest W. Ogram, Jr.
Georgia State University

It seems reasonable to project a steady rise in the value of U.S. and global exports over the next several decades. If the rate of increase of post World War II trade continues, world exports in 1988 will approximate $500 billion, an expansion of two times the 1970 level.

Against this background of expanded markets we are continually seeing progress which is directed toward a one-market world. This is reflected in the continued, and apparently inexorable, growth of multinationalism in international business through the multi-market multinational corporation which is oriented and structured to produce and sell a wide range of goods and services in many different countries.

International companies evolved rapidly after World War II and now the wave of the future seems to be the multinational corporation. Many will quarrel with the term "multinational" because they do not find it easy to define. Various other terms have been used to describe this most recent entry into the field of international business. It has been called a supranational corporation, a transnational corporation; an extranational corporation, and someone recently coined the term cosmacorp.

By whatever name, it is the type of company that is ideally suited for the most efficient application of technology to the problem of economic development and raising standards of living throughout the free world. It operates in a one-planet millieu; it conducts research, produces, advertises, distributes and sells worldwide.

Such an enterprise creates its own international community; and thus, it bridges communications gaps among nations by helping to reconcile differences through a viable network of commercial relationships.

What Is It?

A working definition of the nultinational corporation[1] is as follows:

1. It is a company that has a global outlook on markets. Basic decisions with respect to marketing, finance, production, and research are made on the basis of the alternatives open to it anywhere in the free world.

2. The term also signifies international ownership and control of parent company stock.

Concerning the first point, such companies generally make no distinction between domestic and international investments. They concentrate their production internationally in the country or countries where costs are the lowest and sell in the market where the sales and profit potential are the highest.

A company having a worldwide outlook on markets that is characterized by international ownership and control of parent company equity has several advantages.[2] First, by broadening the ownership base the firm materially reduces nationalistic opposition. Second, it increases global interest in the company's products. Third, it may reduce domestic capital participation by the parent company if additional shares are offered in the national market of the host country. Although in this latter case, the parent company could be accused of draining locally scarce savings away from possible host country investments.

What Are Its Distinguishing Characteristics?

It is likely that the multinational firm of the future will be characterized by a greater use of multinational management. The best man for the job, whether he is from the country of the parent company, the host country, or a third country, will become the rule rather than the exception. There will undoubtedly be exceptions to this rule in the case of the developing countries. Strong feelings of nationalism in these countries may preclude effective utilization of foreign nationals at levels of top management.

As overseas sales and profits as a percentage of total sales and profits become more important, it is likely that there will be a decline in the autonomous power of the subsidiary president. His power base will erode as greater centralized control of product, marketing, and financial planning becomes a necessity. This becomes important for top management when country sourcing of component parts becomes a necessity to carry through the corporate objectives of global marketing and international production.[3]

In all probability this centralizing tendency will accelerate in the years ahead. This assumes trade and tariff barriers continue to decline and it becomes economically feasible to a greater degree than is presently possible to organize the exchange of products and components on a country-by-country basis.

There are very few companies who are able to integrate their international operations to the extent that Massey-Ferguson, for example, is able to do at the present time. The company has been able to integrate to such a degree its production facilities that it utilizes a French made transmission, an engine produced in the United Kingdom, a Mexican-made axle along with U.S. made sheet metal parts to produce in Detroit a tractor for sale in Canada.

A final distinguishing characteristic of the multinational corporation will be the increased emphasis placed on the pooling of research talent along a regional basis as research and development costs increase in the future.

The Impact of Environmental Variables

Population

Demographers tell us that there will be a 50 percent increase in world population within the next two decades and the chances are that these are conservative estimates.

Realizing the market potential that will result from this vast increase in population, many American firms are beginning to look seriously at the possibilities for effective demand, market tastes, and industrial needs of both the developed and underdeveloped areas of the world.

There are strong possibilities that twenty years from now the entire European area and the Latin American countries will each have a single unified market. If we add Japan, whose GNP in 1968 surpassed that of West Germany, to these two regional areas the combined market of all three regions will be larger than the U.S. market. It is also reasonable to assume that by the 1980's the U.S. market will have doubled in size.

Markets in the Developed and Underdeveloped Countries

It has also been estimated that by the late 1980's the proportion of total world production of wealth as between the developed and underdeveloped countries will not change from its present distribution. The underdeveloped share will remain approximately 17-to-18 percent of the total. Thus a company that devotes more of its time and energy to cultivating the markets of the developing countries than it does to the developed areas of the world will be misallocating its resources. At the same time, corporate planners must consider the fact that the growth in production in developing areas will be roughly double that of its population expansion. Therefore, while the developing areas cannot be given the main attention neither can they be ignored.

There are other factors that are important, too. First, the world's population, particularly in the developing areas is becoming younger all the time. In Venezuela, for example, half of the population is 16-to-18 years of age, or less. Even in the U.S.S.R. and the U.S., fifty percent of the population is under 30 and this trend seems to be increasing. Clearly then, the special needs and desires of the young will continue to become a prime element in effective demand which no American firm can afford to overlook.

Urbanization

Another phenomenon concerns the almost unbelievable trend toward urbanization of all economies. Although this is not new, there is considerable evidence that the trend is accelerating. Therefore, the international corporation of today or the multinational corporation of tomorrow will be confronted with the kind of world in which marketing activities, product design, and development must be oriented toward huge urban conglomerations or megalopolis. The firms of the future must be prepared to cope with the problems and the challenges that such urbanization will create in areas such as housing, water and air pollution, and transportation. They in all probability will be participants along with local governments in assisting the latter in providing facilities for such high population-density areas.

Affluence and Leisure

Equally significant for the multinational corporation of the future is the likely impact of affluence and leisure time. What will happen to individuals and societies when the age-old motivations of the necessity to work to ward off starvation or cold subsides? Although affluence is coming at a much slower pace in developing countries, there are already signs that a middle class is emerging in a number of these areas.

It is doubtful that we will see the developing areas recapitulate the Western experience as they move into the modern world. The activities of American Labor unions will almost assure that they will leap the centuries in terms of the work week and not go through the 16-to-18 hours a day characteristic of the Western world during the Industrial Revolution of the 18th and 19th centuries. Nor can we, in all cases, expect the expanding populations of these countries to travel the Western road in terms of our consumption patterns for goods and services. Many of them are likely to go from nothing to acromycin and not just to aspirin.

Traditional Cost Patterns not as Important

From what production sources will the global company of the future serve their markets? In attempting to answer this question, corporate planners will need to make one fundamental assumption about the future—namely, that traditional cost patterns for factors of production may become a thing of the past by the 1980's.

Although traditional sources of energy are in good supply for future generations, they are not uniformly distributed throughout the world and their supply could be cut off suddenly in case of war or political disagreement. Hence today and in the years ahead, great technological emphasis will be placed on such scientific phenomena as fission, fuel cells, and solar energy. As breakthroughs occur in these areas in terms of lower costs of power production, there must result a significant trend toward uniformity of power costs throughout the world.

This same trend may be found in other areas such as non-energy resources. The extant shortages in basic minerals in the United States, for example, are resulting in more extensive technological interest in developing by-products, substitutes, and alloys of non-energy materials.

Even the cost of labor, at least in the developed areas of North America, Europe and Japan, may begin to show this same trend toward harmonization. In the developing economies, once it is economically feasible to install automated equipment and computerized production lines, labor costs in these countries will move toward equality with their more highly developed industrialized competitors.

It is reasonable to assume, therefore, that in the years ahead the determination of the location of plant facilities will not be determined, as in the past, by measuring comparative differences in costs. Instead, as these differences are eliminated, greater attention for structuring production in the international market will be focused on the determination of market accessibility, government attitudes and corporate flexibility in adopting to changes in consumer tastes. Thus, it is realistic to contemplate multinational corporate planning for production and distribution in the 1980's as being centered within a global framework of integrated markets. In this manner they will be able to obtain maximum efficiency in terms of production runs for finished products and component parts.

Worldwide Satellite Systems

The beginning of satellite communications is now at hand. When global satellite systems are fully operational by the early 1970's, communication costs will be significantly reduced. Experts agree that the actual cost of transmission across the Atlantic over the next five-to-ten years will be cut to a fifth or even lower compared to what it is at the present time.

Such a worldwide communications network will be not only able to handle television transmissions but many other types of communications, such as telephone calls, telegrams, transmission of weather reports, and scientific and business data for computers. The tie-in between computers and satellites in the instantaneous transmission of business reports at much lower costs will add a new dimension to the international operations of many companies. Computers will be used not only to analyze the existing flow of current activities but also to assist in organizational, financial, and personnel planning for the future. Furthermore, the close relationship between computer and satellite systems will provide marketing research specialists with an invaluable tool to study changing market variables.

The overall effect will be to increase the potential of international trade and investment. In the case of the developing countries, dependence on former mother countries for international communications is bound to diminish. No longer will a call from one African country to another have to be routed through London or Paris to be completed.

Major Problems Inhibiting Expansion

Multinational firms will be confronted with several obstacles in the years ahead as they attempt to achieve their corporate objectives. These problem areas can be divided into external and internal barriers. They are external or internal in the sense of having their stimulus either outside or inside the business system itself. The former would include nationalism, ineffective monetary and fiscal policy, legal problems, political instability, and increasing government participation in economic affairs. Internal barriers such as limited management horizons, a shortage of young qualified management talent and methods of communication are internal in the sense that they are more amenable to change within the business community itself.

Nationalism

The problem with its many ramifications can be expected to be with us indefinitely. This is not only true in the developing countries, but in the developed areas of Western Europe, Japan, and the United States. American investment insofar as it involves equity participation in foreign countries will in all probability receive only a qualified welcome. This will pose many difficulties and problems for top management of multinational firms.

One of these problems is the attitude of United States and foreign governments concerning trade and investment policy. It is naive to assume that the Nixon Administration (no more than the case with previous administrations) can make foreign producers of textiles and other products "voluntarily" curb sales in the American market without America's paying a high price in terms of restricting international trade and investment. The Japanese would automatically stiffen their resistance to U.S. demands that they ease restrictions on foreign investment in automobile manufacturing.

The extreme resentment in some European countries against American investment in the Common Market can be attributed in part to political nationalism. It can also be attributed to a reluctance to come to grips with American competition or to a fear economic domination on the part of American companies, both of which tend to inhibit the growth potential of U.S. multinational firms.

Ineffective Monetary and Fiscal Policy

Chronic inflation in Latin America and elsewhere has caused many countries in these areas to deflate subsidiary earnings by requiring purchase of foreign exchange for payment of dividends at higher exchange rates. Thus dividends remitted by an American subsidiary abroad to its parent company after being converted into dollars are worth much less than they would have been if the inflation had not caused the country's currency to depreciate.

Legal Problems

From multinational business activity in the future we should realize significant developments in international business law. World treaties regarding the adjustment of country tax laws and agreements among nations, corporations, and individuals with respect to business ethics, unfair trade practices, and a commercial code should be commonplace within the next two decades.

To make a one-world market operate more effectively, we will need improved machinery for the settling of disputes. As increased trade and investment help to contribute to world economic growth, there are likely to be involved greater opportunities for commercial and investment disputes.

Fortunately progress is being made in many of these areas already. In 1968, for example, the U.N.'s Commission on International Trade Law held its first meeting and included in its agenda a full discussion on procedures and regulations covering payment for international transactions. There is also growing interest concerning the establishing of machinery for the arbitration of global investment disputes. Along this line there was recently established the International Center for the Settlement of Investment Disputes (ICSID), which is under the auspices of the International Bank for Reconstruction and Development.

Political Instability

A perplexing problem that will continue to impede multinational firms in the international market is political instability. Over fifty-eight countries have been born since the end of World War II and many of these lack the historical and ethnic foundations necessary to achieve a stable and viable economy. Even though political instability will continue to be a way of life for many generations to come, their market potential cannot be neglected. Insofar as the ramifications of such political instability can be provided for by flexible planning within the corporate structure, the multinational company will survive and prosper. The company that stays by the domestic market almost exclusively will find it increasingly difficult to compete not only in international markets but also in the home market. By the 1980's it is altogether possible that domestic business may be subsumed under international business.

Government Participation

The increasing participation of governments in economic affairs, as unpalatable as this fact may be, has to be recognized as a possible fact of economic life for the future. Today, the overwhelming trend is for governments all over the world to assume increasing responsibility for rising incomes, employment, and growth.

At the present time, the United States is one of the very few countries in the free world that does not have a national economic plan. Whatever the outcome of this issue in the United States, there is not much doubt that the role national governments abroad will play will be one of a greater degree of involvement in economic endeavor in the areas of research and development, wages and prices, and to some extent, even influencing what goods and services can be produced and in what geographic areas they can be produced.

Limited Management Horizons

The general feeling of many corporate officials[4] is that if American firms maintain a shortsighted, parochial point of view and focus their attention solely on competition within the domestic market to the exclusion of anything beyond the horizon of our own coastline, then the future of the multinational enterprise is severely limited. George Bryson in his *Profits From Abroad* states that although many U.S. firms are finding that their biggest competitive threat is coming from abroad, "they refuse to look into the possibilities of going into these same foreign countries and defeating this competition on its home ground."[5]

Qualified Management Talent

A shortage of young qualified management people willing to serve in the overseas market poses a serious threat to multi-nationalism is business. Part of this can be explained as a result of an apparent lack of interest on the part of junior executives in accepting overseas assignments if it involves the possibility of having to move their families abroad for a two to three year period. This apathy is in turn reinforced if management itself downgrades the overseas operations of the company and makes it clear that the way to top management is through the domestic rather than the international side of business.

Methods of Communication

This is another potential problem area. The complexities and ramifications of diverse markets, alternative sources of funds, and dissimilar cultural patterns increase the possibility of a breakdown in the communications link between the home and overseas offices. Thus the inward and outward flow of information must of necessity be on a regular and frequent basis to provide for sound and well timed business decisions.

Conclusion

The multinational firm also has a unique opportunity in helping to create a favorable image in foreign countries of the American system of free enterprise.

Like it or not, the multinational corporation is part and parcel of the future. In this regard it should and must challenge the imagination of the business community. There can be no doubt of its being successful in the years ahead provided it meets its social responsibilities in host countries and at the same time remains fully competitive at home and abroad.

This global type of corporation may well mean the inauguration of a new era in the utilization of the resources of the free world, with the attendant possibility of an increase in human welfare for all of mankind.

FOOTNOTES

1. The definition is based on an inductive research study by the writer undertaken in New York City in the summer of 1964. A number of board chairmen, presidents, and other senior officials of major U.S. forms heavily engaged in overseas operations were interviewed. The intention of the personal interviews was to arrive at a consensus of the views of recognized leaders of the international business community. The study, *The Emerging Pattern of the Multinational Corporation* was published in 1965 by the Bureau of Business and Economic Research, Georgia State College.

2. The disadvantages are possible loss of domestic management control and problems of taxation of dividends and dividend policy.
3. Judd Polk, Economist, U.S. Council of the International Chamber of Commerce, has stated that the " internationalization of production is the most important structural event to have occurred in many years and very likely on a par with the Industrial Revolution." U.S. State Department Conference, held in Washington, D.C. on February 14, 1969, on "The Implications of the Multinational Corporation."
4. See Ernest W. Ogram, Jr., *The Emerging Pattern of the Multinational Corporation*, p. 22.
5. George Bryson, *Profits From Abroad*. New York: McGraw Hill Book Company, 1964, p.5.

From Multinational Corporation to World Government?*

Richard D. Robinson
Massachusetts Institute of Technology

Over recent years, it would appear that U.S. firms have demonstrated a remarkably consistent ownership policy in respect to their foreign operations. A 1971 study reports that approximately 60 percent of the new enterprises established by U.S. firms overseas over the past ten years had been wholly-owned (including branches which, by definition, must be wholly-owned), 8 to 9 percent majority-owned, 7 to 8 percent minority-owned (the remaining 13 to 15 percent were unknown). There has been remarkably little variation from year to year.[1]

By way of contrast, it is reported that Japanese direct investment overseas is more inclined to be on a minority basis (37 percent), somewhat less on a majority basis (34 percent), and even less on a wholly-owned basis (29 percent).[2] This conclusion is supported by the relatively low rate of income repatriated to Japanese parents (3.3 percent of the estimated outflow in 1969 as contrasted by 9.8 percent for the U.S.). Also suggestive is the fact that for the 560 Japanese foreign investment projects, or 96 percent of the total approved by the Japanese Government to the end of 1967, 67 percent of the investors gave as one of the principal reasons for the investment either the export of components and materials or the import of foodstuff and raw materials. That is, for the typical Japanese direct foreign investor major profits are expected to be derived either from the import into Japan of raw materials or the

*Reprinted from *The Atlanta Economic Review*, Vol. 22, No. 9, September, 1972 by special permission.

sale out of Japan of components. In the U.S. and U.K. cases, the data suggests that considerably less than 50 percent of the output of U.S. or U.K.-owned enterprises overseas is imported by the parent companies. But for Japan, this proportion is 80 to 90 percent. Thus, U.S. and U.K. investors are more interested in securing a maximum dividend flow for their capital and skill; they are reluctant to share it. But the Japanese can afford to share the dividend flow because they perceive the major benefit to be derived from export or import. Hence, the Japanese share in equity tends to be relatively low. There are other reinforcing reasons: (1) more Japanese investment is located in less developed countries (possibly 63 percent as of 1968),[3] where alien ownership tends to be restricted, (2) Japan's own restrictive policy in this regard and (3) Japanese sensitivity to cultural differences.

The view is gaining currently among Japanese business circles that indeed, the 50-50 equity relationship should be promoted as a world-wide standard in the sense of a permissible maximum for the foreign investor. One Japanese editorialist wrote in late 1971:

"Only the U.S. is insisting on the full implementation of the principle of 100 per cent liberalization by every country. However, this stand is a close reflection of the interest of the country's own multinational corporations. . .

The reason Japan has been staying with the principle of 50 percent foreign entry is the conviction that this is the smoothest way to achieve co-prosperity of alien and domestic interests. It is believed in Japan that jumping to a 100 percent liberalization policy from the beginning may cause unnecessary confusion in national economic policies and management of business because economies and ways to run business differ from country to country.

Despite the recent inte.national economic developments, it is inappropriate for Japan to immediately abandon its principle of 50 per cent foreign entry. Rather, it should be re-emphasized that this principle offers a most reasonable and realistic way to achieve harmony with domestic interest and to avoid frictions owing to nationalistic emotions in developing countries.

As a proponent of the establishment of a "world business charter," Japan is in a position to present its own version of a code of behavior for multinational enterprises. In such a proposal, the 50 per cent liberalization principle should be advanced as a cardinal rule for foreign business entry into developing countries."[4]

Indeed, it seems to me that we are witness to the unfolding of two somewhat different international business scenarios, one based largely on ownership of physical assets (the North American and

Western European), one based essentially on contract (the Japanese).

What I shall do now is to describe what I perceive to be an important, ongoing process of change in the international business system, *starting* with the multinational firm, not ending with it as so many are prone to do. To me, the multinational firm is a defineable category of firms, distinguishable from the international, which typically preceeds it in time, and from the transnational, which may follow it in time. I say *may,* because that is where to the two scenarios diverge in plot.

The essence of the multinational firm is the fact that it has assigned *global* responsibilities to its top staff and line management, whether it be organized on a regional basis, a product line basis, or a functional basis—or three, which is possible with a matrix type management system. The domestic market is just one more market. Nonetheless, ownership and top corporate management remain essentially in the hands of parent country nationals. To the extent that management can do so psychologically and legally, decisions are made without national bias. The attempt is made to allocate corporate resources optimally on a worldwide basis, although one has to bear in mind that the structure does impose psychological and legal restraints. National loyalties remain and highly nationalistic world perceptions persist. So likewise, does responsiveness to national law and foreign policy.

The *multinational* corporation is very likely to have evolved out of an *international* corporation, the characteristic hallmark of which being the international division. Typically, the international division faces a set of domestic product divisions and staff departments, none of which get very excited about overseas activities. Nonetheless, virtually all of the technical skills required for establishing and maintaining a manufacturing facility are embedded in these domestic divisions, and embodied in people with no foreign experience and typically an exaggerated notion as to the superiority of their own nationality, national business system, and technical competency. As overseas activity other than exporting grows, the conflict between the international and domestic divisions is likely to become critical; it is a case of divided loyalty. It is largely to release this conflict that the multinational corporate structure is introduced, but also to build in greater sensitivity to foreign environments. The international division disappears. As one leading U.S. executive put it, "If we split the company strictly between foreign and domestic business, we would have ended up with two general staffs. And if people grew up in only one area of the company, we would have lost the advantage of being able to interchange them freely."[5] The comment by another, "There is considerable tendency on the part of international executives to guard closely the activities of their divisions or operations. In doing so, they divorce themselves from the rest of the organization. Cooperation between domestic and international divisions becomes more difficult and any desire on the part of domestic personnel to become more familiar with the international operations gradually dies."[6]

As was the case of the international corporation before it, the *multinational* corporation has built into it the seeds of its own destruction. It is not in stable equilibrium either with itself nor with the environment. Point one: although corporate personnel are given multinational responsibilities, characteristically they have had little international experience and no relevant technical-professional training. Point two: being members of a corporate headquarters peopled almost entirely with fellow nationals, the executives with new global responsibilities possess a set of values and world perception that is very likely to bias their decision-making. Although they may possess a *willingness* to allocate corporate resources optimally on a global basis, in fact, they are psychologically and legally incapable of doing so. Point three: given the nonavailability of headquarters personnel equipped to operate effectively overseas, and the lower cost of employing *local* national managers abroad rather than home country expatriates, plus the rapid rate of expansion often characteristic of the multinational stage, the firm employs largely local nationals to manage its new foreign facilities. It may also enter into a number of joint ventures. Hence, the firm suffers a loss of effective central control.

Although perhaps initially inclined for these reasons to permit greater autonomy—if not compelled—to its associated foreign firms than did the *international* corporation, the multinationals—as they mature and gain international experience at the center—eventually begin to reverse the decentralization process. The benefits to be derived from integrating the world wide movement of corporate resources becomes increasingly apparent·as the contribution to corporate profits from overseas activity mounts and as the skill to effect such integration appears in corporate headquarters. The corporation then begins to try to recapture control at the center and to buy up partially-owned affiliates so as to remove conflict of corporate interest inherent in local equity involvement. These trends are, I submit, on a collision course.

On the one hand, we have competent and now experienced local national managers moving upward toward their respective national subsidiary ceilings in terms of promotion. On the other hand is the fact of increasingly centralized control within the multinational corporate headquarters. The local manager may respond by pushing for greater autonomy of his own operation, which is often signalled by a breakdown in communication between subsidiary and headquarters, an exaggerated importance given to environmental factors in decision-making, and continued inability of the firm to centralize effective control. Or, the local manager may leave the employ of the firm. Host governments tend to support the local manager's desire for greater autonomy, for the pressure to increase external control over the allocation of domestic resources sooner or later becomes politically unacceptable. The environmental factor thus, in fact, becomes blown up.

Eventually, the multinational headquarters perceives the cost inherent in the communications' breakdown, loss of control, mounting political pressures, and possible loss of key foreign managerial personnel. As it does so, nationality barriers are removed, and foreign nationals are likely to begin appearing in responsible managerial spots outside their respective national subsidiaries, first in regional headquarters if there be such, then in corporate headquarters itself. (This is where the model begins to diverge from the Japanese, because it is almost inconceivable that non-Japanese managers could work effectively at high levels within the corporate headquarters of a Japanese corporation, particularly when one considers the system of permanent employment and relatively permanent work groups, still characteristic of large Japanese corporations. How can the non-Japanese manager be thrust into such a situation horizontally and be expected to relate effectively? Returning to our non-Japanese model, one should note that several forces combine over time to multinationalize the *ownership* of the multinational corporation. Among these for the U.S.-based multinational are the U.S. controls over direct foreign investment, which program encourages the swap of U.S. parent company stock for foreign assets, the foreign sale of debentures convertible to parent company stock, and the listing of parent company stock on foreign stock exchanges. For the European-based multinationals, the relatively small size of the local capital market pushes in the direction of multinational ownership, including the appeal of cross-order mergers and of repeated joint venturing among multinationals. In addition, both in the more and less developed countries one may be compelled to recognize host society demands—often translated into political pressures—for a share in the profit derived from its market.

Many firms are now in this transitional state between the multinational firm and the truly transnational firm. The latter is simply a corporation which has lost its national identity except insofar as legal restraints may impact upon its decisions and operations. It is owned and managed by the nationals of more than one country. I suggest that a necessary—if not sufficient condition for maximum corporate growth in the future is likely to be multinational ownership and management at all levels.

Thus, it is the transnational corporations which will continue probably to grow most rapidly. Those with annual gross sales of between $5 and $160 billion will soon not be uncommon. In fact, it has been predicted that there will be some 300 of such corporations by 1985 controlling a very large part of the fixed industrial assets of the free world. But will they? Their sheer size—and absence of all national loyalty inherent in their multinational ownership and management—brings these transnational corporations onto a collision course with the nation-state. Indeed, there is considerable evidence that even though governments may be promoting *national* merger and industrial concentrations, increasingly they are resisting mergers and arrangements among the giant multinationals and transnationals. It is U.S. antitrust policy to prevent mergers, wherever they take place or whatever the nationality of the merging companies, if the effect of the merger would be to reduce competition significantly within the U.S. or within the foreign trade of the U.S. The European Community seems to be setting precedent barring the further acquisition of important national companies by large multinationals or transnationals. The Japanese have been restrictive in this regard for some time, and I see no reason why they should shift direction. But to achieve *effective* political control of such giant multinational and transnational firms requires new international institutions, particularly in regard to the transnationals because of their greater growth potential and absence of any national loyalty or bias. No national government, or even an international regional agency such as the EEC, can claim the right to determine the law under which a multinationally-owned and multinationally-managed corporation, with resources strewn around the world, can operate.

Therefore, the next stage in the evolutionary process may be the appearance of the supranational firm. Such entities must necessarily rest on special intergovernmental agreements or treaties, which in each case provides the legal basis for a governing body. The only prototypes at the moment are public (the International Bank for Reconstruction and Development) and quasi-public (Intelsat). One can expect two further near-term developments: (1) the emergence of a European corporation chartered and controlled—if not taxed—under an EEC law and (2) the appearance of an international seabed authority which will charter, control, and possibly tax corporations operating on the bed of the deep sea. Various proposals have been made for a *general* international convention, under which some sort of commission would be created for the chartering, controlling, and taxing of corporations satisfying certain conditions in respect to multinationality of ownership and management.

Consider the politically intolerable size of the giant transnationals within the next decade, the degree to which economic power will be concentrated in the hands of decision-makers virtually unreachable by any government, the inability of single nation-states—or even regional groupings—to regulate these firms. The common interest of nation-states almost compels them to participate in a harmonization of national policy in regard to anti-trust, taxation, corporate law, and restraint on resource allocation. The common interest becomes irresistably compelling if one adds the mounting pressure to internationalize *political* decision-making as we approach the finite limits of our global environment. Obviously, the rate of resource usage, energy consumption, atmospheric and oceanic pollution can only be resolved on a global basis. Finally, there is no evidence leading one to believe that the giant transnational corporation will voluntarily incorporate any mechanism rendering it socially responsible other than through the market place, which even nationally we perceive as inadequate when it comes to anti-trust, consumer safety, education, health, and environmental considerations. It would appear that either the nation states in concert dominate the giant transnational or the reverse will occur. Bear in mind that the former implies an international convention which creates a body of basic law and a representative body with adequate resources to control these corporations. If so, we are very close to effective world government. The international corporate law may specify, for example, that national shareholders will be represented in the corporate board by a government appointee approved by those shareholders. Given such a system of international law and control, the possibility of a truly *supranational* corporation appears.

If nations find it impossible to collaborate to this degree, they are very likely to act to restrain further transnational corporate growth, first by forbidding further mergers and acquisitions and—if this is seen as an inadequate impediment to further growth—then by expropriating local assets. Most vulnerable, of course, would be integrated plants in mature industries serving primarily the local market, and which belong to transnational corporations in which there is little or no local equity involvement.

Or, it may just be that the pattern emerging in Japan for some of the reasons already suggested will prove so profitable that the large North American and Western European-based multinationals and transnationals will be induced to change their structure. What seems to be developing in Japan is the multinational *association*. At the center is a Japanese owned and managed corporation, which is linked internationally by a web of contractual relations with largely locally-owned and managed associated firms. The center supplies capital-intensive, scarce resources—such as new technology (that is, research and development plus the training of local nationals), also management and managerial training, international marketing services, purchase and sale contracts, debt capital, and possibly initial high-risk equity (entrepreneurial) which is later withdrawn. The associated, eventually largely locally-owned and managed firms, produce. Such an association could become transnational if the central corporation were owned by the associated foreign firms. The increase in public-sector or profit-sharing enterprise in both less and more developed countries, whether ideologically socialist or otherwise, also suggests that this pattern may indeed be the wave of future, that the multinational and transnational corporation as presently conceived will prove to be a relatively short-lived transitional form. Both legal restraints and higher profit levels to be realized by those firms concentrating on providing the scarcer, more capital-intensive inputs via contract likewise lead one to this conclusion. The higher profits appear because the firm based in an industrially developed country can concentrate its resources in producing those services in shortest supply and which, therefore, should command the highest prices. In economic terms, it is maximizing its monopoly rent on these relatively scarce factors of production. One might suggest that it is also minimizing its political risk for, from the point of view of the recipient country, benefits and costs would be specifically linked and not generalized in a stream of dividends. The contract route also permits systematic periodic renegotiation as the benefit-cost ratios shift, which, for instance, would be signalled when another firm is prepared to provide comparable inputs at less cost. It is for this reason that I fully expect to live to see the disappearance of many of the giant multinational and transnational firms as presently constituted.

One is thus driven to the conclusion that either a mechanism is created for providing international political control over the giant transnational firms, which could constitute an important next step in the long road to effective world government, or—as I suspect—the Japanese model of multinational associations will dominate. As the associations become transnational in nature, at which point, the

Japanese may find themselves at a disadvantage, the need for some form of international political control will again arise. Such control is also dictated by the environmental problem and the global resource allocation process such implies. So, following either route, the pressure of world business is likely one day to force the nation-states into a posture of cooperation thus far unknown. I hope that I am not being unduly optimistic. Global conflict and catastrophe is always an alternative. The issue, I suggest, is being forced by world business.

FOOTNOTES

1. A. Booz, Allen & Hamilton study, reported in *Business Abroad*, June 1971, p. 9.
2. Gregory Clark, "Japanese Direct Investment Overseas," (unpublished manuscript, 1971), Table II.
3. According to Japan Economic Deliberation Council, *Shihon Jiyuka to Kaigai Kigyo Shinshitsu* (Liberation of Capital Movement and Overseas Expansion of Business), (Tokyo: 1969), p. 137, quoted in *Transfer of Technology from Japan to Developing Nations* (New York: UN Institute for Training and Research, 1971), p. 8.
4. *The Japan Economic Journal*, September 7, 1971, p. 10.
5. William Blackie (President of Caterpillar Tractor) in "CAT Bounds Ahead in Foreign Markets," *International Management*, October 1966, p. 59.
6. Richard J. DeBottis (Assistant to the President, Eriez Magnetics) in "The International Division—Growth Patterns Vary," *International Trade Review*, March 1964, p. 12.